THE COMPLETE COMPACT DISC PLAYER

THE COMPLETE COMPACT DISC PLAYER

Martin Clifford

Prentice-Hall, Inc., Englewood Cliffs, New Jersey 07632

Library of Congress Cataloging-in-Publication Data

Clifford, Martin (date)
　The complete compact disc player.

　　Includes index.
　　1.　Compact disc players--Maintenance and
repair.　I.　Title.
TK7881.75.C57　　1987　　　621.389′3　　　86-25470
ISBN 0-13-159294-7

Editorial/production supervision
　and interior design: Sophie Papanikolaou
Cover design: Photo Plus Art
Manufacturing buyer: S. Gordon Osbourne

Printed in the United States of America
10　9　8　7　6　5　4　3　2　1

ISBN 0-13-159294-7　　025

Prentice-Hall International (UK) Limited, *London*
Prentice-Hall of Australia Pty. Limited, *Sydney*
Prentice-Hall Canada Inc., *Toronto*
Prentice-Hall Hispanoamericana, S.A., *Mexico*
Prentice-Hall of India Private Limited, *New Delhi*
Prentice-Hall of Japan, Inc., *Tokyo*
Prentice-Hall of Southeast Asia Pte. Ltd., *Singapore*
Editora Prentice-Hall do Brasil, Ltda., *Rio de Janeiro*

TO MY INSPIRING GRANDCHILDREN
MICHAEL and STEPHEN FITZPATRICK

CONTENTS

2   *Pulse Code Modulation*   19

3   *Signal Processing*   41

6 The Compact Disc Player: The Control Path   130

10   *Maintenance and Testing*   221

11   *Operational Analysis*   245

12   *Quick Troubleshooting*   270

13   *Digital Audio Tape/Player*   293

Index   304

PREFACE

Both Philips (NV Philips Gloeilampenfabrieken) of the Netherlands and Japan's Sony Corp. made individual contributions to the production of the compact disc and player. Philips began efforts to develop a compact disc in 1969, but it required ten years of effort before it could show the first working system to the European press.

Philips' contribution was the creation of a video disc system using tracking by means of a laser beam. With this as a basis, Philips then developed a more compact version for sound reproduction. Sony added to the technology through its research on data coding and error correction circuitry. Without these advances by Sony, reproduction of the audio signal would not have been possible. Error correction circuitry helps to ensure correct reproduction of sound even when the compact disc is plagued with fingerprints due to disc handling, dust, scratches on the discs, and defects occurring during manufacturing.

Since Sony and Philips were the prime movers toward the compact disc format, we can better appreciate their efforts as shown in the following timetable.

DEVELOPMENT OF THE COMPACT DISC: A HISTORICAL PERSPECTIVE

1928	Harry Nyquist establishes mathematically that the sampling rate of an analog audio waveform must be twice the highest frequency of the wave being sampled.
1939	Pulse code modulation invented by H. A. Reeves.
1969	Philips Research Laboratories begins work on optical disc recording of video, audio, and data.
1972	First public demonstration of optical disc recording (VLP, the future LaserVision).

1973/1974	Requirements established for video, audio, and data recording. Philips' associate, Polygram, producer of first laser-read discs becomes full participant.
1974	Sony develops stationary-head digital audio recorder.
1975	Philips begins development of industrial disc mastering equipment.
1976	Sony produces first digital audio disc system based on FM video format. The disc rotated at 1800 rpm, supplied 30 minutes of music on one side, and used an optical readout system.
1976	Conception of small diameter (compact) disc defines digital audio project parameters.
1976	Sony announces digital audio processor to be coupled with a video tape recorder for 12-bit quantized, two-channel recording and playback.
1977	Sony creates the first consumer digital audio processor. It was called the PCM-1 and it recorded digital pulse signals on video cassettes.
1977	JVC develops its first pulse code modulation digital audio processor. The company begins to provide professional digital recording technologies used in recording studios throughout the world.
1977	In cooperation with NHK, Sony develops a digital audio processor for use with a professional U-matic videocassette recorder.
1977	Sony markets the world's first consumer digital audio processor for use with the Betamax home videocassette recorder.
1977	Sony makes available a digital audio disc system employing a pulse code modulation direct recording method. The disc rotated at 900 rpm and supplied 1 hour of recording and playback per side. It used an optical readout system.
1978	After further technological advances, Philips defines Compact Disc as a digital audio system to reproduce one hour of stereo sound on one side. Efforts continue to develop commercially viable lasers, optics, ICs, disc mastering, and production equipment.
1978	The world's first broadcast of digitally recorded programs is made through Japan's four major FM networks.
1978	Sony develops a long-playing digital audio disc system with the disc rotating at 450 rpm. The unit used an optical readout system and played 150 minutes per side.

1978	Sony announces the development of a stationary-head digital audio recorder using $1/4$-inch tape.
1978	Sony announces a stationary-head, 24-channel digital audio recorder for professional applications using 1-inch tape. In the same year Sony developed a digital reverberator for professional use.
1979	Philips shows working model of their Compact Disc player to press at Eindhoven, The Netherlands. Five months later and ten years after research began in Eindhoven, Sony signs agreement to cooperate in further system development with the aim of making Compact Disc the world standard for digital audio.
1980	Philips, Polygram, and Sony agree to Compact Disc System and submit it to Digital Audio Disc Committee in Japan.
1980	Sony announces the compact disc digital audio system, jointly developed by Sony and Philips at the Japan Audio Fair. In their research program, Philips investigated the basic operating principles and designed the hardware. Sony's contribution centered mainly on the development of software including the signal processing method.
1981	With several digital audio disc systems being promoted, Matsushita adopts the Compact Disc. It is now certain to be a world standard.
1982	Virtually all the world's major audio manufacturers are among 30 player and 10 disc licensees. Development of car Compact Disc started by Philips.
1982	Compact disc players, also known as digital audio disc (DAD) players, launched in Japan in October 1982.
1983	Compact Disc arrives on the commercial market. Players and discs are offered for sale throughout the world.
1985	More than 90 system partners worldwide; 54 hardware and 38 licensees.

An achievement that may be just as extraordinary as the development of the compact disc and its player is the fact that all discs and disc players (with the exception of multidisc players) are standardized worldwide. This means that all compact discs are compatible and can be used in any player. However, it does not mean that all compact discs are manufactured in exactly the same way and to identical quality standards. Nor does it mean that all CD players use identical circuitry and that all have the same features.

At the time of the introduction of compact discs and players, there were many competing systems and a distinct possibility that we would have two or more noncompatible disc types and players. One of these was Telefunken/Teldec's MiniDisc (MD).

The disc was encoded by a string of binary digits but its player did not use a laser beam for scanning the encoded disc. Another was known as an Audio High Density Disc (AHD), a JVC product. In still another technique, a card was used instead of a disc. The card was encoded with digital data but remained in a fixed position and was scanned by a moving laser beam.

Martin Clifford

ACKNOWLEDGMENTS

Not unexpectedly, manufacturers of top quality compact disc players and accessories were ready to supply detailed information about their units, were quick to point out notable points of superiority and were just as willing to supply a detailed look at the circuitry behind the front panel.

While all compact disc players do use both analog and digital electronics, there are substantial differences between the "me too" units and those that represent electronic professionalism at its best.

I would like to acknowledge with sincere thanks, the extensive cooperation supplied by the following top ranking companies.

Aiwa Co., Ltd.

Akai America, Ltd.

Alpine Electronics of America, Inc.

Analog & Digital Systems, Inc.

AudioSource

Audio-Technica U. S. Inc.

dbx, Div. BSR North America, Ltd.

Denon-Nippon Columbia Co., Ltd.

Discwasher, Div. International Jensen Inc.

Dynasound Organizer, Div. Hartzell Manufacturing, Inc.

Geneva Group of Companies, Nortronics

Marantz Company, Inc.

Monster Cable

Nakamichi U.S.A. Corporation
Onkyo Corporation
Philips Auto Audio/Amperex
RCA
Sanyo Electric, Inc.
Sherwood, Div. Inkel Corp.
Signet
Sparkomatic Corporation
Studer Revox America, Inc.
TEAC Corporation of America
Technics
Toshiba America, Inc.
Yamaha Electronics Corporation, USA

SPECIAL ACKNOWLEDGMENTS

I am appreciative of the substantial amount of material supplied by Sony Corporation of America and both encouragement and data from Marc Finer, Product Communications Manager for Sony's Consumer Audio Products and now associated with Communications Research, Inc. as a consultant for Sony. Marc Finer supplied me with two White Papers supplied by Sony, one on the subject of Compact Disc Players and the other on Digital Audio Tape. Chapter 13 is substantially extracted from this latter named White Paper.

Special thanks to Radio-Electronics and Josef Bernard.

My thanks also to Kyocera International, Inc. Chapter 12, Quick Troubleshooting, is based on the unique flowcharting techniques they use for servicing their compact disc product line.

Martin Clifford
North Lauderdale, FL. 33068

1

WORKING WITH BINARY NUMBERS

The study of the compact disc and its associated compact disc player, how they are made, how they work, how to maintain and repair them, and the circuits they use, starts with binary arithmetic. The difficulty in working with binary numbers is that we are not accustomed to them, for we have been trained to think decimally.

Everything we do involves decimal numbers, ten digits ranging from 0 to 9. We are paid in decimal numbers and every price tag we see is in decimal numbers. We use decimals for counting, for our savings, our investments, and our taxes. We may begin our education in decimal arithmetic by counting on our ten fingers.

Working in binary arithmetic, a system that consists of only two numbers or symbols, 0 and 1, means we must arrange our thinking to accommodate this strange concept. But it is through our use of binary arithmetic that we have developed computers, and it is also through binary arithmetic that we now have an alternate sound source, one that supplements the phono record and which has the potential to replace it. It is through our use of binary arithmetic and the compact disc that we will ultimately have a purity of music reproduction never before achieved.

In electronics, binary will not replace decimal arithmetic but will supplement it, and these two arithmetic systems will work together. It may seem strange to begin a technical book on how compact discs are made and how compact disc players work with a brief analysis of the binary number system, but without an understanding of that system there can be no understanding of either the disc or its player.

WHAT IS ANALOG?

Analog (or analogue) is defined by *Webster's New Collegiate Dictionary* as "something that is analogous or similar to something else." The key word is "similar" but it does need some explanation. If you were to measure a voltage, whether DC or AC, you could describe that measurement by writing about it or by talking about it, but possibly the best technique would be to picture it in graphic form. That graph is an analog of the measured voltage. If you were measuring an audio wave, the graph of that wave would be a pictorial representation of the voltage or current for successive moments of time and is its analog (Fig. 1-1). The odometer in an automobile supplies data about the speed of the car. The numbers that are shown are comparable to, or analogous to, the rate of rotation of the wheels.

Most components used by in-home electronic systems are analog units. The voice coil of a loudspeaker receives a varying audio current. The movement of its cone is analagous to that current. The cone could also be used to drive a graphic recorder and the waveform that is produced is an analog of the voice-coil current. A phono record's sound output is an analog of the modulated signal in the grooves cut into that record.

In the case of a microphone, its electrical output is an exact (or fairly close to exact) replica of its input. The input is sound energy, the output is a voltage. Because that output is an "electrical carbon copy" of the input, it is the analog of the input. Although sound energy and electrical energy are two different forms of energy, one can be a duplicate or an analog of the other and often enough are interchangeable. We can convert sound energy to its electrical equivalent, and then reconvert it to sound.

ADVANTAGES OF DIGITAL TECHNOLOGY

We live in a world of analogy and so to move away from it there had to be a deliberate attempt. The reason for this is the need for greater precision which is something that digital systems can give us. Analog systems are basically imprecise and efforts are frequently made to improve them. A speaker system, as mentioned earlier, is an electronic analog system for converting electrical audio currents to a corresponding cone movement, and despite the many years speakers have been in existence, considerable efforts are still being made to improve the accuracy of this analog setup.

Figure 1-1 Analog waveform of an audio voltage.

Digital is more accurate than analog. As a simple example, a digital watch is more accurate than one that is analog. A picture transmitted to earth of another planet via radio may be analog to begin with. It can be improved and made more accurate by digital processing. The analog recording of sound on a phonograph record can be made far more accurate by using digital techniques.

BINARY NUMBERS

The arithmetic system we are most familiar with is the decimal and as its name indicates, it uses ten symbols ranging from 0 to 9. All other numbers in this system such as 153, 1986, and 9032 are combinations of the basic symbols.

The decimal system is just one of many possible systems, such as the binary (used for digital audio and in computers), the ternary, quaternary, octonary (better known as the octal) and the hexadecimal.

Radix

The radix (pl. radices) of a number system is the number of symbols it uses. For all arithmetic systems up to the decimal, the symbols are digits. For a system such as the hexadecimal, the symbols are alphanumeric and consist of numbers and letters of the alphabet.

The radix of the decimal system is 10 since it uses ten symbols; that of the binary system is 2 for its only symbols are 0 and 1. The digit 2, or any digits other than 0 and 1, cannot be used in the binary system and if such numbers do appear or are used, they are incorrect.

Every number system has a radix, also called a base. In the quinary system, the radix or base is 5 for five symbols are used. The radix for the decimal system is 10, and the digits in this system could also be called denary numbers. There is only one digit that is common to all numbering systems and that is the number 0.

The value of the radix is always one greater than the value of the largest symbol used in the number system. Thus, in the binary system the largest symbol value is 1; the base or radix is 2. In the decimal system the largest symbol value is 9; the radix is 10.

A radix point is used to separate the whole number portion from a fractional part. In the decimal system, the radix point is known more familiarly as the decimal point. In the binary system, it is the binary point. For compact discs, only whole number binaries are used.

Integers are sometimes referred to as fixed-point numbers since the radix point is omitted. A decimal number such as 689 can also be written as 689. but as a fixed-point number the decimal point is not necessary. A binary number such as 1011 is also a fixed-point number and can be written as 1011. but here also the radix point is ignored.

WHAT IS DIGITAL?

Technically, any number system, whether binary, octal, decimal, or another, is digital since it makes use of digits or numbers. However, when the word "digital" is used, it is only in reference to the binary system.

LEAST SIGNIFICANT DIGIT

In any row of whole number integers, the rightmost digit has the lowest numerical value and is referred to as the least significant digit, abbreviated as LSD. In a decimal number such as 685, the digit at the right (5) has the least value. Digit 6 is actually 600, digit 8 is 80, while digit 5 is simply 5. In a binary number such as 1001, the digits have a value (as in the case of decimal numbers) depending on their position in the number group. In the binary number just supplied, digit 1 at the far right has the lowest numeric value.

MOST SIGNIFICANT DIGIT

The most significant digit (MSD) is the digit positioned at the extreme left in a group of numbers. In a decimal number such as 6583 the digit at the extreme left (6) has the highest value and is known as the most significant digit (MSD). Similarly, in a binary number such as 1100, the number 1 shown at the far left is the MSD.

THE BINARY NUMBER SYSTEM

The compact disc, the compact disc player, and predecessor components such as pulse code modulators use the binary system either completely or in association with analog. These all make use of a unit called the binary digit.

Binary Digits

Since the radix of the binary system is 2, using the symbols 0 and 1 only, each of these are referred to as binary digits. Utilizing the first two letters of the word "binary" and the last two letters of the word "digits," we get the formation of a new word—bits. The number 0 in the binary system is a bit and so is the number 1. The number 1011 is a four-bit number; 10001 is five bits (Fig. 1-2).

Reference is rarely made to a single bit but rather to groups that appear in sequence. A group of four bits is called a nibble, with eight bits referred to as a byte (sometimes called a symbol). Sixteen bits which follow each other directly is a half word; 32 bits is a word and 64 bits is a double word. The relationship of nibbles, bytes,

0	ONE BIT
01	TWO BITS
101	THREE BITS
1010	FOUR BITS
01110	FIVE BITS
101011	SIX BITS
1011011	SEVEN BITS
01011101	EIGHT BITS
111001011	NINE BITS
1011001101	TEN BITS
01110101001	ELEVEN BITS
111000101100	TWELVE BITS
0110110101011	THIRTEEN BITS
10111011000101	FOURTEEN BITS
110010101100011	FIFTEEN BITS
0110101100011010	SIXTEEN BITS

Figure 1-2 In a binary number, both 0 and 1 count as a bit.

half words, words and double words is the same as the place value of bits, that is, 64, 32, 16, 8 and 4.

Binary numbers are sometimes called machine language, for it is with binary numbers that we give a computer its instructions. The computer makes use of an analog to digital translator called a processor to make the transition from the English language and the decimal number system to machine language. The output of the computer is a device that converts binary to a printout in English, using words and decimal numbers.

When binary numbers are used for voice or music, the information input (the voice or music) is initially analog. It is converted to digital and must be finally converted to its analog form. We hear in analog; digital is just an intermediary step. Its sole purpose, in the case of a high-fidelity system, is to supply an improvement in the reproduction of sound.

Binary Exponents

Exponents can be used in the binary system, just as in the decimal system, but with the base 2 instead of 10. The equivalent decimal value of positive powers of 2 are shown in Figure 1-3. In each instance the exponent indicates the number of times the base is to be multiplied by itself. $2^4 = 2 \times 2 \times 2 \times 2 = 16$. As the value of the exponent is increased, each preceding decimal equivalent is multiplied by 2. As an example we have:

Power of 2	Meaning	Decimal Equivalent
2^5	$2 \times 2 \times 2 \times 2 \times 2$	32

2^7	2^6	2^5	2^4	2^3	2^2	2^1	2^0
128	64	32	16	8	4	2	1

Figure 1-3 Binary exponents and their decimal equivalents.

Binary Numbers and Decimal Equivalents

When working with compact discs, we move between binary digits and their decimal equivalents. Since binary numbers can be expressed only in symbols such as 0 and 1, a binary number can look like 1010 or 110010.

As in the case of decimal numbers, binary numbers are arranged horizontally to show their positional values. Thus, a binary number such as 111 has a total amount of: $2^2 + 2^1 + 2^0$. $2^2 = 4$; $2^1 = 2$ and $2^0 = 1$. The decimal equivalent of binary 111 is $4 + 2 + 1 = 7$. As another example, 1111 is the binary form of $2^3 + 2^2 + 2^1 + 2^0$ or $8 + 4 + 2 + 1 =$ decimal 15.

As indicated earlier, the MSD is always found at the left in any binary grouping. However, it must always be the symbol 1. If a 0 occupies that position, it has no value and may be disregarded. Thus, in a digital number such as 0110101, the zero at the left can be dropped and if there is more than one zero, they can be discarded also. A digital number such as 000101010 has the same numeric value as 101010, and the leftmost 1 is the MSD.

The LSD is the first digit at the right that contributes to the total value of the number. As an example, consider this binary: 10001111000. The LSD is the 1 that appears in the 2^3 position at the right. Thus, the MSD has a value of 2^{10} and the LSD a value of 2^3. In binary, the least significant digit is sometimes referred to as the least significant bit (LSB), while the most significant digit is known as the most significant bit (MSB).

$$1\ 0\ 0\ 0\ 1\ 1\ 1\ 1\ 0\ 0\ 0$$
$$2^{10} \qquad 2^6\ 2^5\ 2^4\ 2^3$$
$$2^{10} = 2 \times 2 \times 2 \times 2 \times 2 \times 2 \times 2 \times 2 \times 2 \times 2 = 1024$$
$$2^6\ \ = 2 \times 2 \times 2 \times 2 \times 2 \times 2 = 64$$
$$2^5\ \ = 2 \times 2 \times 2 \times 2 \times 2 = 32$$
$$2^4\ \ = 2 \times 2 \times 2 \times 2 = 16$$
$$2^3\ \ = 2 \times 2 \times 2 = 8$$
$$1024 + 64 + 32 + 16 + 8 = 1144 \text{ (decimal)}$$

Only the 1s shown above are raised to some power, but not the 0s. Since zero raised to any power is equal to zero, the binary number 10001111000 could have been written decimally as:

$$1024 + 0 + 0 + 0 + 64 + 32 + 16 + 8 + 0 + 0 + 0 = 1144$$

As in the case of decimal numbers using decimal fractions, it is also possible to have binary fractions or numbers following the binary point. However, the compact disc and the compact disc player do not make use of binary fractions and all the numbers involved are binary whole numbers.

In the conversion of a decimal number to its binary equivalent, if the decimal number has a fractional portion, that portion is disregarded and the number is truncated. Thus, a decimal number such as 601.3 becomes 601 with the decimal part omitted.

Maximum Decimal Value of Bits

The maximum decimal value that can be represented by four bits is $1111 = 8 + 4 + 2 + 1 = 15$. The bit on the extreme left of the 1111 group has a decimal value of 8. If you add to it the value of the bit minus 1, you will have the maximum decimal value of all four bits. Thus the bit on the left is 8. Add to it $8 - 1 = 7$. $8 + 7 = 15$. This is the maximum value of the four bits.

To find the maximum value of five bits without changing every bit to its decimal equivalent, write the decimal value of the bit at the extreme left (the highest order bit) and add to it the value of the bit minus 1. The bit at the left has a value of 16. $16 - 1 = 15$. $16 + 15 = 31$. The maximum decimal value obtainable with five bits is 31. Note, however, this is applicable only in instances in which there are no zero value bits in the string of bits. Since the low order bit is $2^0 = 1$, the maximum sum of all bits is always an odd value (Fig. 1-4).

Number of Bits	Maximum Binary Value	Maximum Equivalent Decimal Value
1	1	1
2	11	3
3	111	7
4	1111	15
5	11111	31
6	111111	63
7	1111111	127
8	11111111	255
9	111111111	511
10	1111111111	1023
11	11111111111	2047
12	111111111111	4095
13	1111111111111	8191
14	11111111111111	16383
15	111111111111111	32767
16	1111111111111111	65535

Figure 1-4 The maximum binary value and the maximum decimal equivalent are obtained when all the bits are 1s.

Placeholders

Since zeros at the left of a binary number can be dropped without affecting the total value of the number and since the number zero has no bit value, it might seem its inclusion is not necessary. However, consider a number such as 1101. The decimal equivalent of this number is $(1 \times 2^3) + (1 \times 2^2) + (1 \times 0^1) + (1 \times 2^0) = (1 \times 8) + (1 \times 4) + (1 \times 0) + (1 \times 1) = 13$ (Fig. 1-5). Multiplication by zero always results in zero and so the term written as (1×0) is equal to zero.

But if it is equal to zero, perhaps it can be omitted. We would then have the binary number as 111. This is equal to $(1 \times 4) + (1 \times 2) + (1 \times 1) = 7$. The digit zero used in 1101 is known as a placeholder and by using it, each binary digit has not only its correct value but its correct decimal equivalent. While the number zero does

Decimal Value	Binary Value				
	16	8	4	2	1
0	0	0	0	0	0
1	0	0	0	0	1
2	0	0	0	1	0
3	0	0	0	1	1
4	0	0	1	0	0
5	0	0	1	0	1
6	0	0	1	1	0
7	0	0	1	1	1
8	0	1	0	0	0
9	0	1	0	0	1
10	0	1	0	1	0
11	0	1	0	1	1
12	0	1	1	0	0
13	0	1	1	0	1
14	0	1	1	1	0
15	0	1	1	1	1
16	1	0	0	0	0
17	1	0	0	0	1
18	1	0	0	1	0
19	1	0	0	1	1
20	1	0	1	0	0

Figure 1-5 Decimal numbers and corresponding binary values.

not contribute to the total amount, its use ensures that all the other digits do have the correct place value.

DECIMAL AND BINARY NUMBER IDENTIFICATION

Since the binary system has two symbols (0 and 1) also used by the decimal system, it is sometimes possible for confusion to exist between the two systems. There is no doubt that 643 is a decimal number, not to be confused with binary, since none of these integers exist in binary. But 1101 binary could be misinterpreted as 1101 decimal. Subscripts are sometimes used in connection with binary and decimals and with other number systems as well, for identification purposes. 1101_2 is binary and is recognizable as such by the subscript 2. 1101_{10} is decimal because of the subscript 10. However, subscripts are used only when there is some possibility of confusing a decimal with a binary number.

PULSE REPRESENTATION OF BINARY NUMBERS

An analog waveform is a graphic representation of a large number of decimal digits in rapid succession. The graph of a wave is obtained by plotting instantaneous values as shown in Figure 1-6. If enough of these values are used, they can be connected across their peaks to supply a fairly smooth graph.

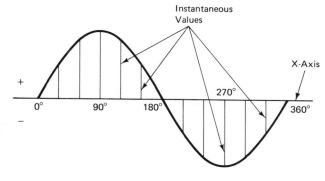

Figure 1-6 Instantaneous values of a sine wave.

0 1 0   0 0 1   0 1 1   1 1 0

Figure 1-7 Pulse representation of binary numbers.

A graph of binary values can also be obtained through the use of pulses of equal amplitude. A pulse indicates the digit 1; the absence of a pulse indicates the digit 0. A pair of adjacent pulses representing binary 1 1 simply takes up twice the space of a pulse representing binary 1. The absence of a pulse, or binary 0, has the same width in the graph as a pulse representing binary 1. Two zeros will take up twice the space (Fig. 1-7).

THE DIFFERENCE BETWEEN ANALOG AND DIGITAL SIGNALS

An analog signal is smooth, continuous, with no breaks in the waveform even in the presence of large, short-lived transients. The digital waveform is characterized by sharp breaks, evenly spaced timewise, known as discontinuities. These are the transitions from one sampled pulse to the next. But while pulse waveforms are discontinuous, the reconstructed waveform is not. We do not hear in digital but in analog only (Fig. 1-8).

(a)

(b)

Figure 1-8 Analog waveform (a) and a portion of its binary pulse equivalent (b).

DATA REPRESENTATION

Information, such as music or speech, can be recorded in two different ways: analog and digital. The analog method is the technique that has been used since the time of Thomas Edison, inventor of the cylindrical phono record, and Emile Berliner, inventor of the flat phono record, techniques now more than one hundred years old.

An analog audio signal is not only continuous but varies in amplitude. Digital consists of a sequence of rectangularly shaped pulses. Digital is represented by encoding the analog waveform as a series of binary numbers, 0 and 1. While the digital format used for high-fidelity sound reproduction is comparatively new, it has been used and is still being used for non-high-fidelity sound functions in calculators and in computers.

Information in one of these formats, such as analog, can be converted into the other, a process known as analog to digital conversion (A/D). The reverse process is also available whereby digital signals can be converted to analog (D/A).

WEIGHTED CODES

A weighted code is one in which there is an arithmetic relationship between the bits. In the binary code used for compact discs, each higher order position is two times as large as its adjacent lower order position. This holds whether the binary digit is a 1 or a 0. In a binary number such as 1111, the value of each bit doubles as we move from right to left. Thus, 1111 is the equivalent of 8 + 4 + 2 + 1 counting from the most significant digit.

If one of the bits is a zero, as in 1101, the zero bit works as a placeholder and counting from left to right we have 8 + 4 + 0 + 1. The digit 4 exists just as though its following digit consisted of a 1 bit instead of a 0 bit. The difference between each bit varies as a power of 2.

The code used for compact discs is not the only code possible. Some codes do not have any arithmetic relationship between the bits, since values assigned to each of the bits can be arbitrary. Instead of relying on some rule for the formation of bit values, the only method for remembering the weight of each bit is through memory. The weighted code used for compact disc binary bits is more convenient since the decimal equivalent of any group of binary bits can be easily calculated.

A series of pulses used for some specific purpose is called a pulse code. Pulses used to indicate binary 1 are sometimes called positive logic; pulses to represent binary 0 may be termed negative logic.

Pulse formation is not a new concept but its use for compact discs and compact disc players is a fairly recent development. A television broadcast signal contains pulses for the control of picture formation in a home television receiver. The signals sent along a wire by a telegraph key are pulses, but these are pulses of two different widths.

The On-Off Concept

A pulse indicating binary 1 is sometimes called an on pulse while binary 0 is an off pulse. For compact discs and their players, however, it is better to think of binary pulses in terms of digits which represent the binary equivalent of a decimal number. As indicated earlier, a waveform of a voltage or a current can be represented numerically using either the decimal or binary number system.

Figure 1-6 shows a sine wave and a few instantaneous values. These could be in decimal form and could possibly have values such as 5; 12; 18; 12; 5 and 0. These numbers can then be converted into their binary equivalents and could be: 00101; 01100; 10010; 01100; 00101 and 00000.

The drawing shown in Figure 1-8(a) is an analog representation of a wave. We can take a fairly large number of instantaneous values of that wave, initially in decimal form, and convert them to binary values. We can then redraw the wave so that it is in binary form, rather than an analog equivalent, and it would appear as shown in Figure 1-8(b).

Note how this is done. We start with an analog wave and then take a number of instantaneous voltage values which are in decimal form. We then convert these decimal amounts to their binary number equivalents. From the binary numbers we can draw the pulse waveform. The amplitude of the binary waveform can be as shown in the drawing or can be smaller or larger, since the pulse amplitudes have no meaning. A 0 pulse rests on the zero base line; a 1 pulse rises above it. Each pulse is of the same width.

What we have then is a series of constant amplitude pulses corresponding to binary digit 1, and a series of spaces between pulses corresponding to binary digit 0. Figure 1-7 shows a number of such waveforms. If a pair of binary 1s are adjacent, then the pulse has a double width. If a pair of binary 0s are adjacent, then we have a double spacing between pulses. Similarly, we could have triple or quadruple width pulses or spaces, depending on whether binary 1s or 0s are involved.

There are definite differences between analog and binary waveforms. The analog can be a continuous wave, a wave of constant frequency and amplitude; it can be one of variable frequency and constant amplitude, or one in which both frequency and amplitude are variable. However, in all cases the wave is continuous in the sense that there is no space between any parts of the wave and an adjacent part.

As far as the binary waveform is concerned, we can regard it as a series of discontinuous pulses with variable spacing between pulses and with the pulses having constant widths. The waveform is a discrete type; there is always a pulse for binary digit 1 and there is always the absence of a pulse for binary digit 0.

THE ANALOG TO BINARY CONVERSION PROBLEM

The problem with a drawing of a waveform such as a sine wave is that it gives the impression of being fixed. The wave is repeated a large number of times, and in the audio range extends from 20 Hz to 20 kHz.

However, pure sine waves make boring listening leading us directly to the complexity of a nonsinusoidal audio wave. Such a wave not only has a varying amplitude but a varying frequency as well. Converting such an analog waveform to its binary equivalent raises the question of how often to make amplitude measurements. The higher the frequency, the smaller, the time existence of the audio waveform. At a frequency of 20,000 Hz the time duration is $T = 1/f$ and for the top frequency end, it is 1/20,000 of a second.

QUANTIZATION

The conversion of a sample or instantaneous amplitude value of an analog signal into binary form is called quantization which is a measurement of the instantaneous peak value of a wave that is constantly changing. Theoretically there is no limit to the number of instantaneous values of an analog signal. There can be a difference between a pair of adjacent values. This difference is sometimes referred to as a quantum but the same word is also used to describe the single instantaneous value of an analog wave. For two or more of these instantaneous values, the reference word is quanta.

The drawing in Figure 1-9 illustrates the concept of quantization of an audio wave. The instantaneous amplitude of this signal is the voltage of the signal at a single specific point in time. The value of the instantaneous amplitude is indicated by vertical bars and is expressed in binary form at the left. The equivalent of the instantaneous decimal values of the analog wave is shown here as 4 bits, but it would be 16 bits in an

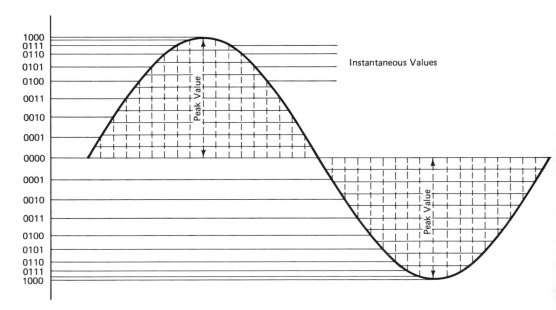

Figure 1-9   Instantaneous values quantized with a 4-bit code.

actual quantization process. With only 4 bits the maximum equivalent decimal value is 15, whereas with 16 bits it is 65,535.

SAMPLING

The quantization of an analog waveform is done repeatedly with the process referred to as discrete time sampling, but more often simply called sampling. Discrete time sampling means it is done at precisely spaced time intervals. It is essential for the sampling frequency to remain constant and therefore the circuit that does this work is crystal controlled.

By agreement, the sampling frequency is always 44.3 kHz. This is standard but multiples of this standard frequency such as 88.6 kHz and 177.2 kHz are also used.

The basic sampling frequency of 44.3 kHz is obtained from a quartz crystal cut to resonate at 0.0443 MHz. Crystal control is used to make certain that the sampling frequency remains constant so that the voltage of the positive and negative peaks of the analog waveform are measured at precisely timed intervals.

Twice the basic sampling frequency can be obtained through the use of a frequency multiplier (a frequency doubler or a circuit that will supply some multiple of the original sampling frequency) (Fig. 1-10). However, even with a frequency multiplier, the circuitry is still crystal controlled. The crystal circuit is an oscillator, while the following multiplier is an amplifier and is tuned to an even order harmonic, either the second or the fourth. The second harmonic is 88.6 kHz and fourth harmonic is 177.2 kHz.

The analog waveform does not remain fixed during sampling but varies in frequency and amplitude. Sampling involves attempting to make an extremely large series of voltage measurements with that voltage constantly changing. Further, this is not a single one-time measurement, but as indicated earlier, consists of a minimum of 44,300 measurements every second. Moreover, the number of measurements can also be two times or four times this amount.

The basic sampling frequency is a little more than twice the highest audio frequency of the analog waveform, generally considered to be 20 kHz. Harry Nyquist, a Bell Laboratories engineer, determined mathematically that the sampling rate of an audio wave should be twice its highest frequency. While 20 kHz has been adopted as the top end of the audio spectrum, the scanning frequency has been set at 44.3 kHz. This leaves a guard band of 4.3 kHz between twice the audio frequency upper limit and the scanning frequency (44.3 kHz − 40 kHz = 4.3 kHz).

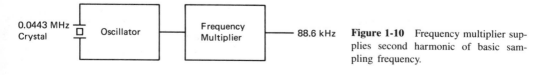

Figure 1-10 Frequency multiplier supplies second harmonic of basic sampling frequency.

THE BINARY WAVESHAPE

While only binary 1 results in a pulse waveform, for the sake of convenience, both binary 1 and binary 0 are referred to as pulses. A binary 0 has as much significance in a binary pulse waveform, and the accidental absence of a binary 0 can result in a substantial difference in the total binary value of the waveform.

Each instantaneous voltage value uses 16 binary bits when quantizing an analog waveform. If each of these bits has a binary value of 1, the sum of all these bits will be the digit 2 raised to the 16th power (2^{16}). This is equivalent to decimal 65,535. In effect, with 16-bit sampling, the analog waveform can be considered to be divided into 65,535 parts. No binary fractional parts are used and if the peak amplitude of any instantaneous value results in a fractional binary, it is truncated to the nearest whole number. Thus, if the decimal amount of an instantaneous value is 47,638.23, the decimal amount (0.23) is dropped. As you can see, 0.23 is an extremely small percentage of the number.

These two factors, a high sampling rate which is more than twice the highest audio frequency (20 kHz) and the use of 16 bits for the binary representation of successive instantaneous amplitudes of the analog wave, mean that this representation is highly accurate. The result is an extremely high dynamic range and in specs usually appears in excess of 90 dB which is far superior to the dynamic range claimed for phono records or recording tape.

ALIASING

Aliasing is the development of beat note products due to heterodyning between the sampling frequency and ultrasonic audio harmonics. It is referred to as intermodulation distortion (IM) but is generally not included in the specs of a CD player.

BIT STREAM

The quantization of an analog wave results in a long series of digital bits with a space between each group of 16 bits, a space that has been established as 22.7 microseconds. A series of bits is sometimes referred to as a bit stream, a data stream, or as a string.

DECODING

The conversion of decimal analog values to equivalent binary number values is called encoding. Sound is first converted to its electrical equivalent by a microphone, but this electrical equivalent consists of an analog waveform. This waveform is then quantized and converted into its binary equivalent. At some time in this process that binary equivalent must be reconverted to its original analog shape. This is necessary, for example, to be able to drive a speaker which requires an analog current through its voice coil. Since this process is the reverse of encoding, it is called decoding. A circuit which changes analog to digital is known as an analog/digital converter, abbreviated as A/D converter. In the reverse process, a digital/analog converter (D/A converter) changes binary to analog.

The technique used in encoding and decoding involves going from a large series of decimal numbers representing momentary instantaneous amplitudes along the envelope of an analog waveform, to their binary equivalent. It is from these equivalent binary numbers that the on/off pulses of the binary waveform are constructed.

A number of errors are possible along the way. The wrong binary number may be derived from a particular analog value. With the tremendous amount of binary digits representing an analog waveform, it is possible to have one or more binary pulses missing. When this happens we get a wrong decimal value during reconstruction, possibly leading to a wrong tone. The output of the device used for producing binary values from decimal, a pulse code modulation unit delivers its derived binary signals to a tape deck. If the tape being used has dropouts (missing magnetic particles on the tape), some binary numbers will be missing.

Quantization Distortion

During the conversion of decimal to binary form, it is possible to have a form of distortion called quantization distortion, also known as quantization noise. A wave in its analog form, possibly representing some varying voltage or current, is smooth. The wave may have sharp, sudden peaks but at no point is the waveform discontinuous. When digitization takes place, the waveform is sampled but it is possible for a particular sample to fall between the specific digital values made available for the conversion. For example, if we have a pair of instantaneous values measuring 4 millivolts and 5 millivolts, it is possible that the instantaneous voltage being converted to binary form will be somewhere between these two. This does not mean the pulse representing the instantaneous value will be omitted. It will be included but there will not be an exact correspondence between the resulting binary pulse group and the precise amplitude of the analog waveform. The resulting distortion is called quantization error.

BIT QUANTITY

The larger the decimal value of a number, the greater the amount of bits required to represent that number. A decimal number such as 3 requires only 2 bits and the binary equivalent is 11. Another relatively small number such as decimal 20 requires 5 binary bits and its binary equivalent is 10100. A still larger decimal number is 601 and its binary value is 1001011001. To divide the audio signal into 65,536 parts would require 16 bits. This is the number of bits commonly used for quantizing an audio waveform.

Codes can be represented by the number of bits they use for quantization. The code could be a 4-bit code, 8-bit, 16-bit, and so on. Codes used in CD are 8 bit and 16 bit.

PULSE ANALYSIS

Just as an analog waveform can have various characteristics such as frequency, amplitude, and transients, so too do quantized pulses have electronic patterns of their own.

Pulse Amplitude

All pulses used for compact discs have identical amplitudes. The fact that a group of pulses could have higher amplitudes than another group is of no significance. The binary representation of a pulse is dependent solely on whether it exists or not. Thus, the pulses shown in Figure 1-11(a) represent the same binary number as those illustrated in Figure 1-11(b). Consequently, there is no advantage in having higher amplitude pulses.

It is also possible to have a series of pulses whose amplitudes are not constant but which vary, as in Figure 1-12. The increases and decreases in pulse height are of no significance.

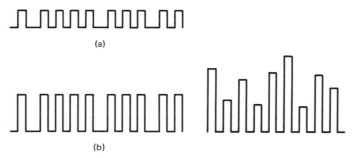

(a)

(b)

Figure 1-11 Pulse amplitude does not affect binary equivalent.

Figure 1-12 The binary equivalent remains the same independently of pulse amplitude.

Pulse versus No Pulse

The absence of a pulse is as significant as its presence, so much so that the absence of a pulse is sometimes referred to as a zero pulse. As indicated previously, the absence of a pulse works as a placeholder. Binary 1001 is equivalent to decimal 9. If the zeros in this binary number were eliminated, we would have binary 11 with a decimal equivalent of 3.

Pulse Width

All pulses in the binary representation of an analog wave have the same width, or the same time duration. This time width applies equally to pulses equivalent to binary 1 as

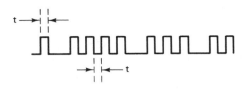

Figure 1-13 All 0 pulses and all 1 pulses have the same time duration.

well as to no-pulse conditions indicating binary 0. As indicated in Figure 1-13, if we let t represent a discrete unit of time, then all pulses or no pulses exist in time t.

Pulse Separation

There is no time separation between pulses whether they represent 0 or 1. Consequently, a pair of adjacent pulses have the equivalent of a single pulse of double-time width. However, such pulses should not be regarded as a single pulse having double width but rather as individual pulses each having a time width t.The same thinking applies to no-pulse conditions.

Counting Pulses

All pulse groups are counted in binary starting at the extreme right and moving to the left. As indicated earlier, while one or more zeros at the right do not contribute directly to the overall value of the binary number they represent, they do work as placeholders. A binary such as 1010010 does not have the same binary value as 101001. Any binary, however, with zeros at the left can drop those zeros without changing the overall value of the binary. A binary such as 0110101 is the same as binary 110101.

Pulse Groups

Pulses for CD applications based on quantized audio waveforms work in groups consisting of 16 bits or 8-bit pairs forming the equivalent of 16 bits.

Pulse Applications

These statements regarding binary pulses are intended only for those used in connection with the production of compact discs and their use in compact disc players. In other applications, such as the Morse code, for example, information is transmitted by the use of narrow and wide pulses. Pulses can also be used to turn circuits on or off and in such an application, the amplitude of the pulse is important. Not all pulses represent binary numbers and can be combined with analog waveforms. A broadcast television signal consists of an analog waveform preceded and followed by a series of constant amplitude pulses.

Graphic Representation of a Digital Code

A pulse code can be represented graphically by using binary numbers, a technique widely used in the CD industry and for that reason in this book as well. A method less often used is to have a period indicate the absence of a 1 pulse. In this case the digital code, for example, could be represented as 1..1....11. The successive double absence of a pair of 1 pulses would be a pair of dots.

2

PULSE CODE MODULATION

Ultimately, whether we make an analog recording or one that is digital, we must use a tape recorder to deliver the signals to a machine for making phono records or compact discs.

THE PULSE CODE MODULATOR

A pulse code modulator (PCM) is a component for converting an analog input signal to one that is digital. The input is two channels of recorded sound, the left and right channels of stereo. The output of the PCM is a sequential string of data in bit form ready for recording on a master tape using a tape deck, with that tape deck as an integral part of the PCM or external to it. The master tape produced as a result of the PCM is used for the production of the compact disc. While the PCM can also be used as a step toward the manufacture of digitally encoded analog phono records, our interest is primarily in how it works for CD.

The PCM samples the analog signal, quantizes the results, converts those results to binary form, changes the two channels of sound to a single consecutive string of bits, makes error corrections, preparing the results of these steps for recording on a magnetic tape. The input to a PCM is analog sound recorded on tape; the output of the PCM is a binary pulse code, recorded on tape. The output of the PCM is delivered to a tape deck as illustrated in Figure 2-1(a), or the PCM and the tape deck can be an integrated unit as in Figure 2-1(b).

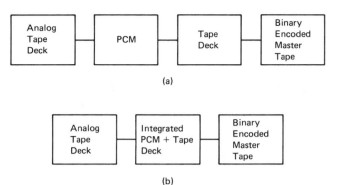

(a)

(b)

Figure 2-1 PCM is followed by a tape deck (a) or can be integrated with it (b).

ANALOG VERSUS DIGITAL TAPE RECORDING

The advantage of the compact disc versus the analog phono record begins with the tape recorder. A tape recorder has definite recording limitations for both digital and analog. Analog recording tries to live within these limitations; digital recording circumvents them.

Magnetic tape has a definite restriction on the amount of signal energy it can accept. Once that level is reached, the tape begins to saturate and any signals recorded beyond that point are distorted. The problem is that this restricts the dynamic range of the input signal, and the operator must either ride the gain control or use some form of signal compression.

At the opposite end of the dynamic range, the input sound to the tape recorder for analog is restricted by the noise floor of the tape. The noise floor is the noise produced by the tape in the absence of an input signal. Magnetic tape supplies its own signal energy and we hear this as hiss. If we have two tones, one of which is substantially louder than the other, the quieter of the two tones will not be heard—a condition known as masking. With loud sounds tape hiss will be inaudible but it will be heard when the input to the tape recorder consists of low signal level passages. For analog, magnetic tape not only sets restrictions on the recording of low and high level sounds but on the frequency range as well. Tape recording has a rolloff at the bottom and top ends of the audio spectrum.

THE BASICS OF DIGITAL RECORDING

To understand the basics of digital recording it is necessary to understand the reasons for the transition from the analog system. With analog sound, energy is converted into its electrical equivalent, also in the form of analog, and it is this analog form that is recorded on magnetic tape. But despite considerable advances in tape and in tape recorders, four major problems remain: limited dynamic range, imperfect frequency response, relatively high harmonic distortion, and measurable wow and flutter.

Substantial efforts have been made to reduce these, and in quality equipment they are low indeed, but the fact remains they have never been eliminated in analog equipment. Digital recording has either made these inaudible or immeasurable.

Sound in digital form can be recorded in any one of a number of different ways, but whichever method is used they all have a common characteristic. They do not represent sound in its analog form and instead supply the binary equivalent. The problem here is that, for analog, magnetic tape can only handle a limited signal. An analog signal can have strong variations in amplitude, something that is not a characteristic of a digital signal.

Pulse code modulation (PCM) requires the tape to handle pulses only, or more precisely, pulses (ones) and the absence of pulses (zeros). In pulse code modulation, the analog output of a microphone (or microphones) is sampled 44,100 times a second. This analog signal is then quantized or converted into a binary digital code with 16-bit quantization. In this form, music is composed of 1,400,000 bits of information per second. This is the digital signal that is recorded on the magnetic tape. However, this digital signal must ultimately be converted to analog in a CD player, for our hearing mechanism is geared for sound in analog form.

By recording digitally the problems of recording on tape in analog are eliminated, including wow and flutter, inaccurate frequency response, harmonic distortion, and low dynamic range. When recording digitally on tape, the problems of upper and lower signal level input do not exist. Digital pulses all have the same amplitude and can be delivered to the tape deck so that recording is above the noise floor and below the saturation level. Consequently, the limitations of tape on dynamic range are no longer of any significance.

Print-Through

The recording of high-level analog signals on magnetic tape can bring along with it the problem of print-through, a condition that results in the production of an echo effect or a ghost-like sound in the background during tape playback. With high signal level recording, some of the signal can be impressed on one or more layers of tape in addition to the one on which recording is taking place. The only way to eliminate this problem is to reduce the level of signal input, but this in turn reduces dynamic range. It would seem, then, that the relationship between digital recording and magnetic tape is perfect, but there is one serious flaw, and that is tape dropouts.

Tape Dropouts

When magnetic tape is manufactured, it is coated with billions of tiny metallic particles. These adhere to the tape binder, an adhesive coating on the tape. However, when dealing with particles in the billions, it is inevitable that some of them will fall away, or may not be impressed on the tape in the first place. Most dropouts are very short—on the order of about a dropout at a rate of approximately one every 1/5,000th of a second. Tape contains literally thousands of these dropouts. For analog recording, such a dropout rate isn't a serious factor. However, for digital recording they can change the binary code, and while this change is extremely brief, it can affect the sound adversely by causing an error in the decoded signal. This problem is solved through the use of an error-correction system.

One of these systems, the Cyclic Redundancy Check Code (CRCC) is so accurate that it detects 99.9985% of all dropout errors. During recording, the CRCC system records an error-correcting word (32 bits) and a check word for every six words of musical signal. Then, during playback there is a constant comparison between the check words and the music. Any discrepancy appears as a code error caused by a dropout. The error-correcting words are then used to reconstruct the proper word.

In the event that CRCC fails to correct a dropout, a system of word interleaving and linear interpolation takes over. This system merely interleaves, that is, shuffles the digital words before they are recorded. Upon playback, de-interleaving restores the proper order. Neighboring words remain intact even if a large section of tape is destroyed by a dropout, since different pieces of tape house adjacent words. Then, using linear interpolation to average the value of the preceding and succeeding words, we get an approximation of the missing information that is so close it is difficult to detect this system's operation.

THE ANALOG MASTER

The initial steps toward the production of a compact disc and those for making analog phono records are the same. The sound is recorded by a tape recorder and, of course, it is in two-channel form. At this stage it is an analog signal and because it has been tape recorded, it carries along with it any noise supplied by the recorder plus any signal compression due to the electrical characteristics of the tape. The tape is referred to as an analog master tape. Prior to the use of this tape, the sound may have gone through a mixdown process. But however simple or elaborate and regardless of the number of tracks used by the mixer, the signal input to the analog master tape is only two channels.

PULSE CODE MODULATION

Music, words, and numbers are referred to as intelligence and sometimes also known as data. Data may consist only of letters arranged in random, sequential order or in groups of two, three, four, and so on. But whatever the arrangement, they are identified as alphabetical.

When numbers are used to convey information, they can belong to any arithmetic system but are most commonly binary or decimal. Each arithmetic system has a specific group of symbols. In the decimal system, these symbols range from 0 to 9 and there are no other symbols in this system. In the binary system there are only two symbols, 0 and 1. Data transmitted through the use of arithmetic symbols is called numeric.

It is also possible to use a combination of letters and numbers with such an arrangement called alphanumeric. While any numeric system can be used, ordinarily alphanumeric data include letters of the alphabet and decimal numbers.

Alphabetic data can consist not only of letters but of words. The Morse code used in telegraphy is an example of the transmission of data in the form of words, but it can also be used in other forms, such as alphanumeric.

Data can be sequential or interleaved, with interleaving as an important error correction technique in compact discs. Sequential data could consist of words so that reading or hearing the words conveys the meaning. A sentence such as "Please ship order today using fastest available transportation" is sequential data. In interleaved form it could read as "Please order using available ship today fastest transportation." The meaning is not immediately obvious and so it must be decoded. With some data transmission single words can be used to represent entire sentences with the data consisting of scrambled letters.

Data can be rearranged or modified for a particular purpose. A microphone, for example, takes spoken or musical data and converts it into a new form, the electrical equivalent of that speech or music. But although changed in the way it exists, it is still data. The data can be converted to pulses, and those pulses and the spacing between them are data, although the original form has been changed.

PULSE CODE

A pulse code (PC) is made up of a succession of pulses representing data. These can consist of pulses having varying widths and amplitudes and can also have different amounts of spacing. Typical examples are the Morse code, the Baudot code, and the binary code used in computers.

For compact discs the pulse code that is used consists of pulses of equal amplitudes and equal spacing. This does not mean that the code is simply a series of individual pulses followed by equally individual spaces. One, two or more pulses may follow each other with no spacing between them. Similarly, one, two or more spaces may follow each other uninterrupted by pulses.

BASIC PULSE CONCEPTS

There are two fundamental types of pulses: random and ordered. You can send pulses of current to a light bulb by operating a switch. These pulses are random and the order in which they are used is of no significance.

An ordered pulse is one that conveys information, also called data or intelligence, and does so in a specific pre-arranged manner. A sequence of such pulses is called a code. A prime example and the oldest of the family of codes is the Morse code, named after the inventor of the electric telegraph, Samuel F. B. Morse. The Morse code consists of a series of dots (dits) and dashes (dahs), but these are not random and each group represents a specific letter of the alphabet or punctuation.

Modulation

A modulated code is one that carries information and any code that does so can be said to be modulated. Current pulses that are triggered when a light switch is turned on and off repeatedly is a nonmodulated code, for the pulses of current do not carry a message. The Morse code used in telegraphy should have been originally identified as a modulated code, but at the time it was introduced the concept of modulation was far in the future.

The word "modulation" is commonly used in connection with AM, FM and television broadcasting but it is also applicable to any code used for carrying information. Carrying information, as used here, is not synonymous with portability. It does mean that the information or data available are converted from their original form into pulses whose arrangement is a representation of the data.

Figure 2-2 Random pulses are not modulated since they cannot be interpreted in terms of data.

A series of pulses can be produced (Fig.2-2) but these pulses, although of uniform amplitude and spacing, are random in the sense that they do not represent data. However, pulses can be changed in amplitude, in width, in spacing, in frequency, for example, with these modifications produced by sound. And when this is done, the pulse code changes from one which is random to a modulated code. Subsequently, the data can be extracted from the code with the data then returned to their original form.

Oddly enough, our earliest use of an electric current for the transmission of information was digital. Pulse codes for such transmission can be said to have started with the patent for a telegraph system obtained by Samuel F. B. Morse in 1840. The first message over the first telegraph line was sent from the U.S. Supreme Court in Washington, DC, on May 24, 1844, to Baltimore by Morse.

The pulses he sent via a wire consisted of a code made up of a series of long and short dashes, with each representing a longer or shorter flow of current. The data contained in the pulses represented letters of the alphabet. The strength of the current in the pulses has no effect on the transmitted data. The only difference was that pulses having a greater current amplitude could travel a greater distance (Fig. 2-3).

With the subsequent inventions of the phonograph and radio broadcasting, analog waveforms were used extensively. This was a natural development because we hear in analog. In the case of the telegraph system, the dots and dashes of the codes were changed mentally, with the brain working as a digital to analog converter.

Until 1983 high-fidelity sound systems were exclusively analog. The delay in using digital for audio sound systems was not by choice, for the technology that has

A	· —	N	— ·	Á	· — — · —	8 — — — · ·
B	— · · ·	O	— — —	Ä	· — · —	9 — — — — ·
C	— · — ·	P	· — — ·	Ė	· · — · ·	0 — — — — —
D	— · ·	Q	— — · —	Ñ	— — · — —	, (comma) — — · · — —
E	·	R	· — ·	Ö	— — — ·	. · — · — · —
F	· · — ·	S	· · ·	Ü	· · — —	? · · — — · ·
G	— — ·	T	—	1	· — — — —	; — · — · — ·
H	· · · ·	U	· · —	2	· · — — —	: — — — · · ·
I	· ·	V	· · · —	3	· · · — —	' (apostrophe) · — — — — ·
J	· — — —	W	· — —	4	· · · · —	- (hyphen) — · · · · —
K	— · —	X	— · · —	5	· · · · ·	/ — · · — ·
L	· — · ·	Y	— · — —	6	— · · · ·	parenthesis — · — — · —
M	— —	Z	— — · ·	7	— — · · ·	underline · · — — · —

(A) (B) (C)

Figure 2-3 Morse code and pulse equivalents representing the letters A, B, and C.

made digital sound recording and reproduction possible was not ready. In other areas digital techniques were applied in missile guidance, in calculators, computers, television, in security systems and telemetry data transmission.

ANALOG MODULATION

The most commonly used forms of the modulation of an analog waveform are in AM, FM and TV broadcasting. AM and FM are abbreviations for amplitude and frequency modulation. In all three systems, AM, FM and TV, the audio signal is superimposed onto a high frequency carrier wave. For TV, both audio and video signals are used to modulate a carrier. In these systems a separate carrier wave is required since the modulated waveform is to be broadcast.

PULSE MODULATION

In pulse modulation one of the characteristics of AM, FM and TV modulation, the carrier wave, is eliminated for use in connection with compact discs. A high frequency carrier wave is not required because the audio wave will not be broadcast.

Pulse modulation consists of the transmission of data in the form of rectangular pulses. In this case, transmission simply means the movement or transfer of the data by wire or cables or by magnetic tape from one component to another. The data can be conveyed by changes in the amplitude of the pulses or the time span they occupy, that is, by their widths or their position with respect to other pulses. Since these changes in the pulses correspond to the analog audio waveform, the process is referred to as modulation.

The different kinds of pulse modulation are known as pulse amplitude modulation (PAM), pulse duration modulation (PDM), pulse position modulation (PPM), differential pulse code modulation (DPCM), delta modulation (DM) and pulse code modulation (PCM) which is also known as linear pulse code modulation (Fig. 2-4).

Delta modulation is a variation of differential pulse code modulation. Of these different forms, the one used for compact discs and compact disc players is pulse code modulation. PCM was not selected arbitrarily but because of its many advantages over the other forms. PCM has virtually eliminated crosstalk, an operating condition in which sound from one of the stereo channels (either left or right) leaks into the sound in

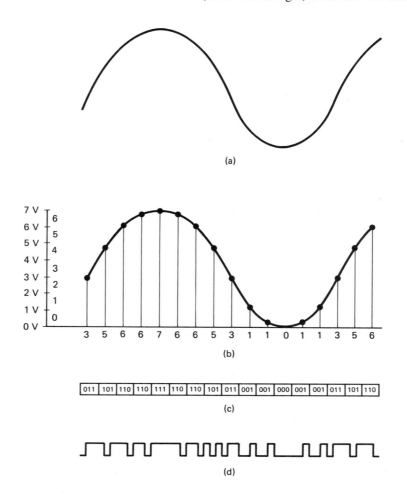

Figure 2-4 Formation of a digital pulse code: (a) analog waveform; (b) sampling; (c) analog-to-digital conversion; (d) corresponding digital pulse code.

the other channel. Dynamic range is considerably enhanced to such an extent it is frequently in excess of 90 dB; wow and flutter are so reduced that they usually cannot be measured. Further, pulse code modulation lends itself well to error correction. PCM systems are used by all branches of the military, Comsat, Intelsat, NASA, and private and public communications companies, including the Bell System.

The Pulse Carrier

In amplitude and frequency modulation, a separate high frequency carrier wave is generated. Thus, for both types of modulation two waveforms are involved: the audio modulating waveform and the carrier. For pulse modulation of any type, no separate carrier is required. Instead, the pulse waveform is produced by quantizing and sampling the analog audio wave.

Figure 2-5(a) shows a possible series of pulses resulting from sampling and quantizing an analog audio wave. The illustration refers to these pulses as a pulse carrier. They are obviously pulses, and they are a carrier in the sense that the number of

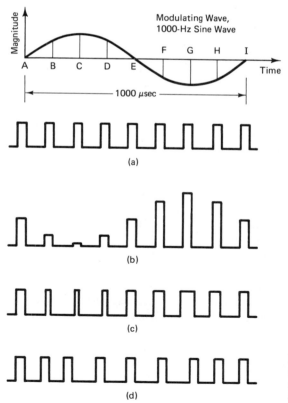

Figure 2-5 Types of pulse code modulation: (a) pulse carrier; (b) pulse amplitude modulation; (c) pulse duration modulation; (d) pulse position modulation.

pulses and nonpulses is a representation of the audio wave. These pulses are equivalent to a 1 kHz audio wave.

Figure. 2-5(b) shows the pulse shapes for pulse amplitude modulation (PAM). The pulses are equally spaced but their individual amplitudes correspond to the instantaneous voltages of an audio wave.

Figure 2-5(c) illustrates pulse duration modulation (PDM). In this case all the pulses have identical amplitudes but the width of each pulse is a representation of the instantaneous voltage strengths of the analog waveform. Thus, a wide pulse could represent a large voltage point; a narrow pulse a smaller voltage point.

The drawing in Fig. 2-5(d) shows pulse position modulation (PPM). A relatively large instantaneous signal voltage could mean a wider separation between pulses than a smaller voltage. The varying separations between pulses correspond to the voltage points of the audio wave.

Delta Modulation

The theory behind delta modulation (DM) is fairly complex but basically differs from PCM in the quantization technique used. With the delta system, quantization of a number of instantaneous voltage points on the analog waveform provides the basis for approximating the voltage points of succeeding values. If the approximation falls below the actual value at any sampling point, it is increased by a suitable amount, delta (δ). If the approximation is higher, it is reduced by an amount δ. The assumption is made that the audio signal does not change too rapidly from one measured point to the next. Distortion is produced when the size of δ is too small for a good approximation, while noise occurs when δ is too large.

It might seem that too many opportunities exist for δ to be too large or too small. However, with delta modulation, the analog audio waveform is sampled at 10 to 50 times the highest audio frequency. Using 20 kHz as the upper limit of the audio band, the sampling frequency could be 200 kHz to 1 MHz.

Obviously, the delta modulation technique must have considerable advantages for it to be considered competitive with PCM. The circuitry that would be used in a delta modulation type of CD player would be much simpler. There would be no need for high precision, fast-settling sample/hold circuits, nor would there be any requirement for a sharp low-pass filter to prevent aliasing.

Unfortunately, the delta modulator has limitations which presently preclude its use in CD technology. Its dynamic range, while adequate at low frequencies, drops at 6dB/octave throughout the audio range.

The meaning of pulse modulation, then, is some variation of a continous series of pulses based on instantaneous voltage values of an analog audio wave. In all of these, whether PAM, PDM, PPM, DM or PCM, sampling and quantization of the audio waveform are required. The resulting pulse structure depends on the type of modulation that is desired.

BINARY PULSE BANDWIDTH

The bandwidth of an unmodulated audio signal conventionally is taken to be 20 Hz to 20 kHz. By contrast, the bandpass of a video signal ranges from about 20 Hz to 4.3 MHz. The bandpass of a binary pulse signal is the product of the number of bits in the binary multiplied by the quantizing rate. Assuming a sampling frequency of 44.1 kHz and a string of 14 bits, the bandpass required would be $14 \times 44,100 = 61,740$ Hz or 617.4 kHz. By increasing the number of bits to 16, the bandwidth required increases. We then have $16 \times 44,100 = 705,600$ Hz or 705.6 kHz.

The trend in sampling, however, is to oversample using either two times or four times the sampling frequency of 44.1 kHz. For two times oversampling, the required bandpass for a 16-bit string becomes 2×705.6 kHz or 1,411.2 kHz, or approximately 1.4 MHz. For four times oversampling, the bandpass needed rises to 2.8 MHz. However, these numbers are minimum bandpass requirements for they do not take into consideration those bits that are used for special purposes, such as error correction codes.

No audio cassette deck or open reel deck can accommodate signal bandwidths that are this large. It can be done, however, by exposing the maximum amount of tape area to the record/playback heads of the deck and by using tape having the maximum particle density. Exposing the maximum amount of recording tape area to the heads can be done in several ways. The speed of movement of the tape past the heads can be increased, but this has the disadvantage of requiring large amounts of tape. Another method is to use a tape that has greater width, possibly one inch in preference to half-inch tape. Still another is to work with tape that has a higher particle density, with far more particles per unit area than ordinary tape. Other techniques include making the head gap narrower, or by moving the recording head and the tape in opposite directions.

However, there is an existing tape deck that can be used and that will easily accommodate the bandwidth needed by the binary signal and that is the video cassette recorder/player. This unit obtains maximum scanning of the tape by using rotating scanning heads which move against the tape in a direction opposite that of the tape itself. With this arrangement it is possible to utilize signals having bandwidths ranging up to a little more than four megahertz. Even if the scanning rate is increased by a factor of four ($44.1 \times 4 = 176.4$ kHz), this is well within the capabilities of a VCR, whether Beta or VHS format. Consequently, video tape decks can be used as a step toward the manufacture of compact discs.

THE PULSE CODE MODULATION TAPE RECORDER

The output of the master analog tape recorder delivers its recorded left- and right-channel sound signals to the L and R input of another component variously called a pulse code modulation tape recorder or a digital audio processor (DAP). Immediately following the input are a pair of low-pass filters (LPF). A low-pass filter (Fig. 2-6) is one which passes all frequencies below a selected value and attenuates higher frequencies. As the frequency is increased, the reactance of inductor L rises while the reactance of the capacitor C decreases. It is this combined L/C action which causes a rolloff of higher frequencies. The beginning of the rolloff point is determined by the selected values of L and C.

The effect of the low-pass filters is to eliminate aliasing noise. Aliasing noise signals can be caused by harmonics of the audio signal heterodyning with the sampling frequency. It is possible for the difference frequency (sampling frequency minus audio signal harmonics) to fall within the audio range. One of the advantages of oversampling, whether double or quadruple, is the much smaller likelihood of aliasing.

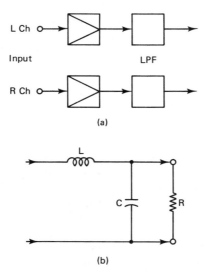

Figure 2-6 Input to a pulse-code modulator (a); low-pass filter (LPF) (b).

Sample and Hold

The left- and right-channel output of the low-pass filters are delivered to a pair of sample and hold circuits (S/H). At this time the analog left- and right-channel audio signals are sampled (Fig. 2-7), either at the basic rate of 44.1 kHz, or multiples of two times or four times this frequency.

The sample/hold circuit is controlled by a crystal oscillator, a timing generator. The hold circuitry can be compared to the charge and discharge times of a capacitor. In this case it is triggered by the timing generator. The function of the S/H circuits is to delay signals when required to make certain the left- and right-sound signals remain in phase or to keep any phase differences to a minimum.

In early PCMs samples were expressed in terms of 14-bit binary numbers, but later this gave way to 16 bits. Since this is an increase of just two bits, it would seem that such an increase would be insignificant. However, each bit value increases expo-

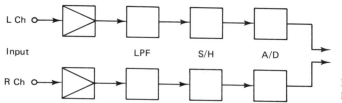

Figure 2-7 Dual sample/hold circuits follow the low-pass filters (LPF).

nentially rather than linearly with the digit 2 as the exponent. Thus, a 14-bit number when expressed decimally has a value of 16,383. However, if this is increased to 16 bits, the decimal equivalent is 65,535, an increase of four times the 14-bit decimal.

THE 16-BIT FRAME

It would seem that sampling the audio waveform must necessarily omit some part of the wave. There is a definite amount of time between each sample and, therefore, those parts of the wave between sampling periods are not quantized. As a result, some portion of the analog audio waveform must be missing in the binary equivalent, and so it is.

Now consider a motion picture. The picture is not actually in motion but consists of a series of still frames. When these are presented in a sufficiently rapid succession, we get the impression of motion. But in between each frame, there is a picture that we do not see because it is not recorded.

Each frame of a motion picture is comparable to quantization and each group of 16 bits corresponding to a single quantization could be referred to as a frame. The movement from one quantized point on the analog waveform to the next is so rapid we are not conscious of the absence of sound between such points.

Data not only consists of music but of pulse strings that control the operation of the disc player. These pulses are used for timing, for indexing, for locating the start and finish of musical bands, for turning preemphasis on or off, and for locating the first and last tracks on a disc. This type of data is arranged in the form of frames with the bits in the frames known as channel bits. A complete frame consists of 588 channel bits. The reason for organizing data into the form of frames is to enable the compact disc player to recognize the data, to recognize the differences between sync words, audio data, and parity bits. As far as audio is concerned, a frame is the amount of time required for six audio samples. But since we are working with stereo, we have six audio samples per channel for a total of twelve. These samples are delivered to the sample/hold circuitry in 22.7 microsecond intervals at the sampling frequency.

Analog to Digital Converter

Following the sample/hold circuitry, the left and right sound channel signals are led into a pair of analog to digital (A/D) converters. These converters accept the quantized signals and change them into strings of binary digits composed of 0s and 1s. It is here that the analog signal becomes a 16-bit pulse code modulation signal.

It is at this stage that the advantages of digital circuitry become apparent. All the A/D circuitry is involved in nothing more than a determination of whether the input signal at any moment is a 0 pulse or a 1 pulse. As far as electrical noise is concerned, or wow and flutter, or print-through, it is as though these did not exist for they do not appear in the A/D output.

The output pulses are not used immediately but are put into storage in the memory area of a small computer, with the release of the pulses precisely controlled by a quartz crystal controlled oscillator circuit.

If we are to reap the benefits of digital electronics, we have no choice but to use A/D converters. Everything has its price, however, and these converters are no exception. The conversion process always results in some inaccuracies, as the output is not a perfect representation of the input. The circuits are also capable of allowing random, unwanted information to leak into the system.

The Clock

Basically, a clock is a crystal-controlled oscillator and circuits of this kind are noted for the frequency stability of their signal output. Since frequency and time are related, the oscillator can be used to control the timing of associated circuits, either turning them on or off at precisely timed intervals (Fig. 2-8). The clock, also known as a clock

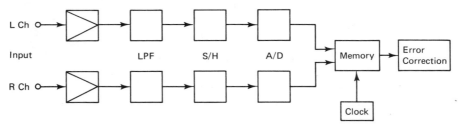

Figure 2-8   The binary pulses are temporarily stored in a memory, with the output controlled by a clock, a crystal-controlled oscillator.

generator or timing generator, has a sine wave output, and this wave can be modified into the form of a sharp pulse that triggers the on/off time of one or more circuits. If several circuits are triggered by the clock, they can be made to turn on or off at precisely the same time. Clock generators are used to control the on/off operation of sample and hold circuits, multiplexers, and A/D converters.

Subcoding

There are analog turntables equipped with programming features so the user can predetermine musical bands to be played or skipped. But this feature is not a part of the phono record and is handled by circuitry external to the disc.

In the case of the CD, however, various operational features are controlled by data that are encoded on the disc along with the musical information. To differentiate them from the codes used to represent musical data, they are known as subcodes and of course are in pulse form. Subcodes are used to control operational display information that appears on the front of the CD player; they are used to identify the time separation between musical selections; they are used for the search of specific musical bands and for repeat playing. Some compact discs are made with pre-emphasis, while others are not. Therefore, a subcode can be used to turn on a corresponding de-emphasis circuit in the CD player, or not, as required. Subcodes are used to control a display indicating the amount of remaining playing time or the time duration of musical bands on a compact disc.

Subcoding does not add audible sound to playback nor does its inclusion result in any sound distortion. Subcodes are added in the PCM in the form of 8-bit strings. Since subcodes will be in the output of the PCM they will be on the master tape used in the manufacture of the compact disc.

Multiplexing

Multiplexing is commonly known through its use in FM broadcasting and is a technique for the broadcasting and reception of FM signals. To emphasize that their receivers are capable of handling stereo channels, manufacturers refer to such receivers as MPX (multiplex) types. Multiplexing circuitry is used in the PCM for intermixing left and right sound channels so that these channels follow each other correctly—that is, left channel, right channel, left channel, and so on. The output of the multiplexer is then a single stream of data. Prior to multiplexing, the data were handled on a separate channel basis with the left and right channels of the sound processed individually. It is the multiplexer that merges these two channels so they form a single interleaved consecutive string.

Signal Output

Basically, the pulse code modulator is a device for sampling and quantizing an analog audio signal, adding control bits, and multiplexing the left and right channels into one. Following this processing, the output can be brought into a tape recorder. It is the output of this recorder that is used for controlling the data that is put on the compact disc.

The VCR Recording Method

A video cassette recorder (VCR) can have a bandpass capability in excess of 4 MHz and therefore is well suited to the recording of a pulse code modulated signal. The VCR, however, is designed for the recording of a standard NTSC television signal and it cannot accept any ordinary baseband signal. Consequently, a pulse code modulation unit whose output is to be fed into a VCR as the recording medium must be equipped with circuitry that will permit the pulse code to be modulated so it becomes the equivalent of a broadcast TV signal (Fig. 2-9). This means that the modulated audio pulse code occupies the position normally used by the video waveform. Sync and blanking pulses remain as part of the wave. The only difference between this wave and the usual NTSC signal is the substitution of the pulse code signal for video data. For example, if you were to connect the output of the VCR used in this manner to the input of a television set you would see the pulse data on the screen instead of a TV picture.

The block diagram of the PCM in Figure 2-9 is intended for producing a master tape that can be used for the manufacture of compact discs but its playback system can also supply an analog output signal for phono records. Such records are often labeled digital but are digital only in the sense that the analog signal has been processed by a PCM. This is the only relationship that such records have to compact discs.

One of the circuits used in the playback section of the PCM is a deglitcher. Glitch is a term borrowed from computer technology. It means a pulse or a burst of noise that results in errors due to signal dropouts. A deglitcher is any circuit that will work on a glitch, either eliminating it or suppressing it to some degree.

A glitch can happen when the value of the binary pulse changes from one value to another. As an example, assume the input is 0111111111 and changes to 1000000000. If the transistor in the digital to analog converter switches off faster than on, there can be a moment when the binary signal will drop to zero and will appear as 0000000000. This extremely large momentary decrease will show itself as a spike in the waveform. A deglitcher, then, can be be considered as being a member of the error correction family.

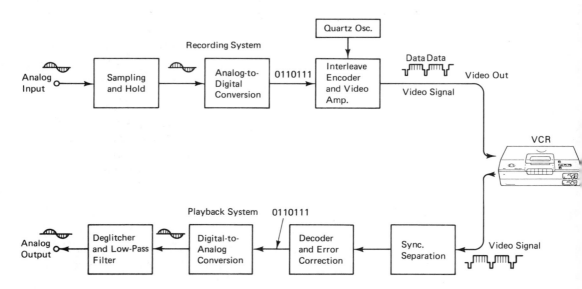

Figure 2-9 Basic PCM for producing a master tape for compact disc and analog phono record manufacture.

Figure 2-10 supplies more details of the dual purpose PCM. The pulse code produced by sampling and quantization is modulated onto a video carrier with the audio data taking the place of the video signal. The output of the PCM is supplied to a video cassette recorder and this unit supplies a master tape for making compact discs. That same tape can also be used for making phono records but the data on the tape must first be reconverted to analog form.

The block diagram of the video type PCM (Fig. 2-11) has two-channel input with the user having an option of a microphone (mic) amplifier or a buffer amplifier. There are a pair of mic amplifiers, one for left-channel sound, the other for the right channel. There is also provision for sound input from an analog turntable. This arrangement is used for the conversion of analog phono records to CDs. The single-pole, double-throw switch marked "input selector" is used to switch from mic input to turntable input.

Pre-emphasis can be used or not, as required, and is added to the input signal as it passes through a line amplifier. This is followed by a dither generator. Dithering is a signal processing technique and is a form of signal energy dispersal. It can be consid-

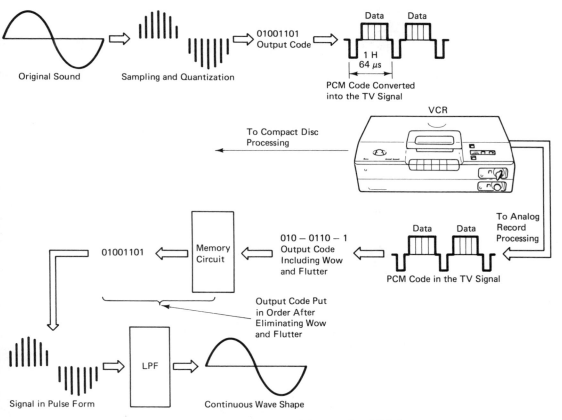

Figure 2-10 VCR used for recording PCM data.

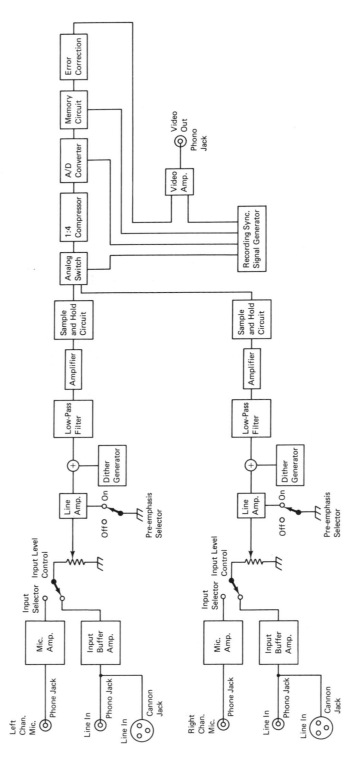

Figure 2-11 PCM for use with a VCR.

ered a form of modulation, but instead of using a sine wave, it employs a triangular waveform. The purpose of dithering is to spread the sound signal energy more uniformly over its band. Because the signal energy is no longer lumped, that is, concentrated at certain frequencies, there is less chance of left-right stereo channel interference. The signal is then passed through a low-pass filter, is amplified, and then delivered to a sample and hold circuit.

The two streams of data for the left and right sound channels are now made into a single stream of interleaved 8-bit data strings. Sync signals, including horizontal and vertical sync and blanking pulses as well, are fed into the A/D converter from a sync signal generator. The output of the A/D converter is supplied to a video amplifier and from there to an output terminal.

Pulse code modulator units designed to work with VCRs can use either VHS or Beta format types. The key is not whether Beta is or is not better than VHS, but rather on recording speed. In either case, best results are obtained by running the VCR at its highest speed: Beta 11 for Beta format VCRs and SP (standard play) for VHS recorders. Running the tape at a slower speed in order to get more recording time results in sound dropouts and breakup.

While a VCR can be used in conjunction with a pulse code modulator component, and was used during the early days of compact disc manufacturing, it can be regarded as an interim measure. Presently, PCMs are being made for the specific purpose of compact disc recording. A PCM can be a separate component or can be integrated with a tape recorder. In that case, the ouput tape is the master tape from which compact discs can be made.

If the PCM is to be used only for making analog discs a VCR is no longer needed because with analog we return to a 20 kHz bandpass. The composite video signal carrying pulse code information is first supplied to a sync separator circuit. The horizontal and vertical sync pulses and the blanking pulses which are necessary when the signal is to be delivered to VCR are no longer required and so these are stripped away. What remains is the binary pulse string which is supplied to an error correction circuit prior to being fed to the D/A conversion circuit. The binary pulses are supplied to a deglitcher and a low-pass filter. The output is the analog signal which can then be used in the manufacture of analog phono records.

The R-DAT Format

While the VCR was drafted for service as a pulse code recorder, there is also a component made specifically for the recording of digital pulses. Unlike the VCR, the R-DAT uses a small cassette, about one-half the size of a standard audio cassette, measuring 73 mm wide × 54 mm deep × 10.5 mm high. It uses a rotary head scanning system, similar in concept to video recorders. Its quantization is 16 bits linear and recording is in stereo. The tape speeds are 8.15 or 12.225 millimeters/second with a maximum recording time of 80 or 120 minutes, and a possible three hour capability. The key to its wide band recording characteristic is the rotational speed of its drum.

This is 2,000 rpm and the writing speed is 3.133 meters per second. A more detailed description of the R-DAT format is supplied in Chapter 13.

8-track PCM

Instead of recording all the binary data in the form of a single track on magnetic tape, that single track can be divided into eight tracks. As a result, the data transmission speed for each of the eight tracks is reduced to one-eighth that of the original serial signal. Consequently, recording of the digital signal can be done at a tape speed of 38 cm/sec.

This PCM unit (Fig. 2-12) is supplied with a tape recorder, an open reel type whose output can be connected to a disc cutting unit. As indicated in this block diagram, the initial input stages are similar to the PCM units described previously. The left and right sound channels are passed independently through a low-pass filter (LPF), sample and hold circuitry (S/H) followed by a pair of analog to digital converters (A/D). The left and right channel signals are then encoded in a block identified as RSC. Here an error correction code is added to the signal and the two separate channels are combined serially. The resulting signal is then split into eight tracks.

The PCM signal distributed between the eight tracks undergoes modified frequency modulation (MFM) and is then recorded on magnetic tape with a recording density of 797 bits/mm (20,240 bits per inch). The recorded tape that results from this process becomes the master tape and is used for the manufacture of compact discs.

The 8-track PCM can also be used for making digitally mastered analog phono records. The lower half of the block diagram in Figure 2-12 shows how this is done. The advantage in this method is that the demodulated MFM signal is completely free from the effects of wow and flutter.

The eight tracks of binary data on the tape are picked up by a group of playback heads with each head capable of handling two channels of data. The eight tracks are brought into a modified frequency modulation demodulator and are then delivered to a time base corrector (TBC). It is here that the eight tracks are recombined into a single track. The following RSC decoder handles error correction, restoring the PCM signal to its original, error-free form. The signal is then edited and separated into its left and right channels.

The rotation of the capstan of the tape deck is governed by a crystal-controlled servo. The servo control works on the basis of the difference in phase between the PCM playback signal and the basic reference signal in the recorder. This is necessary to make certain that the buffer memory responsible for eliminating the effects of wow and flutter will not be swamped with differences too great for compensation.

SIGNAL INPUT

While it is possible to use only a pair of microphones and to bring their output directly into the PCM as left and right channel sound, more often a number of microphones is

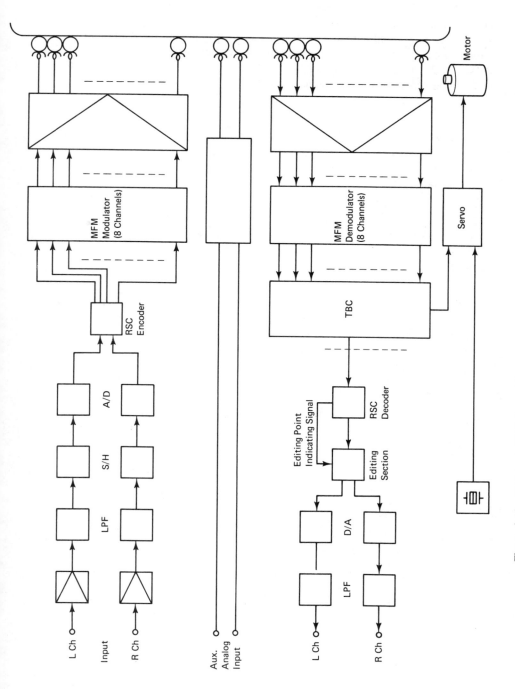

Figure 2-12 Eight-track PCM for making compact discs or digitally encoded analog phono records.

used. The audio voltages produced by these microphones are brought into a mixer and at this time all the sound tracks produced by the microphones are mixed down into a single pair. The sound is recorded on tape at which time controlled amounts of reverberation can be added. The mixer delivers the two channels of stereo sound to a PCM. The PCM may be a type used only for the production of compact discs, or for both compact and analog discs, or only for analog discs.

SIGNAL PROCESSING

The input to a PCM is analog audio and it is delivered by analog recorded magnetic tape. There are various kinds of PCMs integrated with a tape deck on which the output is recorded in digital form, ready for use in the manufacture of a compact disc. The output tape deck may be an external component and can be a VCR. The PCM can encode the audio signal into binary pulse form and then return that signal to analog by using a digital-to-analog converter for ultimately manufacturing analog phono records. But whatever the arrangement of the PCM may be, it includes signal processing circuitry.

Signal processing (Fig. 3-1) covers a wide range but basically it includes signal modification and error correction. Signal modification is usually considered with respect to analog signals and error correction with respect to those that are digital. However, there is some overlap.

One basic difference between signal modification and error correction is that signal modification is partially under the control of the user; error correction is under the control of automatically operating circuitry. Signal modification includes tone control circuitry, equalization (a more elaborate form of tone control), pre-emphasis (including de-emphasis as well), and companding (signal expansion and compression). Error correction includes interleaving, interpolation, parity checking and the Cross Interleave Reed-Solomon Code (CIRC).

ERROR CLASSIFICATION

Errors can be classified in accordance with the way in which they can occur or in the way in which they can be treated. A write error is produced when the PCM encodes its

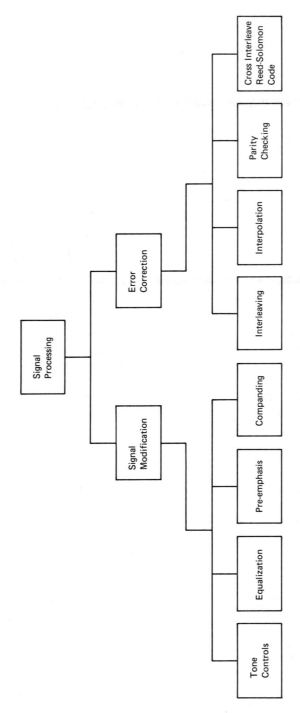

Figure 3-1 Steps in signal processing.

data on the master tape and that tape has dropouts. Another error called read error can be caused by a fault during the scanning of the compact disc by the laser beam in the CD player. Read errors can be subclassified as soft and hard. A soft error is one that can be corrected; a hard error is one in which the original data cannot be recovered. A disc may have a scratch or may be damaged to such an extent that the data that were encoded are lost irretrievably. A search error is one in which the laser beam is unable to locate the beginning of a band or cannot utilize indexing.

TWEAKING

Commonly in analog circuitry tweaking is done to obtain optimum performance from a circuit. This can be done by adjusting a variable resistor, a variable capacitor, by changing the inductance of a coil, or the position of a pair of coils with respect to each other.

Peaking is not required in digital circuitry. Binary pulses represent an on/off condition, so a circuit is either on or off with no in-between possibility. When a digital circuit is functioning, tweaking will not improve performance. This does not mean adjustments are never required but these are done simply to move from a nonworking condition to working state.

ERROR CORRECTION

Theoretically, the bits resulting from the quantization process may be encoded on a disc which may then be used as the original for the reproduction of a quantity of duplicates. But since quantization involves 2^{16} in binary arithmetic or a total value of 65,535, speaking decimally, the chances for error are enormous.

The problem becomes even more serious when you consider we will be working with stereo sound. If we use a fundamental sampling rate of 44.1 kHz per channel, then we will have 88,200 sampling bits per second. This means over 1.4 million bits produced every second (88,200 $\times$ 16). For the hour of music we expect to get out of a compact disc, the laser beam in our compact disc player will need to read over five billion bits.

If we could assume that every manufactured disc would be perfect, that it would never encounter dirt, dust or fingerprints, and that there would never be any quantization errors with each bit always in its proper place, then (and only then) could we record 16-bit groups directly on the disc without further concern.

How serious an error will be in a 16-bit code depends on which bit will be changed. If the change is in the least significant bit then the error is insignificant (Fig. 3-2). But if the error is in the most significant bit (Fig. 3-3), the error is substantial. Here we assume that just one bit will be changed, but it could be two or more bits.

Figure 3-2 There is a small percentage of total error when the error is in the least significant bit.

Figure 3-3 The percentage of error is large when the most significant bit is involved.

Error Correction Techniques

Errors in the binary numbers encoded on the compact disc can occur in manufacturing, by a scratch, particles of dust or by improper handling, by defects in the tape used in the PCM process, and a poor signal-to-noise ratio (S/N). As the S/N increases, the bit error rate decreases. For these reasons, as many as four different techniques are used for correcting errors that can appear in digital coding. They include parity checking, interleaving, EFM and interpolation. These error correction codes are also identified as linear, nonlinear, convolutional and word-oriented codes.

Types of Errors

Bit errors can also be categorized according to the kind of error. For example, it is possible to have a bit error that is not related to other bit errors and, therefore, is called a random bit error. Errors not only involve single bits but groups, with the fault known as a burst error. Since a word involves four groups of eight bits, errors in these are known as word errors. Errors that occur in blocks of bits are called block errors. Some error groups are long; others are short and, therefore, we could have a long-burst error or a short-burst error. Errors can happen in random order where a single recording could conceivably have all the types of errors just listed, although it is possible for a particular type of error to happen repeatedly if caused by a single, specific fault.

The type of error correction system used and the number of different error correction circuits will vary from one compact disc player to the next. Some compact disc players are often guilty of error correction overkill, unnecessarily distorting the program material being played. To overcome this, some players make use of a variable error correction system. In some instances, of course, error correction systems are unable to modify bit structure. It is possible for a three-beam laser pickup not to be able to read signals encoded on a CD because the disc is flawed or damaged. Generally, error correction circuitry will work if a bit, a group of bits or several groups of bits are not in their correct sequence.

Error correction is built into CD players for operation when the encoded program material on a disc is obscured. Without such systems, noise and/or distortion can be introduced. To avoid this error correction circuitry examines the signals surrounding those that are unreadable and fills the gap with information it calculates belongs there. While such systems are needed in CD players they can fill in more data than are actually necessary and are sometimes triggered by problems unrelated to the actual quality or condition of the disc being played.

There are circuit variations in the error correction systems used prior to the manufacture of compact discs and in compact disc players. Some substitute a fixed number of bits of information even when the unreadable data on the disc consists of fewer bits. An alternative error correction system varies the extent of its correction, keeping interpolated data to a minimum. This reproduces as much of the original musical signal as possible and results in more accurate sonic performance.

Interleaving

Interleaving (Fig. 3-4) is just one of the various error correction systems, and as its name implies, it consists in the rearrangement of bits or words so that a new sequence is formed. Obviously, if bits or combinations of bits are put into a new order during the CD manufacturing process, at some point in the handling of the audio signal in the CD player, an equal and opposite function will need to be followed because the bits will need to be restored to their original sequence. Such a process could be called de-interleaving.

Interleaving can be done by splitting a word and transposing the two halves and then repeating the process for all the words that follow. Another arrangement could be done on an individual bit basis using a selected number. For example, if that number is 4, then bit 1 becomes bit 5, bit 2 becomes bit 6, bit 3 becomes bit 7, and so on. If interleaving is done by words, it is then known as a one-word delay, if by two words, a two-word delay, and so on. In the de-interleaving process in the CD player, the signal data are fed into a random access memory (RAM), stored briefly, and then retrieved from that unit in the original sequence.

Manufacturers of compact discs all use some form of interleaving, although the individual interleaving methods may be different. Because of the tremendous number of

T	H	E	I	N	T	E	R	L	E	A	V	I	N	G	P	R	O	C	E	S
1	2	3	4	5	6	7	8	9	10	11	12	13	14	15	16	17	18	19	20	21

1	5	9	13	17	21	2	6	10	14	18	22	3	7	11	15	19	4	8	12	16
T	N	L	I	R	S	H	T	E	N	O	S	E	E	A	G	C	I	R	V	P

Figure 3-4 The interleaving process. The letters represent individual bits or words.

bits that is encoded on discs, it is possible to miss a substantial part of the signal, which is a form of dropout. Interleaving cannot eliminate this completely but it can minimize the results. For example, if there is a gap between two adjacent quantization points, interleaving can restore the quantization data that would have existed in that gap.

While error correction systems are used in the CD player, it is not possible for that player to make changes in the way the data is handled by those systems. In effect, the CD player has no option but to work with the disc in the way in which it was encoded. Generally, interleaving systems tend to favor word and half-word transpositions rather than single bit substitutions.

The significance of interleaving is that consecutive data bits on the recording tape are not in their sequential order on the compact disc. This means that a scratch will not affect data bits which immediately follow each other. As a result damage such as a scratch will not affect data bits which are sequential. For example, if a scratch does damage a series of consecutive bits, the interleaving process separates the series of bits in good condition from those that are not, interspersing good bits with defective ones.

Interpolation

Sometimes a bit error will be so severe that the error correction systems will not be able to cope with it. In that case the error will be overlooked and the processor in the CD player will try to make a smooth move from the last known good data group to the next known good data group. Unless the error is severe and continuous, the transition will be such that the listener will not be aware of what is happening.

Parity Checking

Line power surges and other intermittent electrical activity can cause bits to change their states, that is, a 0 bit can become a 1 bit, and vice versa. This most commonly occurs to only one bit in a string of millions and practically never happens to two closely located or consecutive bits.

Since each data element is either a 1 or 0, it is important that each should be in its correct place within a byte. For this purpose, an additional bit called a parity bit is added to each byte as a reference for checking to make certain the data are unaltered as they move through a system.

When an error occurs in the bits representing a decimal integer, the bit group may be known to contain an error but the particular bit at fault is not known. As an example, consider the decimal number 5. Its binary equivalent is 0101. If one of the pulses drops out, the binary equivalent could become 0001 and its decimal value is 1. Or it could become 0100 and its decimal value is 4.

In the parity checking method of error correction, the number of 1s in each group of bits is counted. An extra bit is then added to the group. If the bit count indicates that an even number exists such as 2, 4, 6, 8, then a zero bit is added to the binary group. If there is an odd number of bits, a 1 bit is made part of the group. The newly included bit is called a parity bit, and depending on whether it is an odd or even bit, calls attention to a possible error.

As an example, consider a group of bits such as 111011. This bit group is an odd order since it has five 1s. Consequently, a 1 parity bit will be added to it. However, if the binary number is 11011, it has only four 1s, and so a zero parity bit will be added to call attention to the fact that an even number of bits exists.

Parity bits do not change the value of a binary group. In the CD player they are recognized as parity bits and are used only as a check on the accuracy of the symbol. They make no contribution to the musical information on the disc. The parity technique just described is sometimes called even parity (Fig. 3-5) since the number of 1s in the binary group plus the parity bit is always an even number.

It is also possible to use an odd parity check and this is exactly the opposite of the even parity method. Figure 3-6 shows decimal integers from 0 to 9 and the corresponding binary code. The parity check will consist of adding a 0 or 1, depending on the total number of 0s in the binary. For an odd number of 1s the parity bit will be 0; for an even number the parity bit will be 1.

Of course, the parity checking method is not perfect whether you are using either odd or even parity bit checking. Further, the method does not determine which bit is missing, or whether a binary group has an extra bit. It does indicate something is wrong, but not in every instance.

To make parity checking more accurate, it is not done on the complete code, but on various combinations of bits in the code, so several parity bits may be used. Groups of bits in a symbol are selected so that the bits are covered by more than one parity check. By evaluating the results using a cross-checking method, it is possible to determine just which bit is in error or which bit is missing. If necessary, the entire

Decimal Integer	8421 Code	Parity Check	Decimal Integer	8421 Code	Parity Check
0	0000	0	5	0101	0
1	0001	1	6	0110	0
2	0010	1	7	0110	0
3	0011	0	8	1000	1
4	0100	1	9	1001	0

Figure 3-5 Even parity code. The binary code for CDs is sometimes called the 8421 code because of the arithmetic relationship of the bits to each other.

Decimal Integer	8421 Code	Parity Check	Decimal Integer	8421 Code	Parity Check
0	0000	1	5	0101	1
1	0001	0	6	0110	1
2	0010	0	7	0110	1
3	0011	1	8	1000	0
4	0100	0	9	1001	1

Figure 3-6 Odd parity code.

groups of bits forming a symbol can be determined. However, even with the most elaborate series of parity checking tests, there are still instances in which parity checking will not be able to determine just which bits are at fault. This could happen because of a scratch on the disc or a dropout on the tape at the time the code is being recorded.

Error Correction Overkill

Error correction is used when making compact discs and also in CD players. It is built into CD players for use when the encoded program material on a disc is obscured. Without such systems, noise and/or distortion would be introduced. To avoid this, the error correcting circuitry examines the signals surrounding those that are unreadable and fills the gap with information it calculates belongs there. Such systems are needed in CD players, but they sometimes fill in more data than are actually necessary and are sometimes triggered by problems unrelated to the actual quality or condition of a disc being played. Some CD players have an error correction system which substitutes a fixed number of bits of information even when the unreadable data on the disc consist of a lesser number of bits. However, a better arrangement is a system which varies the extent of its correction, keeping interpolated data to a minimum in every case. This reproduces as much of the original musical signal as possible and results in a more accurate sonic performance.

Apart from flawed or damaged discs, another reason correction systems are activated is vibration which is the effect of acoustic or mechanical feedback on a CD player's transport. Just as these factors affect analog turntables and induce unwanted motion which causes improper tracing of the record groove, they can be a problem during digital disc playback. This is directly related to vibration of the laser beam transport. In one player the entire laser transport system is mounted on a massive cast alloy subchassis. This is attached to the unit's main chassis by tuned rubber mounts that filter vibrations which could otherwise trigger the unit's error correction circuitry.

Cross Interleave Reed-Solomon Code

Invented by Reed and Solomon, this code is used for error correction. The code consists of a combination of parity checking and interleaving. While quantizing is carried on as a 16-bit process, the 16 bits are treated as a pair of sequential eight bits (or bytes). During the interleaving process, the bits are not interleaved individually but as eight-bit groups. The two halves, consisting of eight bits each, are encoded separately on the CD. The advantage of doing so is that damage to the disc, such as a scratch, will affect only half the recorded signal.

This does not mean the Cross Interleave Reed-Solomon Code (CIRC) can restore a damaged disc to pristine condition. The CIRC code can correct up to about 3,500 bits, a relatively small amount of the billions that are encoded on the disc. However, if a scratch does exist and has a width of less than 2.5 millimeters it can be repaired by the Cross Interleave Reed-Solomon Code.

When the CD's error correction system is at work, its effectiveness can be augmented if the unit has a dual eight-bit microprocessor control instead of the industry standard single eight-bit circuit. If one microprocessor reaches the limit of its ability, it passes the excess workload to the second, assuring smooth operation even in worst-case situations.

Eight-to-Fourteen Modulation (EFM)

The output of the CIRC circuitry is in the form of strings of eight bits and it would be ideal if these could be encoded as is in the process of manufacturing compact discs. But some of the eight-bit binary codes can be troublesome. Thus, it is possible to have such a code in which 1s and 0s follow each other directly. A code such as 10101010 would be representative. An arrangement of bits in this fashion decreases the reliability of playback. To overcome this problem a technique known as eight-to-fourteen modulation (EFM) is used. With this method, each byte (eight bits) has a 14-bit code substituted for it. As a consequence, 1 bits are spaced apart by two or possibly three 0 bits.

The need for EFM is a matter of getting the laser beam in the CD player to distinguish between adjacent pits and flats. The effect of tracking using an eight-bit code (Fig. 3-7) shows that the laser beam scans a pair of flats simultaneously. Note that the beam cannot recognize the transition from the flat identified as No. 1 to flat No. 2. The output should be 010, thus recognizing the existence of a flat between the two bumps. However, by using eight-to-fourteen modulation the effect is as though the pulse waveform had been stretched (Fig. 3-8) and so the laser beam recognizes that it has moved from a pit to a flat.

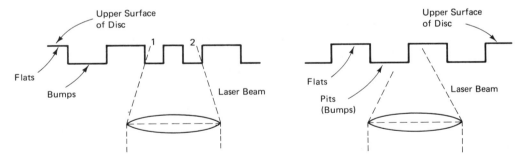

Figure 3-7 Effect of 8-bit code on laser scanning.   **Figure 3-8** Effect of 14-bit code on laser scanning.

The left and right channel audio signals are first sampled at a frequency of 44.1 kHz and then converted into binary representations by undergoing a 16-bit linear quantization process. A frame (Table 3-1) consists of six such sampled signals. Accordingly, each frame cycle is 7.35 kHz or 136 μs. With the EFM system, the sampled

TABLE 3-1. FRAME FORMAT. (Courtesy Sony Corporation of America)

	Data Bits	Channel Bits
Sync bits		24
Control/indication bits	$1 \times 8 = 8$	$1 \times 14 = 14$
Data bits	$12 \times 2 \times 8 = 192$	$12 \times 2 \times 14 = 336$
Error correction bits	$4 \times 2 \times 8 = 64$	$4 \times 2 \times 14 = 112$
Connecting bits & bits for supressing low frequencies		$34 \times 3 = 102$
Total	264	588

signal is first divided into two symbols, one consisting of the lower 8 bits and the other the higher 8 bits, and modulation thereafter is carried out on the basis of each individual symbol. EFM literally implies that each symbol of 8 bits is converted into 14 channel bits. The word "symbol" indicates 8 bits and is synonymous with byte.

The EFM technique has its limitations, as do other error correction techniques. There is no single error correction method that can ensure absolute accuracy in the process of converting from analog to digital form and then back to analog again. If the code is such that we have a pair of ls following each other directly, they must be separated by a pair of successive zeros. Another restriction is that there may not be more than ten successive zeros in any 14-bit string.

The 8- to 14-bit modification is referred to as modulation, since the audio signal represented by the original eight bits out of the preceding CIRC circuitry can be regarded as controlling the 14 bits. Consequently, in the compact disc player we must have a counter process, an EFM demodulator somewhere in the line prior to digital-to-analog conversion.

Using EFM circuitry, the digital output of the PCM is in eight-to-fourteen modulation form and that is the way it is recorded on the digital master tape. This means the compact disc is encoded with the binary data arranged in this manner.

PRE-EMPHASIS AND DE-EMPHASIS

Pre-emphasis and de-emphasis are in the category of signal modification and are not involved in error correction. Pre-emphasis for a compact disc consists of a 50-microsecond boost in the treble region. Its purpose is to improve the signal-to-noise ratio at the upper part of the audio spectrum and is supplied in preparation to making a disc. To obtain a flat frequency response an equal amount of de-emphasis must be produced in the compact disc player. De-emphasis is obtained automatically in the compact disc player and there are no user adjustments or controls. The 50-microsecond boost and counteracting 50-microsecond de-emphasis are standard.

OTHER ERROR CORRECTION CIRCUITS

The error correction circuitry used in a PCM will depend on whether the PCM is used for producing a binary encoded master tape only or whether the PCM is also to be used to produce a master tape for analog phono records. In the latter case the PCM could possibly include a deglitcher.

Deglitcher

A Schmitt trigger circuit can be used in conjunction with transistor-to-transistor logic (TTL) to convert their signals so they are free of glitches. The input signal must be able to pass through a pair of threshold values before there can be any change in the output.

The error correction circuits that have been described are not the only ones that exist. Binary coding was used in computers before PCMs, compact discs and compact disc players came on the scene with error correction circuitry designed for their special needs. Since error correction circuitry must be encoded on the compact disc requiring special decoding circuits in the player, it would seem unlikely that any changes would be adopted that would destroy the compatibility of compact disc players.

CODES AND ERRORS

The generation of an unwanted pulse or the elimination of an existing pulse results in an error. Depending on how serious an error (or sequence of errors) may be, the result can range from a sound change that may not even be noticeable to the inability of the compact disc player to reproduce one or more bands of music.

There are two types of codes: error detecting and error preventing. Codes such as the CIRC, EFM, and parity checking are error detecting codes. The Gray code (also called the cyclic or reflective code), is an error preventing code. It is called cyclic since it changes by only one bit as it goes from one value to an immediately following value. While the Gray code is used in computers, it has no application for compact discs and their players.

BIQUINARY CODE

The biquinary code is another that is used in computers but not in CD players or PCMs. The code is interesting because it supplies automatic parity checking and, therefore, falls into the category of error preventing codes.

The word "biquinary" consists of the prefix *bi* (or two) and *quinary* (five). This coding technique uses seven bits, a string consisting of two bits followed by a sequence of five bits. The two bits can exist in two forms only: as 01 or as 10. The decimal equivalent of the seven bits is the sum of the bi portion and the quinary portion of the code. The biquinary code for decimal integers 0 through 9 appears in Figure 3-9. For the five decimal integers from 0 to 4, the *bi* portion is represented by two bits and these are indicated as 01. For the five decimal integers from 5 to 9, the bi portion consists of two bits, 10.

The quinary portion is made up of five bits. The value of each quinary is increased by one by moving left one column. Examine the quinary corresponding to decimal 0. The 1 bit is at the extreme right. For decimal 1, the 1 bit is moved to the second column. Note also that quinary bits for decimal 0 through 4 are identical to quinary bits for decimal 5 through 9. In the bi portion of the biquinary, 01 = 0 and 10 = 5. The quinary portion can have any value ranging from 0 to 4. Biquinary-coded digits can be used to represent any decimal number and follow the same technique as for encoding decimal values into binary-coded decimal. A decimal number such as 306 can be represented as shown in Figure 3-10.

The disadvantage of the biquinary code as compared to the binary code is that the biquinary requires more bits per word. However, the advantage of the biquinary is that this code makes it easy to detect errors (Fig. 3-11).

Decimal Integers	Biquinary bi	Biquinary quinary	Decimal Integers	Biquinary bi	Biquinary quinary
0	01	00001	5	10	00001
1	01	00010	6	10	00010
2	01	00100	7	10	00100
3	01	01000	8	10	01000
4	01	10000	9	10	10000

Figure 3-9 Biquinary code and decimal equivalents.

Decimal Digit	Biquinary Code bi 5 0	Biquinary Code quinary 4 3 2 1 0	8421 Code 8 4 2 1
0	0 1	0 0 0 0 1	0 0 0 0
1	0 1	0 0 0 1 0	0 0 0 1
2	0 1	0 0 1 0 0	0 0 1 0
3	0 1	0 1 0 0 0	0 0 1 1
4	0 1	1 0 0 0 0	0 1 0 0
5	1 0	0 0 0 0 1	0 1 0 1
6	1 0	0 0 0 1 0	0 1 1 0
7	1 0	0 0 1 0 0	0 1 1 1
8	1 0	0 1 0 0 0	1 0 0 0
9	1 0	1 0 0 0 0	1 0 0 1

Biquinary-Coded Digits Can
Represent Any Decimal Number

3	0	6
↓	↓	↓
0101000	0100001	1000010

Figure 3-10 Comparison of biquinary and 8421 codes.

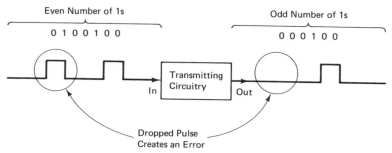

Figure 3-11 Because two pulses must be present, the biquinary code supplies automatic parity checking.

DOUBLE ERRORS

If a string of bits has a double error, an error may still be indicated by a parity bit but the ability to detect the particular faulty bit is lost. An error can also occur in parity digits. In that case it becomes difficult to know if the error exists in the word bits or the parity bits.

MISCELLANEOUS CODES

A code consisting of a sequential string of bits can have any values assigned to the bits. The binary code used for compact discs and compact disc players is sometimes called the 8421 code since these decimal numbers indicate the values of the first four bits, beginning with the bit having the least significant value. Another code is called the 7421 code and is similar to the binary code except that the high order digit has a value of seven instead of eight.

Any decimal value can be assigned to bits and this is done to achieve a particular operating advantage. Thus, it is possible to have a 6311 code, and 6421, 4321 codes, etc. Once a code has been selected, this does not mean the code cannot be modified. Thus the CIRC circuitry in a PCM changes a 16-bit code to an 8-bit code and following EFM circuitry changes the 8-bit code to a 14-bit code.

THE COMPACT DISC

It is now more than a century since the invention of the talking machine, subsequently called the gramophone, phonograph, record player and finally a turntable. Tremendous progress has been made in the intervening time, but the turntable still remains an electromechanical device with a stylus mounted in a cartridge traveling the grooves of a phono record. Tracking force, the pressure of the stylus against the record, is down to the weight of several postage stamps, and yet the wear of both the stylus and the record grooves is inevitable.

The quality of the phono record begins to deteriorate from the first time it is played. Common problems include hiss, hum, crackling and popping sounds and notable enemies include dust, dirt, finger smudges and the possibility of scratches created by the unwanted movement of the diamond stylus across the softer material of the record. To survive, a phono record must be treated very carefully.

The invention of the compact disc (CD) is the first complete departure from the turntable, using a completely different technology. The CD is not an improvement on the phono record; rather it is a complete breakthrough.

INCOMPATABILITY

Phono records and compact discs are not only incompatible physically but electronically as well. A compact disc will not fit onto a turntable and an LP cannot be squeezed into a CD player. Even if the physical interchange could be made, the electronics of the CD player and that of the turntable make compatability impossible. The output of the turntable and the CD player is the closest to which we can get in terms of similarity because both outputs are baseband audio, that is, audio not modulated onto a carrier.

For that reason, both can be a signal source for a stand-alone preamplifier, an integrated amplifier or a receiver with input audio terminals. But even here incompatability exists, for the turntable and the CD player cannot use the same input terminals on these components. The phonograph record is the predecessor of the digital disc so it is safe to say there has been a transition between the two, with many looking on the compact disc as the successor to the phono record.

Phono records are analog; CDs are digital. Their incompatability does not mean that analog and digital are mutually exclusive. What digital has done is to insert itself into the sound reproducing chain. The conversion of sound to its electrical equivalent is via a microphone, a sound energy transducer whose output is an analog representation of the sound input. The analog output of the microphone can be converted into its digital equivalent by an analog-to-digital device such as a pulse code modulator. Ultimately, however, the digital signal must be returned to its analog form for driving speakers or headphones. We can only hear in analog form and so the use of digital technology is only applicable in the high-fidelity system at some point or points prior to the speakers.

THE DIGITAL LP

It is possible to buy LP phono records with the words "digitally recorded" printed on the label, even though such records are analog types. They are analog since the grooves cut into such records are the analog equivalent of the electrical sound waveform. These phono records are called digital, not because of any digital techniques used in making the records which are strictly analog, but because digital methods are used in making the tape recording masters.

A typical tape deck, such as the cassette or open-reel types used in home high-fidelity systems, has analog record and playback components. In the manufacture of phono records the tape recorders may be referred to as digital but this is only because the audio signal is first converted digitally, using binary digits to represent the amplitude of the sound at selected moments. These binary digits, consisting of a sequence of zeros and ones, the only two digits that can be used in a binary system, are recorded on the master tape. It is the arrangement of these digits in a specific sequence that ultimately controls the cutting stylus in the production of a master phono disc. From that moment on, up to and including the pressing of phono records, the process is analog. And it remains analog up to and including the moment the sound is reproduced on a turntable equipped with a tonearm containing a cartridge complete with a stylus.

CD'S OFFICIAL NAME

The official name originally given to the compact disc is Compact Disc Digital Audio but this name was never accepted for popular use, possibly because no acronym could be formed from such a title. For a while they were popularly known as digital audio discs, and while the acronym immediately became the DAD, it too lacked popular acceptance. The acceptable designation today is CD, applied equally to the disc and its player.

ADVANTAGES OF THE COMPACT DISC

The advantages of the CD over the analog phono record are extensive. The compact disc has a wider frequency response, a much wider dynamic range (so wide, in fact, that it sometimes presents a problem), a complete absence of surface noise, lower distortion, especially intermodulation distortion, and longer playing time (one hour on a side compared to less than half that for a phono record). Wow and flutter figures are so low they cannot be measured with freedom from record warp, greater ease in handling, no need for equalization, no stylus wear and no physical contact with the surface of the compact disc so theoretically it should last indefinitely. There is greater accuracy of sound reproduction and less storage space as well. Hiss and record scratch are completely absent. Immediately prior to the beginning of play on a compact disc there is absolute silence and there is complete silence between the playback of the different compositions on the disc. There are no antiskating devices for none are needed. The compact disc is much smaller than the LP and requires less storage space. The compact disc but not the turntable can be used in the car. Stereo separation on the CD is superior to that of the LP. Still, there are critics of the CD claiming musical dissatisfaction. There are also critics of integrated amplifiers that use transistors instead of tubes. And in the early days of hi-fi, enthusiasts of monophonic sound claimed that stereo supplied a ping-pong effect.

THE HIGH-FIDELITY SYSTEM AND THE CD

The growing use of compact discs and compact disc players will inevitably have an effect on all the other components in the high-fidelity chain. Microphone techniques catering to analog records may need to be changed. The number and types of microphones for any recording may need to be modified. Inevitably, the other components including preamplifiers, power amplifiers, speakers, and sound processing equipment such as equalizers, may need to undergo an upgrading process.

WHERE IS THE SOFTWARE?

The various branches of a technology do not move forward in a uniform step. It took a long time for TV broadcasting and the manufacture of TV sets to achieve equality. The sole advantage of the phono record today is the availability of a staggering number of disc releases. Gradually, compact discs will reach that state, but we do have a growing number of categories including pop, rock, Broadway original cast recordings, country music, easy listening, samplers, soundtracks, spoken word discs, jazz, Christmas music, classical, and late releases. It is even possible to buy test discs for the evaluation and testing of CD players.

VITAL STATISTICS OF THE COMPACT DISC

The compact disc is 120 mm in diameter (4-23/32″), and has a thickness of 1.2 mm. The diameter of the disc is divided into several sections beginning with a center hole with a diameter of 15 mm, followed by a spindle support diameter of 50 mm. The storage area of the disc extends from the outer perimeter of this support section almost to the edge of the disc. The amount of data storage area on the disc is surprisingly small when you consider that just one side of the disc is used for this purpose. The working surface of the compact disc that is encoded with data is about one-sixth that of an analog phono record but it has more than twice the maximum playing time. The phono record requires the playing of both sides to have approximately one hour of playing time but the CD does this using just one side. This is an advantage in the playback of musical compositions that require 30 minutes to one hour since phono records need to be turned over while the compact disc does not.

The so-called tracks on the disc (Fig. 4-1) consist of pits and flats representing binary 1 and 0. Each pit is approximately 0.1 micrometer thick, 0.16 micron wide and about 0.2 microns deep, along a 2-1/2 to 7 mile long spiral track. To give you some idea of just how narrow the tracks are on a compact disc, about 60 of them can be put in the area occupied by just a single groove in an LP phono record. A typical compact disc will have 20,000 tracks in its signal area. While the playing time is 60 minutes, this does not use the full capacity of the disc since it has a maximum recording capability of 79.8 minutes on one side. The reverse side of the disc is not used.

The compact disc contains almost six billion digital sound signal bits. These bits are the binary equivalent of the instantaneous voltage values of the original analog audio signal. There are additional bits on the disc used for functions such as speed

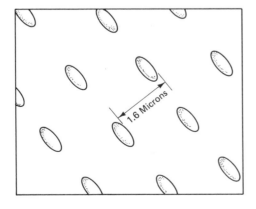

Figure 4-1 Track pitch is 1.6 microns (Courtesy Studer Revox America, Inc.)

control or error correction. The bits are laid out in a continuous helical track with 16 bits representing a single quantization of the analog waveform.

When the disc rotates in its player, its underside surface is scanned by a laser beam from the center toward the rim. Scanning of the pits and flats is at the rate of 1.6 million bits per second and since there are 3600 seconds per hour, the total number of bits is calculated to be 3,600 × 1,600,000 or 5,760,000,000 exclusive of control or error correction bits.

These approximately 6 billion bits are for audio information only and represent a minority of the total number of bits encoded on the disc. These are a little less than 20 billion bits and if we subtract the nearly 6 billion dedicated to the audio signal, the number of bits used for audio control—for error correction, parity checking, synchronization, eight-to-fourteen modulation, and subcodes is quite close to 14 billion. Basically, then, there are two kinds of bits on a disc—audio bits and working bits. The working bits are never heard in the sense that they do not produce sound.

The 20 billion bits used to describe the total amount of encoding on the compact disc will vary from one disc to another, depending on the number of musical compositions and their lengths. Twenty billion is an approximation and is supplied here to indicate the staggering number involved in a disc.

What is fixed, however, is the ratio of the working bits to the audio bits. The greatest number of bits is required by eight-to-fourteen modulation and comprises 41.8%. Following this we have 32.7% used for audio signal, 17.4% are required for the merging bits, 4% for synchronization, 2.7% for parity and finally 1.4% for subcodes (Fig. 4-2).

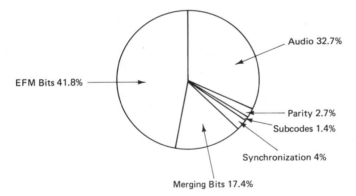

Figure 4-2 Relative percentages of audio and working bits. (Courtesy Josef Bernard and Radio-Electronics.)

BIT FUNCTIONS

If we add the number of working bits we will find they represent 67.3% of all those encoded on the disc. Consequently, bit control represents the greater part of what is put on the disc.

EFM Bits

Originally consisting of 8 bits, EFM represents a conversion to 14 bits. The use of this form of modulation means that it becomes possible to obtain binary zeros and ones more accurately from the encoded disc during playback. A 1 results every time there is a transition from a flat to a bump or a bump to a flat. The advantage of EFM is that it stretches the separation between the flats and bumps. When an 8-bit code is used, it is possible for the laser beam to cover a pair of adjacent transitions at the same time, producing an incorrect reading. This is eliminated, or at least minimized, by the code "stretching" that results from EFM.

Since the total number of bits is changed with EFM, their total digital value changes as well. This modulation takes place prior to encoding; consequently the 14-bit stream must be demodulated to its original eight bit form, a process that takes place in the CD player.

Merging Bits

Each group of 14 bits that result from EFM have 3 bits added, known as merging bits. Merging bits are required so that EFM works correctly.

Synchronization (Sync) Bits

The sync bits have various functions, one of which is to enable the CD player to supply audio data at specific points along a track. During the disc encoding process, a sync generator is used whose output is fed into a channel modulator that controls the recording laser. Sync bits are used to indicate the beginning of a frame.

In the pulse code modulator a recording sync signal generator controls the timing of an analog switcher, the A/D converter and memory circuits. In the CD player sync pulses control the timing of EFM demodulation, interpolation, the channel demultiplexer and the D/A converter(s). The sync pattern of 24 bits is produced by a sync generator.

Parity and Subcode Bits

Parity bits are automatic error correcting bits. Subcoding is explained in detail in Chapter 6. Subcode bits are used as control signals for the front panel display. They are also used to help identify the beginning of a musical selection.

To provide constant linear velocity the rotation speed of the disc is continuously adjusted. It is 500 rpm at the inside to 200 rpm at the outside. Tracking, decoding of the bits on the disc, and the rotational speed of the disc are minutely synchronized by a clock generator in the compact disc player, which in turn is controlled by data encoded in selected tracks on the disc.

In an analog phono record, the two channels of sound are contained in the walls of the groove with which the phonograph stylus makes contact. The stereo channels in the compact disc are sequential. There is just one continuous track, with left and right channel sounds following each other alternately.

STRUCTURE OF THE COMPACT DISC

Figure 4-3 illustrates the details of the structure of the compact disc. The laser beam strikes the underside of the disc, passing through a transparent layer that is 1.2 mm thick and having a refractive index of 1.5. The underside of the disc is the signal surface and it is on this surface that the laser beam is focused.

The spot size of the laser beam on the surface of the disc has a diameter of approximately 0.8 mm but when it is refracted by the transparent layer becomes as small as 1.7 μm at the signal surface (Fig. 4-4). This means that a bit of dust or a scratch on the surface of the disc is only a millionth in size on the signal surface. In fact, any dust or scratch less than 0.5 mm becomes insignificant and causes no error in

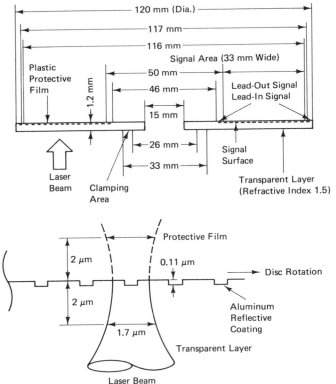

Figure 4-3 Structure of the compact disc. (Courtesy Sony Corporation of America.)

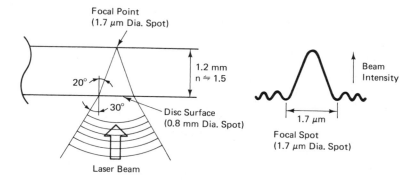

Figure 4-4 Laser beam focusing. (Courtesy Sony Corporation of America.)

signal readout. Accordingly, the disc does not need as much delicate handling as the conventional phono record.

This does not mean that the disc is immune to dirt and scratches. Dust particles aren't uniform in size and there are scratches that can be troublesome.

The signal surface beneath the transparent layer contains a series of tiny pits impressed outward from the inner circumference at a pitch of 1.6 μm. Technically, they are bumps but are often referred to as pits.

A pitch of 1.6 μm means that there are over 20,000 tracks composed of such pits in the signal area. The unusually narrow track pitch of the compact disc means that the center hole and track arrangement must be precise. The accuracy of the disc's track pitch is equal to that of the pattern used in making a large scale integrated circuit. Highly accurate cutting and stamping techniques had to be developed specifically for the manufacture of the discs. In addition, an advanced tracking servo system had to be devised to assure precise tracking by compensating for the slight deviation (within 0.1 mm) in the center hole size.

The pits and reflective surface in the disc correspond to one and zero in digital data. In other words, various digital information is represented by the presence or the absence of the pits on the signal surface.

The height of each pit is a microscopic 0.11 μm. This figure is very close to but slightly smaller than the quotient obtained by dividing the laser wavelength (λ = 780 nanometers) by 4 and then by the refractive index (n = 1.5). One reason for selecting this height of the bumps is to make the tracking error detection easily available.

PITS, FLATS, BUMPS, AND LANDS

Before a compact disc is encoded its upper and lower surfaces are absolutely flat. The lower flat suface is the area that is made highly reflective and it is this surface on which the laser beam is focused. At the time the disc is manufactured, the stamper is applied to the upper surface. The stamper produces a series of depressions in the surface called pits. So what we now have are flat areas, not affected by the stamper, and a series of microscopic depressions. To distinguish between them, the depressed areas are called pits. Thus, we have a succession of flats and pits, but remember this is our view from the upper surface of the disc. This is the surface of the disc to which the label will be attached and this is the surface you will see when you put the disc into the disc drawer of the compact disc player. It is not the working surface of the disc. It is the lower surface that is important, for this is the surface that will be read by the laser beam.

The stamper that was used on the upper surface not only changed it into a series of flats and pits, but affected the lower surface as well. The pits on the upper surface produce a series of bumps on the lower surface but the flat areas (also called lands) will remain unaffected. So what we now have on the lower surface is a series of flats and bumps. The bumps extend slightly above the flats. But since the flats are now beneath the level of the bumps, we call them pits. Remember, however, that these pits are still part of the flat area of the undersurface, are highly reflective and it is on these that the scanning beam is focused.

What is the purpose of the bumps? Since they are not focal points, they act to interrupt the scanning beam, and so what results is a beam-switching action. The important feature of the pits and bumps is that it is the transition from a flat to a bump or a bump to a flat that produces the binary transition from a 0 to a 1 or a 1 to a 0.

DISC GROOVES

The 5 km long information groove of a compact disc contains a complex digital signal consisting of interleaved digital values from two audio channels representing the musical information. Auxiliary information for indicating the selections such as the tracks and playing time is also stored in this information groove. While the word "groove" is used here, there are no grooves on the compact disc and the word is simply a carryover from analog phono records. A better word to use is "tracks" with the understanding that this simply indicates the encoded spiral of data, and that it is not visible as such. Generally, track is used to refer to a complete musical selection. This can be a single selection on the disc, as in the case of a disc encoded with a number of musical compositions, or it can refer to an entire disc, as in the case of a concert or an opera. Sometimes a track is called a musical band, or simply a band, again a carryover from the language used with analog phono records.

Inevitably, comparisons will be made between tape and compact discs. Both have their functions and purposes and there is no reason to believe that having one eliminates the other. The greatest advantage of tape is that it is a recordable medium. Like a blackboard it can be wiped clean and used over and over again. But when considered from the viewpoint of playback, only the compact disc has a much higher recording density; area for area, we can get much more data onto a disc. The disc also has a much higher stability, since it is completely unaffected by extraneous magnetic fields.

From the viewpoint of wear, dirt, handling, and warpage, the compact disc is superior to the analog phono record to such an extent that a myth has developed that the compact disc is indestructible. Like the familiar analog record, the discs can contain manufacturing defects and may even be scratched. During play, even flecks of dust can lead to signal dropouts in severe cases.

DISC LAYERS

The compact disc consists of three layers. A relatively strong transparent substrate is coated with an ultrathin aluminized layer on which the information is encoded. The label listing the contents, the artists, and the disc brand is printed on this layer on the upper surface of the disc. The varnish and the ink applied during the printing process are the only protection of the aluminized layer.

Although the laser pickup scans the opposite side which is more completely protected, a scratch on the printed side of the aluminized layer can interfere with or even prevent playback of the compact disc. The pitch of the information grooves on the compact disc is only 1.6 microns and the average bit length is approximately 2 microns (2/1000 of a millimeter).

THE NEED FOR DIGITAL RECORDING

There are two basic methods of transmitting information: digital, as in the case of telegraphy, and analog, as in the case of telephones. Both have advantages and both are essential, but digital is superior in at least one important respect. Consisting of coded signals, telegraphy is far less subject to electrical interference, noise or distortion. In broadcast communications a coded signal can often get through at times when sound signals become unintelligible.

Similarly, the audio pulse code used by CDs is not affected by noise or distortion. It simply needs the presence or absence of pulses to be able to recover the original analog audio waveform.

THE SIGNAL SOURCE

The initial steps in the manufacture of a compact disc follow the same steps used for making phono records. Two or more microphones (usually more) are used for recording the sound. As more experience is acquired with compact discs, it may be that microphone placement will change with some microphones taking advantage of the wide frequency response of the compact disc.

The electrical signals representing an analog of the sound are brought via cable into a mixing console under the control of a sound engineer who can modify the sound by emphasizing some tones, attenuating others, strengthening the output of some instruments, and weakening others. The individual musical instruments or a group of such instruments are then recorded on a multitrack recorder. Some of these machines have as many as 24 or 32 tracks positioned side by side on the tape. The term "tracks" is possibly an unfortunate choice for they are not visible and are tracks only in the sense that they are recording paths. When using multitrack recording, separate microphones are used for each musical instrument or a small group of instruments supplying sound for a particular magnetic recording track.

These tracks are subsequently mixed down and are ultimately joined into two tracks for stereo reproduction. In this way the music is carefully controlled. The alternative to this process requires extremely careful positioning of the microphones and is sometimes preferred by sound engineers who have considerable microphone experience.

The multitrack method does have its advantages since the musicians need not necessarily perform at the same time and when they do, they can be separated at some distance from each other. Following the mix down process, the signal which has been analog up to this time is brought into a random access PCM editor.

The output of the PCM is brought into a tape recorder and almost ten times as much dynamic energy can be impressed on the tape before tape saturation as compared to analog recording. The pulse signal brought into the recorder is well above the noise floor and well below the tape's saturation level. With the recording of pulses, harmonic distortion and the even less desirable intermodulation distortion are nonexistent. Various modifications are made in the PCM with 50 microsecond pre-emphasis added to the treble end, track numbers and indexes, and subcodes are included.

HOW COMPACT DISCS ARE MADE: AN OVERVIEW

The disc is made of a clear polycarbonate plastic which initially is at a sufficiently high temperature to be in a molten state. It is then molded into its circular shape having a diameter of 220 millimeters. One side of the disc is stamped with millions of microscopic pits and then coated with a fine film of aluminum. The film is then covered with an equally fine layer of plastic. This is the business side of the disc and is the side that is scanned by a laser beam in the compact disc player. It is also the side that faces downward when inserted into the CD player. Scanning is done from underneath. The upper side of the disc plays no part in the reproduction of sound. Alternatively, some discs are made of optical glass instead of plastic. Virtually all CDs are made with a 50 microsecond treble pre-emphasis to improve the high-frequency signal-to-noise ratio. A complementary de-emphasis curve must be applied on playback to restore flat frequency response.

Manufacturing Cleanliness

Cleanliness is as essential in the manufacture of compact discs as it is for phono records. A speck of dust not visible to the naked eye can be like a stalled car on a railroad crossing. A clean room for making CDs has no windows; the air that is brought in completely controlled. It has the dust particles precipitated, and the air is washed and dried, so when it is finally permitted to enter the disc room it may have fewer than two or three particles of dust in a cubic foot of air. The largest of these particles is smaller than a fiftieth of the diameter of a human hair. A meter having a large scale readout in digital form indicates the number of dust particles in the air per unit volume. At times the meter reads numbers such as 3, 2 and 1, and occasionally drops to zero. By comparison, the operating room of a typical hospital is like a sink of sludge.

Imprecision in Recording

When a phono record is made, the undulations in the grooves of that record are an analog representation of the sound. The best that can be said of it is that it is an excellent approximation but never absolutely precise. The cutting stylus in the making of a master record is a physical device and as such is governed by the laws of inertia. It cannot start, stop, or change direction instantaneously.

Digital recording is more precise since it depends on numbers, but this is not to say that digital is completely exact whereas analog is not. Precision is a relative matter. The quantization of a sound wave produces binary numbers which are good approximations of the instantaneous amplitudes of the sound. These binary numbers are whole numbers only and do not have binary fractions, even though the amplitude being measured at any one moment could be represented by a binary whole number plus a binary fraction. As a result the compact disc is not without distortion, although it is much better in this respect than analog phono records.

MAKING THE COMPACT DISC: THE DETAILS

The production of the compact disc can be listed under two main headings: mastering and molding. The mastering process starts with the work of polishing a plain glass optical disc. This disc has an outside diameter from 200 to 240 mm, a thickness of 6 mm and undergoes various cleaning and washing steps, including supersonic cleaning. During its manufacture, the disc is kept under strict quality control with an automatic glass disc inspecting instrument used to examine the surface of the disc and to confirm that defects such as scratches and dirt do not exist. If the disc passes inspection, it is polished (Fig. 4-5).

The glass disc is then coated with a thin chrome film or coupling agent, a step that is taken to produce adhesion between the glass disc and a photo-resist, which is a photosensitive material.

At this time we have two products that are to be joined. The first is the binary coded signal recorded on the compact disc master tape and the other is the glass disc. The data on the CD master tape is now transferred to the glass disc by a laser beam cutting method (Fig. 4-6).

Note the difference here between cutting an analog phono record and a compact disc. With phono records sound grooves are formed on a lacquer disc surface by using a cutting lathe. For compact disc production a laser beam is used. This type of cutting

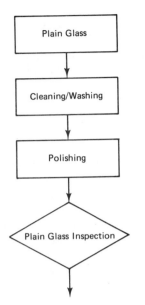

Figure 4-5 Initial steps in the manufacture of a compact disc. In some CD
factories plastic is used instead of glass.

```
┌──────────────────────┐
│ Adhesive Layer Coating │
└──────────────────────┘
            │
            ▼
┌──────────────────────┐
│  Photo Resist Coating  │
└──────────────────────┘
            │
            ▼
┌──────────────────────┐
│  Laser Beam Cutting    │
└──────────────────────┘
            │
            ▼
```

Figure 4-6 Steps preparatory to laser
beam cutting.

has a tremendous advantage since the laser beam does not have the inertia of the mechanical cutter. The impressions caused by the laser beam are applied at a 1.6 micrometer pitch from the innermost circumference of approximately 46 millimeters to the outermost circumference of 116 millimeters. The sound recording device is actually composed of a glass disc rotating system having a constant linear speed of 1.2 to 1.4 millimeters per second and a transfer mechanism that forwards the laser cutting head at a 1.6 micrometer pitch.

Working within such extremely fine tolerances means there must be no deviation of the laser beam. Consequently, the laser beam system is mounted so as to be free of any external vibration. The surface of the disc is still completely flat at this time because no pits have been formed. The pits are formed by photographically developing the glass disc.

The glass disc is now subjected to a nickel evaporation process (Fig. 4-7), a method that makes the surface electrically conductive.

The disc, now known as a glass master, is inspected automatically not only for its electrical characteristics but also for the number of dropouts. Dropouts, as used here, means the lack of formation of pits or the possible development of pits in areas that should be flat.

Following the quality control inspection of the glass master, the next step is nickel electrocasting which is similar to that used in making analog phono records. In the case of compact discs, however, to correctly and faithfully copy the microscopic pits, the work is conducted under environmental conditions several times stricter than those

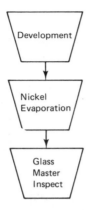

Figure 4-7 A glass master is produced
by a nickel evaporation process.

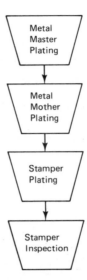

Figure 4-8 Metal stamper is produced
from a metal mother.

applied during the production of phono records. The disc undergoes a series of metal replications resulting in a disc called a stamper (Fig. 4-8). The stamper is equivalent to a photographic negative in the sense that it is a reverse of the final compact disc. That is, we now have bumps where we should have pits. It is the stamper that is used for making the final copies, the compact discs.

Making a master for compact discs can be done only under what should be called laboratory conditions. Extraordinary precision is required since the pits have dimensions measured in millionths of a meter, and further, the number of pits is in the billions. The pits and flats not only carry the music but identifying numbers as well. This indexing permits the user of the compact disc player to find any composition on the disc in a matter of seconds, not necessarily in sequence but in any random manner.

Molding

Using the stamper, discs are then produced by an injection plastic molding process. If we regard the stamper as equivalent to a negative, then the molded disc can be regarded as a positive. What we now have is a plastic disc with its pits and flats. It is then subjected to an aluminum evaporation process which is necessary for several reasons. The pits and flats must be strengthened to avoid any possible deformation of the plastic. Furthermore, a reflective surface is needed since the pits and flats will be scanned by a laser beam in the compact disc player. The aluminum is deposited as a fine film by an aluminum evaporation method. The aluminum is carefully selected to have a high order of reflectivity. To protect the aluminum film, ultraviolet-ray-hardened resin is coated over that film. This type of resin satisfies such requirements as good bonding ability with the aluminum film, excellent surface hardness and erosion or corrosion resistance. Not just one but several coats of the resin, sometimes referred to as plastic, are applied to a thickness of 5 to 6 millionths of a meter. The hardening of the plastic is rapid and takes place in several seconds (Fig 4-9).

The final step is the printing of the disc's label. The printing is applied directly over the protective layer surface with a special kind of ink made of ultraviolet-ray-hardened resin. This, incidentally, is the same resin that is used as the protective layer covering the aluminum film base.

Final Testing

Final testing of the manufactured disc begins with a visual inspection to determine the existence of any foreign matter or scratches on the disc. Ordinarily in the production of analog phono records, the playback of randomly selected records is a matter of routine. Compact discs, however, are not dependent on listening tests. This is because digital recording characteristics incorporated into the compact discs permit automatic inspections through signal reproduction of the error rates, positions of dropout occurrence and other defect factors.

While there is less dependence on listening tests, this does not mean such tests are not done. Such tests are performed on discs selected at random, often out of inventory, as a check on sound quality. CDs that are ready for shipment are housed in plastic cases and are wrapped in thin sheet plastic. None of the discs are exposed, as is often the case with phono records sold in jackets. The intent here is to keep the discs as dust free as possible (Fig. 4-10).

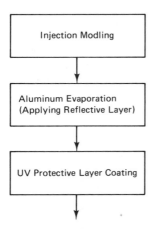

Figure 4-9 Reflective layer is coated with plastic.

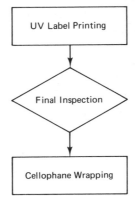

Figure 4-10 Label is printed on top side of disc.

DITHER

The music supplied by a phono record carries along with it the noise of the prior tape recording process. This consists of noise due to the random distribution of the magnetic particles on the tape generating low level signals more familiarly known as tape hiss. As a result, when listening to a phono record we hear what could be referred to as a noise floor most evident when the stylus tracks the unmodulated grooves of the record. During playing of the record, we may not be as conscious of the noise because of masking effect, a condition in which noise seems to become inaudible when in the presence of a much louder sound.

While we can hear a noise floor when listening to LPs, such noise is not present when listening to compact disc playback. Some people who have installed compact disc players find this disturbing and, therefore, digital audio engineers have added random noise to CD masters, a technique known as dither. The choice of this word is unfortunate since it is also used (as indicated previously) for an entirely different purpose.

Not all CD manufacturers engage in dithering, a technique which seems to work at cross purposes with the achievement of the compact disc. The sound supplied by the compact disc is practically identical with that recorded on the PCM's tape deck, an advantage negated by dithering.

COMPACT DISC SOUND

In terms of specs, compact discs and disc players are superior to phono records and turntables. In the final analysis, however, it is what we hear that counts. At one time speakers made in Japan were said to exhibit a characteristic called "Japanese sound" and speakers made in New England as having "New England sound." You will also hear references made to "compact disc sound," a subjective evaluation that seems immune to criticism. As in the case of phono records, the playback capability of a CD will be dependent on the quality and capabilities of the compact disc, the player, the following preamplifier, power amplifier and particularly on the speakers. A poor speaker system or a room with untreated acoustic deficiencies, will not permit the compact disc to deliver the best sound. Whether the CD will replace the phono record is a moot point and perhaps not too important.

DATA STORAGE

A tremendous amount of data is stored on the compact disc and while the music is the most important, it is not the only information. Since the maximum possible digital encoding on the disc is about 70 minutes, it is possible to play long concerts without interruption, something the analog phono record cannot do. However, because the listener is interested in searching for and playing selected musical passages, corresponding information must also be encoded on the audio track. There are two methods of doing this.

For example, if the total musical content on the disc can be subdivided into individual selections, these can be separated by short, silent grooves. On the compact disc these selections are identified as tracks. The information accompanying the disc includes the track numbers and the compositions corresponding to those numbers. A control on the CD player permits selection of any desired track in any order.

A different method of subdividing the musical content of the disc is through the use of indices, with the word "index" used to represent the singular and plural. Indexing is mostly used with classical recordings. With indexing, either a particular selection or some part of the composition can be chosen for listening.

The subdivision of compact discs is determined not by the manufacturer of the compact disc player but by the manufacturer of the discs. On recordings comprising several sections for which no indexing is used, the starting time, referred to as CD time, is specified on the disc's jacket. Each compact disc is also subdivided into minutes and seconds of playing time. Any location can, therefore, be accurately and reproducibly accessed. Accessing by CD time is known as CD Time Mode.

DISC GLOW

The surface of the compact disc glows with rainbow-like colors when the disc is held up to the light. This is caused by the diffraction of light from the micron sized tracks encoded on the disc.

ALTERNATIVE USES FOR THE COMPACT DISC

Because the compact disc is considered primarily as a supplement to analog phono records, or even as an ultimate replacement, it is not generally realized that the CD has potential in other directions.

Four-Channel Sound

What we hear when attending a concert in a music hall, for example, is not only the pleasure of music that is live versus its recorded version, but music with greater depth. We hear the direct sound (also called dry sound) of the music from the performers and also the reflected sound from the walls, ceiling and floor. This reflected sound, or reverberant sound, arriving at our ears slightly delayed in time because of the greater distance the reverberant sound must travel, adds richness and depth of sound. Consider how much more enjoyable sound is in a concert hall than the same sound played outdoors.

Four-channel sound is an effort to recreate a desirable listening condition in the home. While compact discs are made for stereo, they could also be made to supply both dry and reverberant sound. Since the two extra channels would require more space for the additional pits and flats, playing time would be reduced. While CDs for four-channel sound could be made, none are presently being manufactured. CD manufacturing is concentrating on catching up with the much larger number of releases available in phono records.

Compact Disc Video

Although a compact disc can supply a full hour of playback time, this does not mean the total capacity of the playback side has been used. Each CD has unused areas which can be dedicated to other purposes. One approach has been to use a CD still picture adapter. This means the listener will be able to view the accompanying song, lyrics, or musical score possibly accompanied by color illustrations. It will require the use of an RGB (red, green, blue) monitor instead of the usual TV set.

Using a Still Picture Adapter

Also known as CD-Still Frame Graphics, two still picture modes are possible: line graphics mode, supplying one picture every three seconds, and a TV graphics mode (one picture every 12 seconds). Depending on the mode that is selected, each compact disc is capable of holding up to 1,200 pictures in addition to 60 minutes of high-fidelity music.

CD-Draw

This is an acronym for CD-Direct Read After Write and envisions a type of CD that would be recordable. Like phono records, compact discs are designed for playback only.

CD-Cada

Cada is an acronym for cable digital audio. The first two letters, Ca, are taken from the word cable, while da is from the first letters of digital audio.

CD-ROM

The compact disc player is intended for use as a sound source, supplementing a turntable, a cassette or open-reel tape deck, and AM or FM broadcasts. However, its development has opened the way for comparable, but not identical systems.

One of these is the CD-ROM (compact disc read-only memory) using a 4.72-inch compact disc. CD-ROM information can only be accessed by a CD-ROM drive and not by an audio compact disc player. Instead of having its output connected to a high-fidelity sound system, the CD-ROM drive is connected to a microcomputer with the output of the disc shown on the computer's monitor.

The substantial advantage of the compact disc in this application is its ability to work as a large data base, storing up to 550 megabytes. This is comparable to more than 1,500 floppy diskettes. A floppy disc is a magnetic medium; the compact disc CD-ROM is binary encoded data. Instead of using a compact disc player, the CD-ROM requires a CD-ROM drive.

5

THE COMPACT DISC PLAYER

Both the phono turntable and the compact disc player are electromechanical devices but in the phono turntable the mechanical section and the electronics section are fairly independent. With the compact disc player, the mechanical components are controlled by the electronics.

Turntables used for analog phono records are characterized by operating conditions which can only be regarded as flaws. These include record placement, cartridge alignment, physically cueing and searching for tracks, adjusting tracking weight, and antiskating. The rotation of the record produces an electrostatic charge that attracts dust requiring the use of a dust cover. And you do hear noise from the moment the stylus is placed on the beginning track and also between bands. Playing degrades records since some modulated material in the groove walls is inevitably removed by the stylus.

The CD player is totally noiseless and absolute silence precedes each track. The only sounds you will hear are those produced by the motor that operates the disc drawer and you will not even hear that if loading of the disc is handled by a spring-loaded device. You need not be concerned with a center spindle. There is no speed adjustment control for none is needed. You will never need worry about stylus wear and replacement. The compact disc player is not subject to acoustic feedback even if you like playback at high volume levels. You will not need to be concerned if the player is not absolutely level, which is a concern with turntables.

DIGITAL DISC VERSUS ANALOG PHONO: A SUMMATION

While the input to a compact disc system is analog, as is its output, the CD is not simply an improvement over analog but a complete replacement. This is evidenced in

73

the following brief summation (Table 5-1), which is a comparison of their physical and electrical characteristics.

COMPACT DISC PLAYER BLOCK DIAGRAMS

Because compact disc players are so electronics oriented the design of various units can be quite different. Basically, they all use a laser beam for reading the tracks on a compact disc, but the circuitry for handling the data supplied by the disc can be different. Figure 5-1, for example, is a block diagram of a compact disc player but it is somewhat different from the one in Figure 5-2, which in turn has a moderate resemblance to that in Figure 5-3. Figure 5-2 is unique, since it supplies explanatory material that accompanies the blocks. While there are differences in various compact disc players, they are all electromechanical devices. In this respect they resemble analog

TABLE 5-1   DIGITAL DISC VERSUS ANALOG PHONO: A SUMMATION.

	Compact Disc Player System	Analog LP Phono System
Physical		
Disc Diameter	4-3/4 inches (12 cm)	12 inches (30 cm)
Disc Speed	500 rpm at center; 200 rpm at rim. Constant linear velocity	33 rpm and 45 rpm. Constant angular velocity
Playing Time	Approximately 60 minutes for stereo; 35 minutes for quadraphonic. Only stereo presently available. Disc has reserve capacity for video display. Plays one side only.	28 to 30 minutes per side; plays both sides.
Disc Life	No wear from laser beam. Disc should last indefinitely. Disc requires moderate care, cleaning. Disc is covered with protective plastic coating.	Fair to good. Disc wear begins with first playing. Scratch and warp possibilities. Requires regular cleaning.
Vibration Sensitivity	Sufficiently low to permit unit to be installed in cars, RVs, boats, and planes. Also suitable for portable use.	High. Ideal player support should be as massive as possible. Designed for fixed position use only.
Warpage	Negligible	Easily warped
Stylus Wear	Stylus is laser beam, does not wear.	Stylus wear begins with first playback.

turntables but there is no question that the compact disc player is far more sophisticated electronically.

The CD player uses a motor for rotating the disc, but unlike the turntable, rotation varies depending on the position of the laser scanning beam. A turntable depends on constant speed of rotation; the CD player depends on carefully controlled variable disc rotation. The CD player also uses a motor for operating the door used for the insertion of the disc. The CD player requires servo systems for motor control and is operated by a microprocessor.

With a turntable, the signal is delivered directly from the pickup unit to a following preamplifier; consequently, electronic circuitry is external to the unit. The compact disc player makes substantial use of electronic circuitry housed in the player (Table 5-2) for signal processing before delivery of that signal to a separate amplifier. The signal moves from the ouput of the photodiodes (the signal transducer) through a digital signal amplifier, through error correction circuitry, signal synchronization, and

TABLE 5-1   DIGITAL DISC VERSUS ANALOG PHONO: A SUMMATION (*cont*)

	Compact Disc Player System	Analog LP Phono System
Playing Convenience	Excellent. No tracking weight or antiskating adjustments required.	Moderate. Some adjustments required.
Electronic		
Dynamic Range	90 dB to 95 dB	About 60 dB; often less
Frequency Response	From 5 kHz to 20 kHz plus/minus 0.5 dB	Varies. Can be from 30 Hz to 15 kHz, and sometimes to 20 kHz. Low-frequency end limited with high amplitude tones.
Stereo Separation	Better than 90 dB	Average about 30 dB
Wow and Flutter	Too low to be measured	Depends on equipment and can be less than 0.2%.
Signal-to-noise Ratio	90 dB	60 dB and often less
Connections	Can be connected to aux, tape or tuner inputs. Do not connect to phono inputs.	Connect only to phono inputs for record equalization. May require specal preamp or transformer depending on cartridge used.
Disc Availability	Fair	Excellent
Access to Music Bands	Excellent	Fair
Indexing	Excellent	Not available
Positioning	Will play in any position.	Turntable must be absolutely horizontal.
Disc Loading	Top or front	Top only

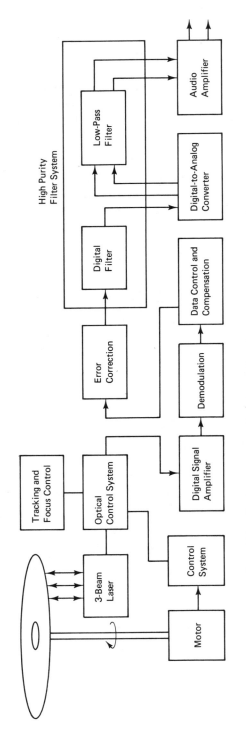

Figure 5-1 Circuit arrangement of a compact disc player. (Courtesy Sherwood, Div. Inkel Corp.)

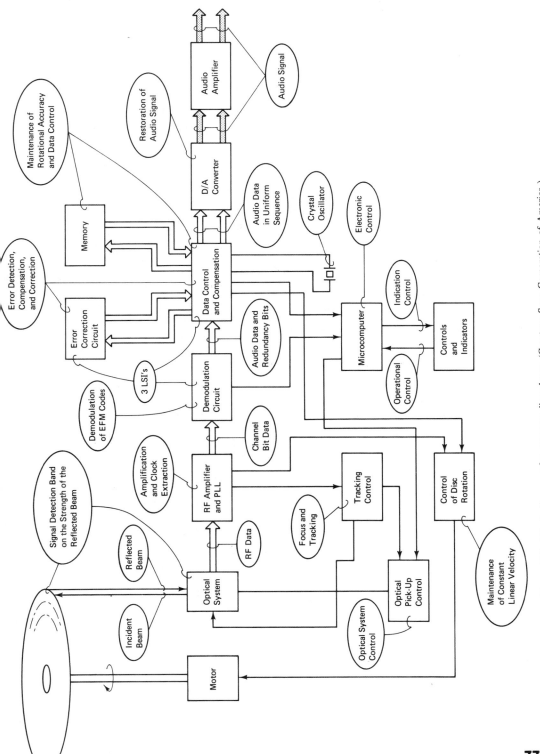

Figure 5-2 Block diagram of a compact disc player. (Courtesy Sony Corporation of America.)

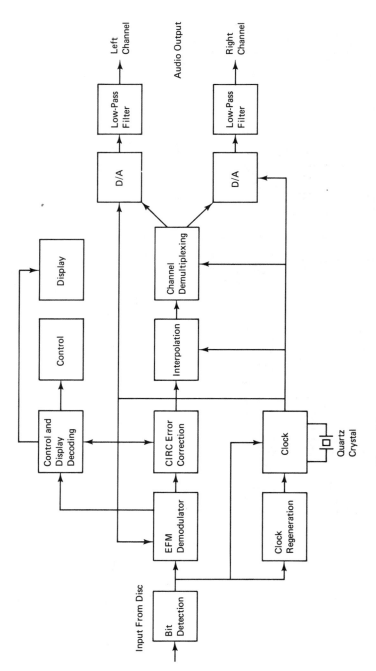

Figure 5-3 Another arrangement of a compact disc player.

TABLE 5-2 SIGNAL FORMAT.

Number of channels:	2 channels (4-channel recording will also be possible at twice the present rotational speed.)
Quantization:	16-bit linear quantization
Quantizing timing:	Concurrent for all channels
Sampling frequency:	44.1 kHz
Channel bit rate:	4.3218 Mb/sec.
Data bit rate:	2.0338 Mb/sec.
Data-to-channel bit ratio:	8:17
Error correction code:	CIRC (with 25% redundancy)
Modulation system:	EFM

then to a digital-to-analog converter. The left and right stereo signals are then supplied to a low-pass filter which is followed by an audio voltage amplifier prior to connection to the audio input of a high-fidelity system.

The compact disc player can be considered a mirror image of the pulse code modulator. In the PCM the analog audio signal is converted to binary form, is error corrected and finally has both audio signals delivered in sequential binary form on magnetic tape. Since the PCM is an encoder device, the CD player is a decoder, ultimately translating the binary code into an equivalent analog waveform. But, as indicated by the block diagrams, one CD player is not a replica of the next. However, all compact disc players are alike in that they all use a laser beam for scanning the encoded tracks on the compact disc. This is quite different from turntables in which a variety of pickups can be used. The laser beams, however, can be controlled and mounted in a number of ways.

The underside of the disc encoded with the tracks is the side that is read by the laser beam. What we have here are two different materials: an aluminized layer containing the pits and flats and a protective layer on top of it. The metal layer is highly polished and is carefully selected to have a high order of reflectivity. Since each section of flat area is a true focal point for the laser beam, it is from this section that the laser beam is sharply returned to an arrangement of photodiodes.

Fiber Optic Technology

Fiber optic technology is now being used to couple the various stages in a compact disc player to prevent the noise and distortion caused by digital signal interference (DSI). One unit uses as many as six fiber optic cables which connect the various stages of the player, eliminating the noise and distortion that can occur with hard-wired designs.

The fiber optic connectors carry digital information only, including the L/R clock signal, the word clock signal, the bit clock signal, digital audio data signal, de-emphasis actuate signal, and the audio muting actuate signal. Data on the disc not only consist of the stereo audio signals but synchronization and identification data as well. Using fiber optics improves performance and sound quality by allowing the digital-to-analog converters to process only the pure digital audio data, preventing conversion errors caused by extraneous noise of the other digital processing stages.

MICROPROCESSOR STRUCTURE

Since the compact disc player contains a microprocessor, it does have some of the capabilities of a computer. Programming is built into the player, and the function keys on the front panel correspond to the keyboard accompanying a computer.

Constant Linear Velocity

Constant Linear Velocity (CLV) signifies a condition in which a uniform relative velocity is maintained between the disc and the optical pickup.

Conventional LP phono records rotate at a constant angular velocity (CAV) of 33-1/3 rpm. Compared with the LP, the rotation of the compact disc varies depending on the position of the pickup for the purpose of assuring a constant linear velocity of 1.25 m/sec. The turntable platter of the CD system rotates at a speed of 500 rpm when the pickup is tracing close to the inner circumference of the disc. As the pickup moves outward, the rotational speed gradually decreases to a minimum of 200 rpm. The CLV servo is designed to control the speed by synchronizing the frame sync impressed in the disc and the frequency of the quartz crystal oscillator built into the player.

With constant linear velocity, any length of track on a compact disc is scanned in the same amount of time as any other identical length of track. This is applicable whether the disc tracks are being read near the inner or outer circumference. Spindle speed is the same for all CD players of all types, whether used for in-home entertainment, in a car, or in a portable unit.

The servo systems in the CD player are very important for the CD player. Only when they operate properly does it become possible to detect digital signals correctly.

SCANNING

Because scanning of the compact disc is from the underside, the scanning beam is focused on the flat portion of the disc (Fig. 5-4) instead of the pits which now correspond to bumps on the reverse (scanning) side. Reverse side scanning is possible since the disc is transparent and does not present an obstacle to the beam. The flat

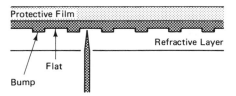

Figure 5-4 Laser beam is focused on flat portion of underside of disc. (Courtesy Sherwood Div. Inkel Corp.)

surface is uniform and lends itself to precise focusing. While efforts are made to control the depth of the pits during manufacturing, it is difficult to do so to extremely close tolerances.

PHYSICAL AND ELECTRONIC TECHNOLOGY

Manufacturers supply operating specs of their compact disc players but these are very limited in the amount of information given. Even operating tests performed by independent laboratories or magazine writeups give no clue as to the way in which a compact disc player is constructed. Probably the only ones who are aware of how well (or how poorly) the physical details may be manufactured are design engineers and service technicians.

A top quality player may use a copper-plated chassis, copper washers on all screws and a pure copper heat sink to reduce the effects of magnetically induced distortion. The audio output terminals may be gold plated. The unit may have a floating transport subchassis and special rubber bushings to minimize any possibility of chassis vibration affecting the audio signal.

Connections inside the compact disc player can be ordinary copper wire, linear crystal oxygen-free copper or fiber optics may be used. Linear crystal oxygen-free copper, abbreviated as LCO-FC is copper in crystalline form and is notably free of oxygen. As a result its conductivity is higher than ordinary copper resulting in a smaller IR (voltage) drop. The signal voltage at the output end of such copper wire is practically identical with the input. It is true that the lengths of wire used in making connections inside the CD player are small and the savings in signal drop are also limited, but it is definitely a step in the right direction.

Circuitwise, the structure of the compact disc is not static. Circuit improvements include independent power supplies for the analog and digital sections, separate printed circuit boards for digital, servo, audio and display circuits, polystyrene capacitors, and close-tolerance metal-film resistors.

REFRACTION AND REFLECTION

The plastic coating covering the disc provides a substance that will refract or scatter the impinging beam. This coating covers both the bumps and the flats and therefore the scattering effect is applicable to both. Thus, the returned beam from the focal point is both reflected and refracted. Most of the refracted beam from the bumps and the flats does not reach the photodiodes and is therefore ineffective. However, enough of the reflected beam from the flats does reach the photodiodes and a definite transition results between the returned beam and a refracted beam. We can consider the flats and bumps as performing the function of an on/off switch as far as the returned laser beam is concerned.

If the disc consisted only of a flat area or only of bumps there would be no switching action. It is the transition from a bump to a flat, or from a flat to a bump, that results in the generation of a binary 1 or 0. As long as the laser beam travels along the surface of a bump or the surface of a flat there is no laser switching.

Laser beam efficiency is the ratio of the reflected light to the incident light. Were it not for refraction that efficiency would be much higher than it is.

LASER BEAM SCANNING MECHANISM

The laser beam scanning mechanism in Fig. 5-5(a) is just one of its type; there are others (Fig. 5-5b). The scanning beam is produced by a low power aluminum gallium arsenide (AlGaAe) semiconductor diode which is made to emit a coherent infrared light beam. Like ordinary light, the beam tends to spread after leaving its source and so it is placed at the focal point of a collimator lens with a relatively long focal distance (Fig. 5-6). This lens accepts the spreading beam, nullifying the spreading out action and forces the beam to follow parallel lines. In some players a combined collimator-focus lens is used.

The beam is then sent through an optical grating, also called a diffraction grating. This grating is based on the fact that light can be bent around edges to a small extent. These effects are emphasized when light is passed through a slit or a multiple arrangement of extremely fine slits, producing the phenomenon known as diffraction. The bending effect is proportional to wavelength.

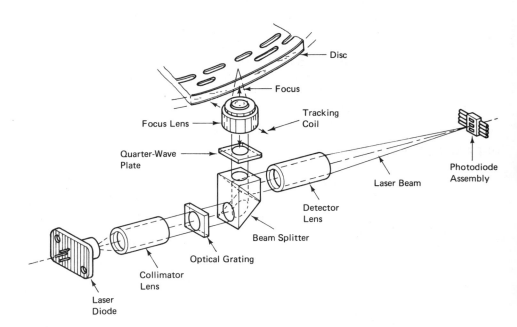

Figure 5-5(a) Laser beam scanning mechanism.

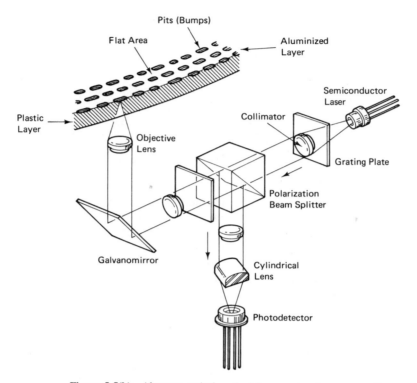

Figure 5-5(b) Alternate optical method for scanning the compact disc.

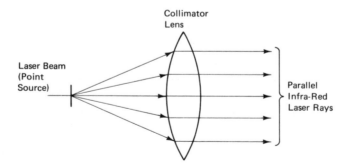

Figure 5-6 Collimator lens forces infrared beam into parallel lines.

    The diffraction grating could be called a beam splitter, for that is what it does. The output of the grating consists of a main or central beam, plus a succession of beams of decreasing strength. For our purposes we are only interested in the main beam and its side beams (Fig. 5-7). The main beam is used for tracking the disc while the side beams are used to keep the main beam precisely on the track it is following.

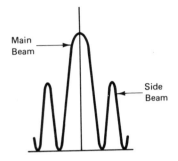

Figure 5-7 Diffraction grating results in a main beam plus a succession of smaller side beams of decreasing amplitude. Only two of the side beams are shown here.

Following the optical grating the three beams, the main beam and its two side beams, enter a beam splitter. This optical component is a partial prism better known as a half prism. The effect of the prism is to force the beams to make a right-angle turn. As indicated in Figure 5-5(a) and (b), if the beams have been traveling horizontally, they now move in a vertical direction. It is from this action that the prism is called half prism, for it now works as though it were a mirror set at an angle of 45 degrees, forcing the beams to make a 90 degree turn.

Wave Polarization

The main scanning beam and its pair of side beams now move upward through a quarter wave plate, a thin section of a doubly refracting crystal whose function is to polarize the beams. Note that from this point the beams moving upward toward the disc will meet the beams being reflected from it since both the incident and reflected beams will be following the same path. To keep them from interfering with each other, the incident beam is polarized by the quarter wave plate.

A pair of transmitted waves can avoid interfering with each other in two ways: They can use different frequencies, and this is the technique used in radio and television broadcasting, or if they must use the same frequencies, they are polarized. Thus, one wave could be horizontally polarized while the other is vertically polarized. This is the technique used for the transmission of signals from satellites to the earth, permitting 24 channels to use the same space otherwise occupied by 12.

While waves can be vertically and horizontally polarized, there is still another possibility known as circular polarization, and that is what is used here. There are two types of circular polarization: one in which the wave is rotated in a clockwise manner somewhat like a corkscrew with the other wave rotating counterclockwise. When this is done the two waves, both operating at the same frequency, can occupy the same space in a noninterfering manner.

Beam Focusing

The main beam and its pair of side beams must now be focused on the metallic, flat area of the underside of the disc and this is done by a focusing lens, also called an objective (or object) lens, a convex type with a focal distance of 4 mm. This lens is as precise as those used in the most advanced microscopes and supplies outstanding brightness. Aberration is non-existent. This lens is capable of moving both horizontally and vertically.

The laser beam is thinner than a human hair, having a diameter of 0.5 micron with each of the tracks on the disc separated by 1.6 microns on centers. On its way from the laser to the disc, the beam follows parallel lines (Fig. 5-8) and like all other light can be sharply focused by a lens. The lens, made of glass or plastic, is a converging type and in CD players is referred to as an objective lens. The focal length of this lens is the distance from the lens to the point at which the originally parallel light rays converge. The distance from the objective lens to the undersurface of the disc is critical.

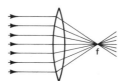

Figure 5-8 Focusing action of the objective lens. The focal point is f.

Because the focal point of the laser beam must be so precise and because of the extremely limited tolerance of that focal point, any warpage of the disc cannot be tolerated. For this reason the discs should not be subjected to surface pressure. While the plastic coating on the disc is vulnerable to thermal deformation, that plastic is reinforced by the aluminum structure of the disc. Unlike phono records whose larger size makes them more prone to twisting torque, the smaller diameter of the compact disc is in its favor.

Beam Reflection

The reflected beam and a much smaller amount of refracted beam now return to the beam splitter by passing through the focusing lens and the quarter-wave plate. At the splitter a mirror action occurs once again and the beams are reflected at a right angle. They pass through a series of lenses made of an assembly of convex, cylindrical, and concave lenses, known collectively as a detector. The converging beams finally reach a photodiode assembly.

An alternative method of laser beam scanning, as shown in Figure 5-5(b), uses a different technique. One modification is that a galvanomirror is used to get the scanning beam to make a right-angle turn instead of depending on a half prism to do this. Instead of a separate quarter-wave plate to achieve beam polarization this is also handled by the beam splitter.

The Photodiode Assembly

The photodiodes are transducers which change the incident light energy to an electrical signal. To strengthen the output of these diodes, the electrical signals are fed into what could be called a preamplifier but is better known as a high-frequency amplifier (HF amplifier). The word "preamplifier," commonly used in high-fidelity systems, would create an inaccurate impression, for the HF amplifier used here is a very wide band type.

When the reflected laser beam from the disc reaches the photodiodes in the beam assembly, it is converted simultaneously by these diodes into electrical signals. The electrical signal output of these diodes is in pulse form and is a representation of the original pulse signal encoded on the disc.

The aggregate signal output of the photo diodes is processed in several steps. These include detection and separation of the synchronization information, separation of the music and information data (for example, track time), generating a control signal from the synchronization frequency and the quartz reference for controlling the platter speed and finally, converting the digital audio signals to their original analog shape.

The photodiode detectors not only supply the digital audio signal for driving the HF amplifier, but also an automatic focusing signal and a signal for an error-signal amplifier. Any error that is detected is fed into a servo circuit which then moves the objective lens to correct the main laser beam position.

All semiconductors are light sensitive and must be enclosed by an opaque substance. Photodiodes, two-terminal devices, are used to take advantage of this characteristic. Since transistors can be regarded as diodes back to back, the photodiode is half a transistor. The photodiode contains a p-n junction with the diode designed so that incident light is focused on or is as close as possible to that junction.

The photodiode is reverse biased so that with no light impinging on the junction current flow is very small and from a practical point of view can be considered nonexistent. This would be the condition upon receipt of the very limited amount of refracted light from the pits on the undersurface of the disc. When the photodiode receives reflected light from the flats, current flow through the diode is proportional to the amount of light entering this component. In this sense, the diode can be considered to be triggered on or off by the light or the absence of light from the disc.

The photodiode arrangement consists of an assembly of four photodiodes. These can supply two types of signals. One of these is the audio signal which is supplied to an audio signal amplifier followed by processing circuits. A large scale integrated circuit (LSI) translates the photodiode derived information from the flashes of laser light. It then analyzes these data and converts them into varying audio voltages. The other is an automatic focusing signal which is delivered to error amplifiers to control focusing.

THE LASER BEAM

While a laser beam is correctly referred to as a light beam, it differs considerably from ordinary light. Such light consists of an aggregation of hues, each of which has its individual wavelength. White light is the most notable example.

The wavelengths of light are extremely small and are measured in nanometers, at one time called the millimicron. A nanometer is 0.000000001 meter or 10^{-9} meter. It is also equivalent to 10 angstroms. An angstrom, abbreviated as Å, is a unit of measurement of the wavelength of light and is equal to one ten-billionth of a meter. The spectrum of white light ranges from 385 to 760 nanometers or 3850 to 7600 angstroms and consists of hundreds of hues, each having a specific wavelength.

The word "laser" is an acronym obtained from *l*ight *a*mplification by *s*timulated *e*mission of *r*adiation. A laser is a device that utilizes the natural oscillations of atoms or molecules between energy levels for generating coherent electromagnetic radiation in the ultraviolet, visible, or infrared regions of the light spectrum. The laser, as distinguished from a laser beam, is an active electronic device that converts input power into a very narrow, intense beam of coherent light. The key component in a laser is an optical resonator used to stimulate atoms to a higher energy level, forcing the atoms to radiate in phase. It is from this in-phase condition that we obtain the description of a laser beam as coherent light.

Laser beams can be generated by semiconductor diodes and the first of these used successfully in 1962 was made of gallium arsenide. The research was conducted by independent research groups at General Electric and at the Lincoln laboratory of IBM. The wavelength of the laser beam produced by gallium arsenide, a semiconductor, is from 8400 to 9100 angstroms. The laser beam is many times thinner than a human hair and has a diameter of 1.6 microns (1.6 micrometers). At its focal point the beam has a diameter of less than one micron (10^{-6} meter). The laser diode is made of aluminum gallium arsenide (AlGaAe) whose output consists of coherent radiation in the infrared region of the light spectrum. The semiconductor laser diode is usually operated by its own independent power supply.

Invisibility of the Laser Beam

As indicated earlier, a laser beam is sometimes correctly referred to as a light beam. However, the words "light beam" seem to imply that the beam is visible. The light of the laser beam has a wavelength of 7800 angstroms and cannot be seen by the naked eye since it is outside the range of our vision. Our vision extends from approximately 4000 angstroms at the blue-violet end of the visible light spectrum to about 7000 angstroms at the opposite, deep red end of the spectrum.

LASER PICKUP ASSEMBLIES

There are two basic types of laser beam pickup assemblies: one which is parallel to the compact disc and another which is vertical to it (Fig. 5-9 and Fig. 5-10). With the horizontal assembly, the laser beam is forced to make a right-angle turn by a right-angle prism, a half prism. The vertical assembly does not need a right-angle prism since the beam is initially directed right at the disc. The system in Figure 5-9 is known as a rotating arm pickup; that in Figure 5-10 is a slide or sled pickup.

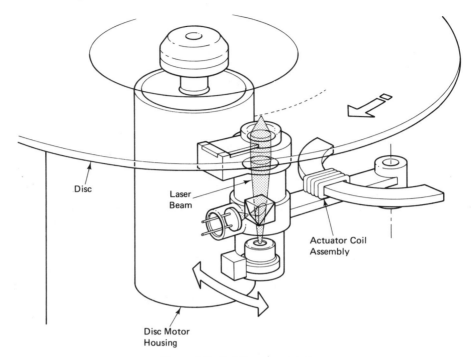

Figure 5-9   Rotating arm pickup.

Slide systems are characterized by a radial tracking coil that is used to move the entire optical assembly to maintain accurate tracking. In the rotating arm system a radial tracking coil moves the rotating arm to which the laser beam assembly is attached. The motor action of the rotating arm pickup is obtained by sending a correction current through a radial tracking coil which surrounds a curved shaft that works like a motor armature. These two optical assemblies are not the only ones that are possible, but they are the most common.

LASER BEAM TRACKING

In the compact disc player the laser beam performs the function of the phono cartridge in an analog turntable, while the laser pickup assembly could be said to correspond to the tonearm. The laser beam does not track grooves because there are no grooves on a compact disc and even if there were, they could not possibly compel the laser beam to track them. In the case of a phono record the grooves exert a physical restraint on the stylus and if the tracking force is adequate, the stylus will remain in the grooves.

The tracking technique uses a main laser beam (Fig. 5-11) and a pair of subbeams with each one positioned on either side of the main beam. The outputs of the two subbeams are constantly compared by special electronic circuitry to keep the main laser

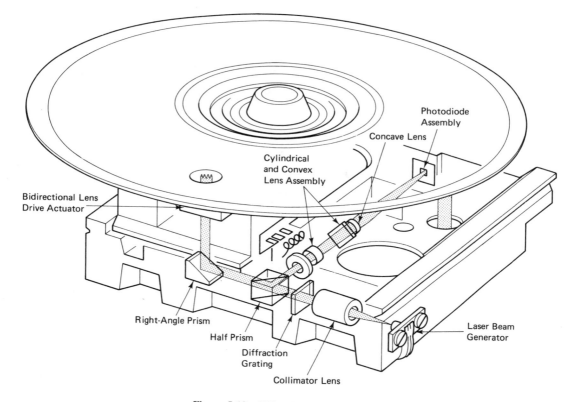

Figure 5-10 Slide (sled) type pickup.

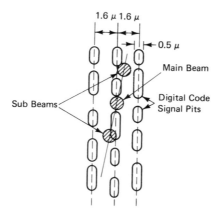

Figure 5-11 Three-beam laser tracking system. (Courtesy Aiwa Co., Ltd.)

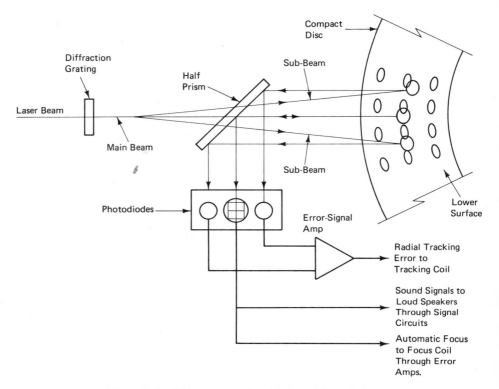

Figure 5-12   Subbeams control positioning of the main beam.

beam directly on course using a highly responsive servo control. The pickup assembly is driven by a linear motor for extremely fast cueing time.

     The subbeams (Fig. 5-12) ride the space between the tracks. Any deviation from precise tracking by the main beam is detected by the subbeams forcing the mechanism controlling the main beam to move left or right. This is handled by an error-tracking voltage fed to a servo which moves the tracking beam mechanism back to its correct position. The action is so rapid and the distance of the correction movement so small it is impossible for a listener to detect any sound changes.

     Early compact disc players used a single laser beam pickup system but even low cost compact disc players now have the three-beam pickup method. This technique ensures accurate tracking.

Tracking Servo Control

There are a number of variations of optical tracking systems used in compact disc players. Figure 5-13 illustrates such a system with a unit based on servo control of the tracking beam. Control of the optics is by a number of bipolar ICs (integrated circuits).

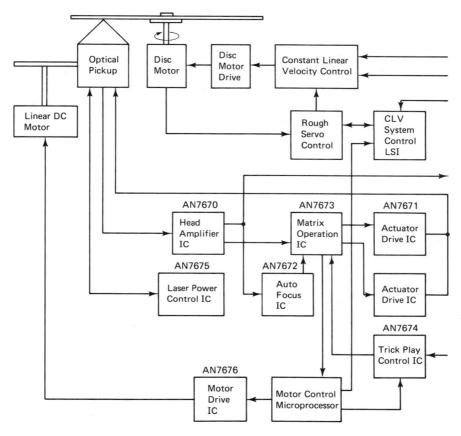

Figure 5-13 Servo systems for a compact disc player.

In this drawing each is identified by the letters AN followed by a number. This is a manufacturer's identification and is used when ordering a replacement.

The block diagram not only illustrates servo control for tracking error but also indicates servos for handling focusing errors, motor speed, and laser power. Laser power is controlled by AN7675, AN7672 handles focusing, and AN7670 tracks error.

FOCUS CONTROL

The laser beam must not only be moved horizontally left and right to perfectly track the pits and flats, but vertically as well so that the beam comes to a fine focal point. The objective lens (Fig. 5-14) can be moved vertically and is designed similar to the mechanical system of a speaker. The lens is controlled magnetically. The coil is stationary and the magnet moves. If the beam is out of focus, a focus error signal is

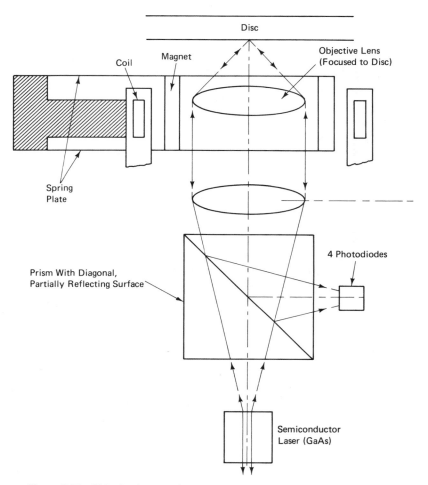

Figure 5-14   Objective lens can be moved to achieve focusing. (Courtesy Revox.)

developed, amplified, and subsequently delivered to a controlling amplifier. Signals from this amplifier cause the lens to move alternatingly up and down. The error voltage that develops when the beam is out of focus becomes smaller as the focal point is reached. No focal hunting is involved. If the beam moves out of focus, the error voltage develops at once, keeping the beam in its correct position. Actually, the focusing lens readjusts for each track and because of this a whistling sound of approximately 12 kHz could develop. This whistling sound is eliminated by a transistorized R-C filter in the control loop. The sound does not exist when the beam is in focus and the filter is active only in the search mode.

Focusing is not a matter of moving the focusing lens any great distance and there would not be a noticeable change in the position of this lens during the search mode. The permitted deviation of focusing is ± 1 micrometer.

In early television receivers focusing of the picture was handled manually via a rotary control first on the front of the receiver and subsequently on the rear. Once focusing was obtained the control was rarely touched again. Focusing of the laser beam in the compact disc player is completely automatic. As indicated in Fig. 5-15, there are four equally spaced photodiodes. As in drawing (a), if the beam is correctly focused, the spot formed by the beam is round, indicating that all four diodes receive the same amount of light from the reflected laser beam and all of the output signals of the diodes have the same strength. The algebraic sum of all these voltages is delivered to an error amplifier but since the input is zero, the output is zero as well. If the laser beam is close to the surface of the disc but does not reach it, the output voltages of the four diodes result in a sum that is greater than zero, as in (b), and the error amplifier supplies a correction signal voltage in its output. If the laser beam focuses on a point beyond the surface of the disc as in drawing (c), the output voltage of the diodes is less than zero or a negative voltage. Again, a correction signal voltage is supplied by the error amplifier, but with a negative polarity. The objective lens is moved forward or backward depending on the polarity of the signal supplied.

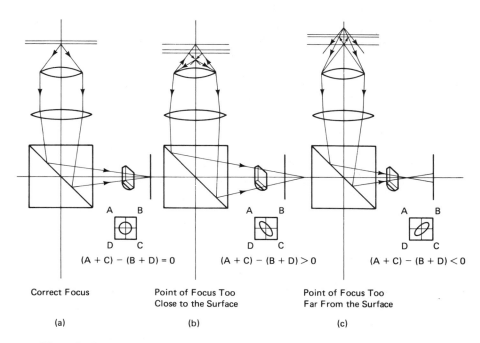

$$(A + C) - (B + D) = 0 \qquad (A + C) - (B + D) > 0 \qquad (A + C) - (B + D) < 0$$

Correct Focus	Point of Focus Too Close to the Surface	Point of Focus Too Far From the Surface
(a)	(b)	(c)

Figure 5-15 Correct focus (a); incorrect focus (b and c). (Courtesy Sanyo Electric, Inc.)

Laser Beam Mount

Vibration can affect not only the laser beam assembly but can trigger a unit's correction circuitry, thereby altering a signal which is error free. Vibration as used here does not refer to mechanical vibration alone, but can be due to acoustic feedback as well. While analog turntables are particularly susceptible and while CDs are used in autos and portables, this does not mean they are completely immune. A factor that could make a CD player prone to mechanical and acoustic feedback is the way the laser transport system is mounted. In one setup the CD's entire laser transport system is supported on a massive cast alloy subchassis. This is attached to the unit's main chassis by rubber feet that filter vibrations which could otherwise trigger the unit's correction circuitry. In another setup the laser pickup and disc drive assemblies are placed on a unitized floating mount.

The type of suspension system used is a problem of mechanical design and its solution depends on the manufacturer. It is in a feature of this kind that so-called bargain CD players differ from those made by top name-brand manufacturers.

MOTORS

There are several motors in the player. One of these is used to operate the disc table and has its speed controlled by a motor servo. There is also another motor for loading and unloading the disc. The third motor is used for driving the laser beam pickup unit. The pickup drive and motor are both servo controlled.

There are various kinds of motors used in compact disc players but these all have similar requirements. They must have sufficient torque to drive a mechanism either directly or via a gear arrangement. They must be responsive to small signal levels, start and stop rapidly, and not do any hunting. Hunting is the motion of a motor on both sides of the zero point of the feedback signal.

Some motors are given special names by compact disc player manufacturers but they are usually linear DC motors, that is, a motor whose rotation is directly and linearly proportional to the amount of drive voltage. Another type of unit is the Hall motor. This motor makes use of the Hall effect to give rotation proportional to field strength. The Hall effect is the development of a transverse electric field in a current carrying conductor placed in a magnetic field.

The Motor Tracking Mechanism

The optical pickup system of a CD player must be able to read the disc's encoded signals quickly and accurately, as well as to provide aid in error correction. For these reasons the laser beam must be servo controlled at the optimum position, regardless of the condition of the disc. Among the various servo control systems, the stability of the tracking servo is of the utmost importance in order for the optical pickup to realize its full potential.

The purpose of the tracking servo is to assure accurate tracking of the laser beam along the microscopic 1.6 μm track even under the most severe disc conditions, including an eccentric center hole. The tracking servo mechanism, therefore, must balance the need to move at a high speed with an accuracy of less than a micron, as well as to move slowly from the inner to the outer track across the entire disc.

In a conventional CD player using a pickup sled, for example, the torque of a DC motor is applied to the pickup through a complicated worm gear and reduction gear assembly. Such systems are difficult to design properly because the mechanism's "play" (backlash, friction, and so on) does not allow an optimum smooth, high-speed movement. Smooth movement depends on having a low gear ratio, while high speed access demands a high gear ratio design.

Poor Trackability

In the event of a condition of poor trackability, the mechanical movement of the pickup sometimes exceeds the limit of the servo control boundary of the two-axes objective lens. The relatively limited servo control area is insufficient to follow these large movements, thus the lens deviates from the center of the laser beam.

The effect of this behavior is a deformed beam on the disc's pits and affects the pickup's ability to read the digital signal. Another harmful result of the off-axis beam is improper operation of the tracking servo and this will also degrade the accuracy of tracking.

DISC MOTOR CONTROL LOOP

The data from the compact disc must be supplied as steadily as possible to the digital signal processing circuit which follows the output of the photodiodes associated with the laser beam assembly. Without motor control of the disc, however, the speed with which data bits would arrive would depend on the position of the laser pickup. If the disc would be allowed to rotate at a constant speed, then the data bits would be delivered to the signal processing circuitry at a variable speed. For example, if the laser pickup reads in the middle of the compact disc, the reading speed is much higher than near the edge. For this reason the disc motor is operated at a variable speed with that speed determined by the location of the laser assembly with respect to the disc. The disc motor speed is constantly adjusted so that the laser pickup reads the encoded data on the disc at a steady rate of 1.2 to 1.4 meters per second.

VIBRATION DAMPING

Like a phono turntable, a compact disc player is motor equipped except that the compact disc player has more motors. Even though the laser beam assembly has lateral and vertical position correction circuitry, it is essential to keep vibration to a minimum.

Furthermore, rotating parts and vibrations inside the player can induce microphonic behavior in high-gain audio circuitry and result in signal transmission errors. Consequently CD players are equipped with vibration damping assemblies with their design varying from one CD player to the next. One player even has its analog audio circuit board mounted on a copper-plated solid steel assembly to stabilize the circuit assembly and effectively damp any internal vibration. CD players to be used as portables and for car installation are especially protected against shock and vibration.

SERVOMECHANISMS

A servomechanism, abbreviated as servo, is an automatic feedback control system. The compact disc player uses three sophisticated servo systems to maintain the accurate flow of data. One controls the rotational speed for constant linear velocity, as opposed to the constant angular velocity of 33-1/3 rpm used by analog turntables. Another keeps the laser beam on-track. The third adjusts beam focus for discs that are not perfectly flat.

There are many types of servos. In the compact disc player they are electromechanical with a feedback signal controlling the forward or reverse rotation of a motor shaft, or the lateral or vertical movement of a device. The servo-controlled motor is sometimes referred to as an actuator. Servos have several distinct advantages. They can be made to be completely automatic and they can control mechanical movements in very small increments. Servos can be analog or digital, depending on the kind of control signal used.

In the servo system an error voltage is developed if the device controlled by the servo motor is not precisely positioned. This error voltage is fed into an integrated circuit in which the voltage is amplified (Fig. 5-16). The error voltage, referred to as a

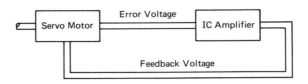

Figure 5-16 Error voltage is amplified in an IC and fed back to the servo motor.

correction voltage or feedback voltage following amplification, is supplied to the servo motor to operate it in a direction that decreases the error voltage. When that voltage drops to zero, there is no further feedback; consequently, there is no further correction movement of the shaft of the servo motor. The feedback error voltage can be DC and can be positive or negative. A negative voltage causes the motor shaft of the servo to revolve in one direction; a positive voltage results in rotation of the servo motor shaft in the opposite direction.

THE DEMODULATOR

The signal output of the HF preamplifier is brought into a demodulator IC (Fig. 5-17). This is a crystal-controlled oscillator circuit with an operating frequency of 8.64 MHz. This frequency is obtained by multiplying the fundamental analog signal sampling frequency by 196. 196 x 44.1 kHz = 8643.6 kHz = 8.64 MHz.

There are two inputs to the demodulator. One of these is from the output of the preceding HF preamplifier. The other is an input marked HFL obtained from a preceding HFL detector. The abbreviation HFL represents "high-frequency low." Its function is to stop signal demodulation if the input signal drops below a previously determined level. That level is about 1.5 volts peak-to-peak. If that input signal should drop to about 350 millivolts or less, demodulation of data will be halted.

The demodulator may also be combined with other circuitry including error detection and the correction of any error signals, and circuitry which can distinguish between 0 and 1 pulses. It may also be responsible for rearranging the data for temporary storage in a random access memory (RAM). For that reason this block of circuits is sometimes called the signal processor, data processor, or data control.

The way in which these various functions are handled, and the IC circuit or circuits used, can be different in various CD players. The general approach may be the same; the specific details may be different.

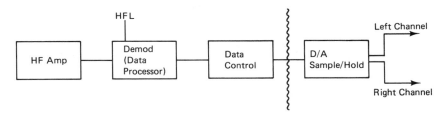

Figure 5-17   Audio signal flow from the HF amplifier.

THE AUDIO SIGNAL PATH

The first step toward recovery of the audio signals in analog form begins with the conversion of the laser beam into an equivalent digital pulse form by the photodiodes. These are connected as shown in Figure 5-18(a) in alternate shunt pairs; that is, diodes 1 and 3 are joined as are diodes 2 and 4. The diodes are DC powered from a 5-volt source.

There is no signal amplification by the diodes and actually there is a loss which can be overcome by following the diodes with an amplifier. The diode output is brought into a pair of ICs identified as photodiode comparators. These are a pair of signal inverting amplifiers.

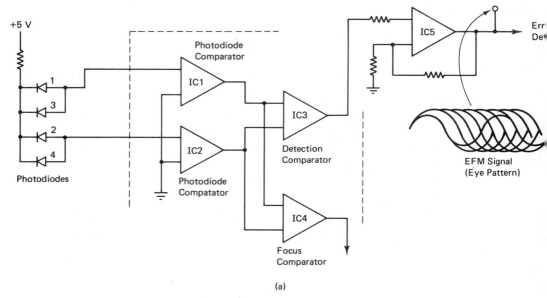

Figure 5-18(a)   Steps toward the formation of the EFM signal.

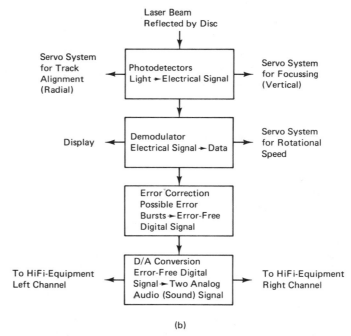

(b)

Figure 5-18(b)   Audio signal path is used to trigger servo control systems. (Courtesy Revox.)

The output of IC5 (integrated circuits in Figure 5-18a) looks like a successive series of high frequency sine waves (HF) but is the EFM signal, also called an RF signal, or because of its appearance as an eye pattern but is actually a pulse signal. The strength of the signal at the output of this amplifier circuitry is about 1.5 volts, peak to peak. The input from the photodiodes is approximately 170 millivolts, peak to peak. If you are accustomed to the movement of an audio signal from the output of a phono pickup in an analog audio system, it might seem that the path taken by the audio in a compact disc player is devious by comparison. This is true since what we are dealing with here is not just the pulse form of the signal but data that were encoded in the disc-making process along with the audio. This is in addition to the fact that in the audio path we also have error correction circuitry and digital-to-analog conversion circuitry. This means the signals in the compact disc player must not only supply left/right audio, but also signals for triggering a servo system for radial track alignment, signals for a servo system for vertical focusing, signals for operating one or more front panel displays and data for controlling a servo system for rotational speed of the disc (Fig. 5-18b).

The reason that this may seem so different is that it more closely resembles the way in which a TV signal behaves. It not only supplies the video signal (comparable to the audio signal in this case) but also pulses which control the start of each sweep line in the picture tube plus vertical movement of the lines as well. This calls for a composite signal, one that is both digital and analog. The video signal is analog; the picture control pulses are digital.

Digital-to-Analog Converter

The digital signal picked up from the compact disc by the reflected laser beam ultimately reaches a digital-to-analog (D/A) converter (Fig. 5-19). In compact disc players the D/A converter is a critical component because it has a significant effect on the sound quality. It is at this stage that the binary digital code recorded on the disc is converted into corresponding amounts of current to make up the analog audio signal.

The D/A converter may be equipped with a conversion error detection/correction circuit, an arrangement which is not integrated with the D/A unit but is external to it. The correction circuit compensates for any errors or deficiencies detected in the digital code by making the proper plus or minus current adjustments (Fig. 5-20). The graph in Figure 5-21 illustrates the effect of conversion error correction and the absence of such correction using a theoretical 100 dB S/N level as a reference.

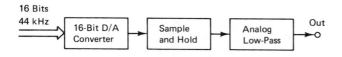

16 Bits
44 kHz
16-Bit D/A Converter → Sample and Hold → Analog Low-Pass → Out

Figure 5-19 Following the digital-to-analog converter the audio signal moves into sample and hold circuitry, followed by an analog low-pass filter.

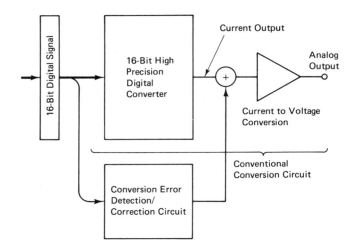

Figure 5-20 Digital-to-analog conversion correction arrangement. (Courtesy Denon-Nippon Columbia Co., Ltd.)

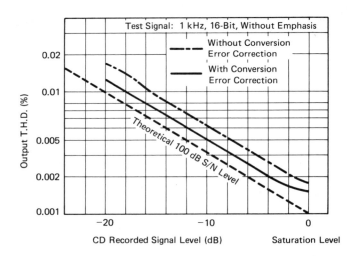

Figure 5-21 Graph indicating effect of digital-to-analog error correction. (Courtesy Denon-Nippon Columbia Co., Ltd.)

Crossover Distortion in D/A Conversion

Audio high-fidelity systems sometimes make use of a Class B amplifier, a circuit in which the output transistors operate alternately in processing the output signal. Since the transistors work one after the other, there is a problem in joining the two output waveforms smoothly without a break point.

We have a comparable problem with the D/A converter because the left and right sound channels follow each other sequentially. Since the digital code on compact discs is alternately coded with left and right channel signals, there is always a time difference of 11.3 microseconds between the signals for each channel. This results in high frequency imaging problems (Fig. 5-22) because of the phase difference between the left and right channel signals. The phase shift is not fixed, as indicated in Figure 5-22(a) but is maximum at 0 degrees, 180 degrees, and 360 degrees, with the evaluation done at a frequency of 2 kHz. However, for higher audio frequencies as in Figure 5-22(b), the phase shift becomes more severe, and at 20 kHz can become as much as 81 degrees at the zero point on the X axis compared with just 8 degrees at the same crossover point when the frequency is 2 kHz.

As a result we could get an output wave somewhat resembling that supplied by a Class B amplifier (Fig. 5-23). The point at which the upper and lower halves of the

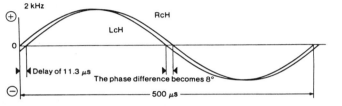

Figure 5-22(a) Phase difference at 2 kHz with left and right signal timing error. (Courtesy Denon-Nippon Columbia Co., Ltd.)

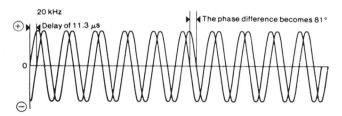

Figure 5-22(b) Phase difference at 20 kHz with left and right signal timing error. (Courtesy Denon-Nippon Columbia Co., Ltd.)

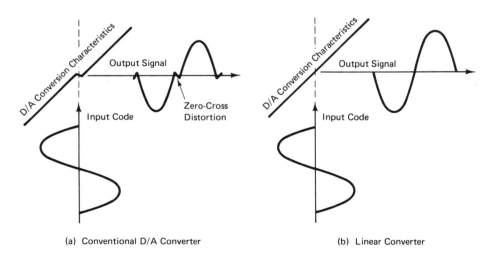

(a) Conventional D/A Converter

(b) Linear Converter

Figure 5-23 Nonlinear D/A conversion (left); linear D/A conversion (right). (Courtesy Denon-Nippon Columbia Co., Ltd.)

output wave in Figure 5-23(a) do not make an unbroken connection results in zero-cross distortion. Zero-cross distortion is so called since it occurs on the X axis and is the point at which the signal changes its polarity.

The drawing in Figure 5-23(b) shows the result of the correction of this fault. The output wave is smooth and continuous and does not exhibit a center break. The technique for overcoming zero-cross distortion is to have not one but a pair of D/A converters (Fig. 5-24). The use of this circuitry not only involves the cost of an additional D/A converter but extra input and output filters. It is one of the factors that accounts for the wide discrepancy in price between top of the line and bottom end compact disc players.

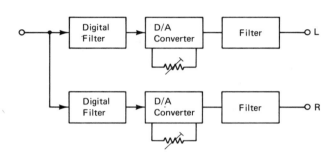

Figure 5-24 Double D/A converter system. (Courtesy Denon-Nippon Columbia Co., Ltd.)

Time Smear

The crossover distortion produced in digital-to-analog conversion is also known as time smear. While time smear can be eliminated by using a dual converter, it is possible to achieve the same results with the help of a unit known as a real time converter.

The real time converter uses three sample and hold (S/H) switches. Since the left and right signals are read alternately on the compact disc, when the left signal enters the first sample and hold circuit, it is kept there until the right signal is received. Then two other sample and hold gates open and the left and right signals are supplied at exactly the same moment. This arrangement avoids time smear in D/A converters not so equipped. The output of the gates is followed by a pair of filters. The usual D/A converter arrangement feeds just a single filter.

SAMPLE AND HOLD

Following the digital-to-analog converter, there are just a few steps remaining before the left and right sound signals are ready for driving a following analog audio preamplifier. These include sample and hold circuitry and signal filtering (Fig.5-25). The arrangement of these circuits and the type and number that are used will vary from one compact disc player to another.

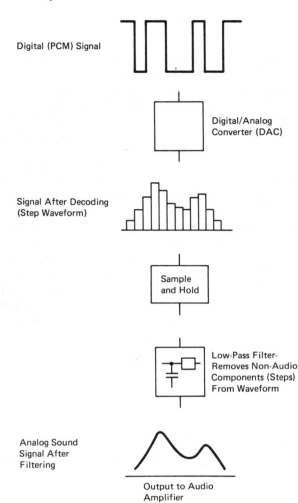

Digital (PCM) Signal

Digital/Analog
Converter (DAC)

Signal After Decoding
(Step Waveform)

Sample
and Hold

Low-Pass Filter-
Removes Non-Audio
Components (Steps)
From Waveform

Analog Sound
Signal After
Filtering

Output to Audio
Amplifier

Figure 5-25 Sample and hold circuitry samples the analog signal and holds it pending the arrival of the next sample. The sample and hold stores the sample in a capacitor followed by an op amp.

The Problem of Single Sampling

Digital sampling is part of the process for manufacturing compact discs and CD players. In the disc-making process it is involved in the conversion of decimal values of an analog waveform to binary equivalents; in the playback system it works in an opposite manner to convert binary numbers back to the original analog waveform.

The problem with sampling in the CD player is that it generates spurious frequencies which must be filtered prior to the delivery of the audio signal to a following amplifier. A procedure in some CD players is to use a sampling frequency of 44.1 kHZ, a frequency that is approximately twice the highest frequency in the audio range (20 kHz).

Effect of Sample and Hold

The effects of the spurious signals produced by the digital-to-analog circuitry can be lessened by following the converter with sample/hold circuitry. Sample/hold, as its name implies, holds each sample until the next one becomes available. The result of this action is the production of a stairstep signal (Fig. 5-26). This signal is not the same as that of an analog signal but more closely resembles a succession of uninterrupted pulse waveforms. Its advantage is that it is closer in its resemblance to analog than the instantaneous values previously indicated (Fig. 5-27).

The quality of sound supplied by a CD player can be affected by the pickup and the filters it uses. Another contributing factor is the switching distortion possible in the sample/hold circuitry. A player may use a class A arrangement to minimize or eliminate this problem.

Sample and hold circuitry can be combined with oversampling. While the oversampling used is most often twice that of the standard sampling frequency of 44.1 kHz (88.2 kHz), a more effective arrangement is to use quadruple oversampling (four times the standard, or 176.4 kHz). The advantage is that noise power is distributed over a band that is four times as wide. While the noise power originally extended to 22 kHz or half the normal sampling frequency, it is now spread over a band that is four times as wide and extends to 88 kHz. The effect is to reduce existing noise within the audio spectrum to one fourth its original amount.

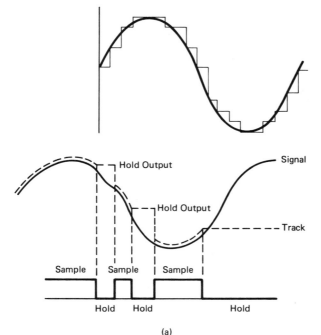

Figure 5-26 The effect of sample/hold circuitry is to produce a stairstep signal that is a close approximation of the original analog waveform.

Figure 5-27 Sample and hold produces a series of approximations of the analog waveform.

Theory of Oversampling

Assume that in the compact disc manufacturing process the sampling frequency is selected to be 44.1 kHz. In the compact disc player the signal obtained after demodulation will contain unwanted remnants of the sampling frequency based on multiples of that frequency. Thus, in addition to the audio frequency band ranging from close to DC (possibly just a few hertz above DC, such as 5 Hz), spurious signals would be arranged as follows: 44.1 kHz + 20 kHz; 88.2 kHz + 20 kHz, and so on. What this means is that unwanted pulsating noise exists at regular intervals beginning at 24.1 kHz (44.1 kHz - 20 kHz) even though the audio spectrum ends at 20 kHz.

Sampling and Filtering

One of the most important factors affecting the sound quality of a CD player is how the player converts the digital signal from the disc back into analog form for output to a following amplifier. That amplifier can be the preamplifier in a high-fidelity sound system or the amplifier input of a receiver.

While top quality CD players use a 16-bit digital-to-analog system for the widest dynamic range and lowest noise, lower cost units may be 14-bit types. To improve their S/N ratios, 14-bit A/D systems may use complex circuitry.

Double Sampling

Double sampling, also known as oversampling, is a technique in which the sampling rate is increased from 44.1 kHz to 88.2 kHz.

By doubling the sampling rate and passing the digital signal through a special kind of filter, this system moves the beginning of the first band of ultrasonic noise in the analog signal from 24.1 kHz up to 68.2 kHz. Since this noise no longer begins so soon after the end of the audio frequency band at 20 kHz, it is possible to use a low-pass filter having a very gradual rolloff.

If we had originally set 25 kHz as our arbitrary hearing limit, then our minimum sampling frequency must be 50 kHz. Adding a guard band to that would bring us to approximately 52 kHz, but a higher sampling frequency is a mixed blessing. It could have made our data storage problem more difficult and it also could have meant encoding more data on the disc.

Frequency and phase response are affected by the filters. Some compact disc players use analog filters but these cause errors both in frequency and phase response with frequency deviations of several dB and phase shifts which in the worst cases approach 180 degrees.

Other compact disc players use digital filtering followed by analog filters that show the same kind of response errors. A good arrangement is to use a combination of digital and analog filters with these optimized for a wrinkle-free frequency response, that is, having a typical variation of less than 0.2 dB and flat phase response of less than 2 degrees at 20 kHz.

Quadruple Sampling

A compact disc player may be equipped with dual signal processors operating at a digital sampling frequency of 176.4 kHz, four times the industry norm. This serves to move spurious ultrasonic frequency components far above the audio band, thus eliminating possible intermodulation effects. The low phase shift achieved by oversampling is reduced to zero by a combination of digital and analog filtering.

The signal path circuitry after the digital-to-analog converter is a source of frequency aberration. With quadruple sampling the analog signal path circuits can be completely direct coupled, eliminating the need for series capacitors and ICs, using high precision metal film resistors right through to gold-plated output jacks.

FILTERS

Filters can be classified in many ways but commonly they are described in terms of what they do. A low-pass filter will pass all frequencies up to a selected cutoff point; a bandpass filter will pass a band of frequencies, and so on.

Filters are also categorized as passive or active. A passive filter has no gain and consists only of components such as resistors, capacitors and inductors. Because the filter is passive there is some amount of signal loss. An active filter is one that is directly associated with a solid-state amplifier and such a filter will either overcome filter loss or may exhibit some gain.

Filters may be classified as simple or complex and one way of doing this is to refer to the filter by order number. The higher the order number of a filter the greater its complexity. Thus, the filter in Figure 5-28 is a second-order low-pass filter. A higher order filter can be obtained by cascading two or more second-order filters. We can take the filter in Figure 5-28 and change it into a fourth-order filter (Fig. 5-29). This fourth-order filter consists of a second-order filter (Fig. 5-28) repeated or cascaded.

Higher order filters are used to achieve certain desired results. Ideally in a low-pass filter, commonly used in the audio chain in compact disc players, we want all

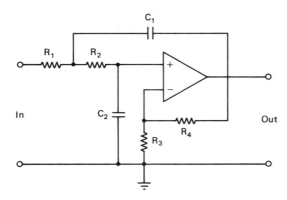

Figure 5-28 Second-order low-pass filter.

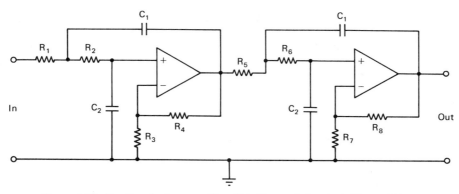

Figure 5-29 Fourth-order low-pass filter. This filter, and the one in Figure 5-28, are active types.

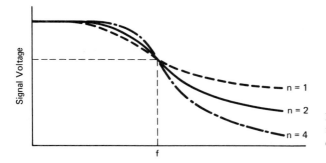

Figure 5-30 The higher the order of the filter (*n*), the sharper the rolloff. The dashed lines indicate an ideal condition.

frequencies passed up until a cutoff point and then we want an extremely sharp dropoff. This is indicated by the rectangle in the graph of Figure 5-30. What we will get will depend on the order of the filter. If we use a first-order filter, we will get the response curve marked *n* = 1. This filter has a very gradual rolloff. If we use a second-order filter the rolloff will become sharper as shown by the line marked *n* = 2. The rolloff becomes even sharper with a fourth-order filter (*n* = 4).

It might seem that this would solve the filter problem quite nicely. Just use the highest order filter needed to do the job, and as a matter of fact that is exactly what some manufacturers do. But the higher the order of the filter the greater its construction complexity, and the greater the need for careful engineering design to make sure the elements of the filter do not interfere with each other or cause other problems. There is also the matter of manufacturing cost, since the higher cost of such a filter must inevitably be reflected in the price of the compact disc player.

The Analog/Digital Filter

The analog filter in Figure 5-31(a) is an L-type low-pass LC filter. The output is obtained with the set time delay and rounded peaks determined by the circuit's frequency response and attenuation characteristics. If the filter is given a certain number of

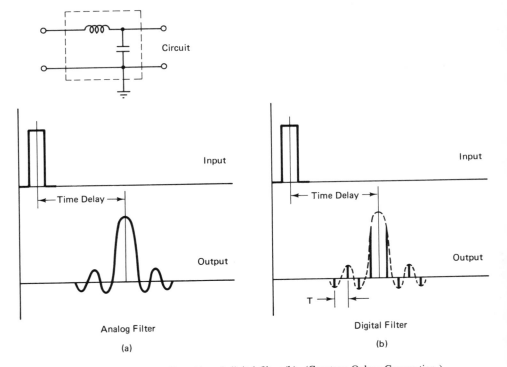

Figure 5-31   Analog filter (a) and digital filter (b). (Courtesy Onkyo Corporation.)

stages and a good multiplication factor, a pulse train output like that shown in Figure 5-31(b) is obtained. In other words this circuit should be considered simply as a filter which acts as an analog circuit filter in a digital circuit. For this reason, it is called a digital filter.

Advantage of Digital and Analog Filtering Systems

Modern technology has made analog filters quite effective but there can be a problem since analog filters by themselves supply limited performance. By combining an analog filter with a digital filter and applying both in just the right way, the limitations found with analog filters are minimized.

Oversampling and the Digital Filter

There are two ways of removing spurious ultrasonic components produced by digital sampling. One is to use a multipole analog output filter having a steep dropoff characteristic; the other is to use oversampling and digital filtering. Whether frequency phase shifts at the upper frequency end of the audio band caused by sharp cutoff analog output

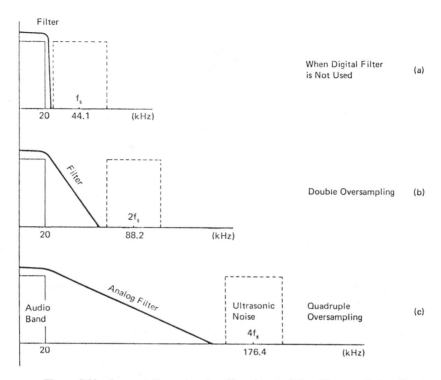

Figure 5-32 Oversampling and analog filter characteristics. (Courtesy Onkyo Corporation.)

filters produce an effect that is audible in the reproduced sound is the subject of some debate. The amount of phase shift may be small and can be measured but whether its effects can be heard or not is subjective.

The relationship between oversampling and analog filters is shown in Figure 5-32. The filter attenuation characteristics in Figure 5-32(b) are not as steep as in Figure 5-32(a) and become still more gradual in Figure 5-32(c). Likewise, the group delay characteristics in the audio band become flatter and the high end phase characteristics also improve. But since it would appear to be logical to go from single sampling to double, would it not be advisable to proceed to quadruple sampling? The improvement in using quadruple oversampling is only marginal in respect to double oversampling.

DOUBLE OVERSAMPLING AND DIGITAL FILTERING

One of the most important factors affecting the sound quality of a compact disc player is the way in which that player converts the digital sounds picked up from the compact disc back into its analog form for delivery to an audio amplifier. Not all compact disc players use the eight-to-fourteen technique (EFM) and use instead a true 16-bit digital-to-analog (D/A) converter for the widest dynamic range and lowest noise. This is preferred to the 14-bit type that requires a complex procedure to artificially bring the S/N ratio back up to that of a 16-bit system.

To further assure that the analog output signal is an exact representation of its digital counterpart, CD players can employ a double oversampling technique and a digital filter. By doubling the sampling rate from 44.1 kHz to 88.2 kHz and passing the digital signal through a filter, this system moves the beginning of the first band of ultrasonic noise in the analog signal from 24.1 kHz to 68.2 kHz. Since this noise no longer begins so soon after the end of the audio frequency band at 20 kHz, it is possible to use a low-pass filter having a more gradual rolloff.

The advantage of the double oversampling digital filtering technique is that there is almost no signal degradation, particularly alteration of phase characteristics that steep filters inevitably introduce around the cutoff frequency of 20 kHz. Sonically, this means that high frequency sounds are clearer and free of the harshness associated with single sampling, giving the music a quality that would otherwise be lost.

If we were to connect each of the peak values (Fig. 5-33), we would have the original analog waveform. However, the fact that we can connect these points in the drawing does not mean that is what we will actually have, at least not without some further electronic effort.

These instantaneous values could be regarded as a series of extremely short-lived voltage pulses. These can shock excite the production of a large series of frequencies which are multiples of the sampling frequency. Thus, if the circuitry in a compact disc player uses the standard sampling frequency of 44.1 kHz, a multiple series of bands of signal voltage will be generated, starting at twice the sampling frequency, three times, and so on (Fig. 5-34). These are not single, fixed frequency voltage points but bands of frequencies centered around the newly generated pulses.

Since these frequencies are well above the top end of the audio spectrum, it might be thought that they could produce no ill effects. However, the instantaneous pulse at 44.1 kHz does have what looks like a lower sideband capable of extending very close to the upper frequency limit of the audio signal. Its effect is to reduce the output level of the audio signal in that frequency region. We can now see the advantage of oversam-

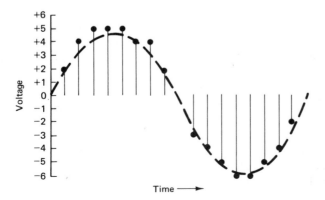

Figure 5-33 Theoretically, connecting the peak values could produce the equivalent of the analog waveform (dashed line).

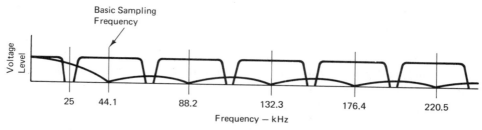

Figure 5-34 Frequency sampling shock excites bands of frequencies around the sampling point.

pling. If the sampling frequency is 88.2 kHz, then the spurious signals that accompany the instantaneous values of the pulse voltages are so far above the high end of the audio frequency band that there is no possibility of interfering with it.

Brickwall Filtering

The ideal low-pass filter would be a first-order type with such a sharp and steep rolloff that no signals having a frequency higher than the frequency at the rolloff point would be able to get through. Such a filter could be described as a brickwall type.

If the sampling frequency is 44.1 kHz, the rolloff frequency would be half this amount or approximately 22 kHz. But no filter, not even one of the higher order types, is capable of immediate and sharp attenuation of frequencies above the passband.

Since we commonly accept 20 kHz as the upper frequency limit of the audio spectrum and if we use a sampling frequency of 44.1 kHz, then we have what could be called a guard band between 20 kHz and the start of rolloff in the low-pass filter. This is 2 kHz obtained by subtracting 20 kHz from half the sampling frequency. We do not use a low-pass filter with a rolloff of 20 kHz since the high frequency end of the audio spectrum would be affected by it.

It can be considered fortunate that 20 kHz was selected as the upper frequency limit of the audio band. Many of us have a hearing limit that is 18 kHz, and more often less than that, so using 20 kHz gives us a guard band, also of 2 kHz, between what we can hear as a practical matter and an outer limit that is idealized. Further, using 20 kHz as that outer limit lets us use approximately twice that frequency as our sampling frequency.

Transversal Filter

The filters previously described are not the only ones that can be used and some are quite elaborate. One of these is a transversal filter, a component that could contain as many as 96 elements. Using quadruple oversampling and a digital transversal filter, spurious signals produced at the sampling frequencies could be suppressed quite effectively.

Quite commonly a digital filter is inserted in the line preceding digital-to-analog conversion with an analog filter following the sample and hold circuitry (Fig. 5-35). A top quality CD player could include a 96th order double oversampling digital filter on a CMOS LSI chip with a 9th order analog low-pass filter. In fact, there is no point in using quadruple oversampling unless an even lower order analog filter is used. However, the use of such a filter will make the circuit more susceptible to noise.

In practice, then, double oversampling has the best overall balance and for this reason, many CD players use it, although a few do use the quadruple form. Very few, if any, CD players work with sampling at 44.1 kHz, although you may find some older CD players using it. With double oversampling it is possible to use a seventh-order active filter which provides better cutoff characteristics without deterioration in high end phase characteristics. The result is a better response at the treble end with smoother rounding off than in earlier components.

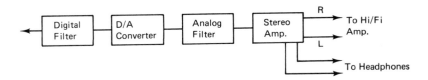

Figure 5-35 Filter preceding D/A converter handles digital signal; that following handles analog.

Conversion Resolution

The accuracy of quantizing the analog signal is determined by the number of binary bits used in the sampling process. If 16 bits are used, and this is commonly the case, the accuracy is superior to a 14-bit rate.

The second factor is the sampling rate. A sampling rate of 88.2 kHz results in better sound translation accuracy from analog to digital than a rate of 44.1 kHz. But even with a high sampling rate, and some are at 176.4 kHz, and using 16 bits, we cannot expect a perfect match between the decimal value of all samplings and their binary number equivalents.

The transition from digital pulses to an equivalent audio waveform seems simple enough for it would only seem necessary to use a digital-to-analog converter. However, the conversion process does present problems because with this basic arrangement it is possible to generate noise and unwanted signals. For these reasons various digital-to-analog arrangements are used plus a variety of filter schemes. The more elaborate these become the higher the cost of the compact disc player. While all compact disc players are basically alike, they can differ considerably circuitwise.

NOISE

Bifilar Winding Noise Filter

Pulses ranging from several hundred kHz to 20 to 30 MHz are generated constantly in the digital section of compact disc players. This pulse group can be passed at low levels via the ground and power supply lines and also by electromagnetic or capacitive coupling to analog circuits where it can affect sound quality. If this pulsed noise is included in the compact disc player's output, sound quality can be affected in many ways in the amplifier to which the compact disc is connected.

This noise can be categorized as two different types: normal mode noise (V_{NMN}) and common mode (V_{CMN}) noise (Fig. 5-36). Although normal mode noise can be removed by regular resistance-capacitance (RC) filters, common mode noise cannot. And if loop I exists the problem is complicated by the common mode noise becoming normal mode noise. The removal of common mode noise, therefore, is important.

The output circuits can be equipped with a bifilar wound filter (Fig. 5-37) for eliminating common mode noise. The filter consists of a coil formed by a bifilar

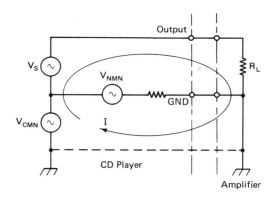

Figure 5-36 Noise group V_{CMN} and V_{NMN}. (Courtesy Onkyo Corporation.)

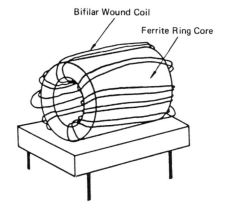

Figure 5-37 Bifilar wound filter. (Courtesy Onkyo Corporation.)

winding on a highly efficient ferrite core. The common mode noise filter is inserted in the line between the analog output and the audio output terminals on the rear of the compact disc player (Fig. 5-38).

In electronics there is always a tradeoff between what is wanted and what is obtainable. Thus, the filter following the digital-to-analog converter should have a slope that is steep enough so that any signals above 20 kHz are removed. The problem is to do so without degrading the signal in any way and to avoid any unnecessary phase shifting. It is easy to assume that this could best be done by using an active low-pass filter instead of one that is passive, but the problem of phase shifting, especially near the cutoff point, will still exist. Furthermore, the fact that the filter is an active type, possibly using an op amp, introduces new problems. The amplifier, for example, can be affected by temperature changes and in time its component values could also increase or decrease.

These difficulties arise from the transition of digital to analog. The output of the digital-to-analog converter does have an analog signal in its output but not in the smooth, unbroken form to which we are accustomed. Instead, it consists of a succession of instantaneous values.

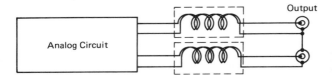

Figure 5-38   CMN filter. (Courtesy Onkyo Corporation.)

Quantization Noise

The difference between the decimal value and the binary value is called quantization noise. However, by using 16-bit binaries and a high enough sampling rate, this noise can be kept to an inaudible level. Each bit used during the quantization process contributes about 6 dB to the signal-to-noise ratio. For a 14-bit system this would be 6 $\times$ 14 = 84 dB and for a 16-bit system would be 6 $\times$ 16 = 96 dB. While a signal-to-noise ratio of 96 dB is obviously preferable, a S/N of 84 dB is considered very good.

Line Noise

Electrical noise in the form of voltage spikes (Fig. 5-39) can ride in on the power line voltage. While the line voltage is nominally 117 volts, the spikes can be in the order of several kilovolts peak to peak and are capable of causing considerable damage to any electronic component connected to a powered outlet. The voltage spikes can be caused by lightning or can be generated by equipment connected to the line.

While the line frequency is 50 Hz or 60 Hz, voltage spikes can be any frequency but are usually much higher than that of the line. Protective filters are commercially available and can be inserted between the line cord of the compact disc player and the power line output (Fig. 5-40). The line filter consists of an L-C network and may

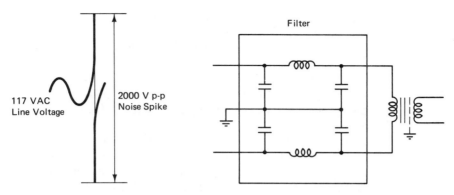

Figure 5-39 High-voltage electrical noise spike superimposed on line voltage (not drawn to scale).

Figure 5-40 Line noise filter.

include a one-to-one power transformer equipped with an electrostatic shield connected to ground. In the L-C circuit the capacitors act to bypass the higher frequency voltage pulses while the inductors have a high reactance to their passage. The values of capacitance and inductance are selected so they have little effect on the much lower frequency of the line voltage.

AUDIO OUTPUT

The output of the analog filter is a continuous, unbroken audio wave in analog form. Before being supplied to the output terminals of the compact disc player, it is supplied to a stereo audio amplifier for strengthening to the point that its amplitude will be adequate for driving an external preamplifier, with that component as a separate unit or integrated with a power amplifier.

Connecting the CD Player

While all compact disc players are equipped with a pair of left/right audio output terminals into which an RCA plug can be inserted, some have two such pairs of jacks. When two jacks are available they will have different impedances and different signal voltage levels. In a typical unit one output jack has an output impedance of 3.75 kilohms supplying a level of 0.5 volt measured at 1 kHz. The other jack has an output of about six times as much and supplies 3 volts at an impedance of 600 ohms. However, the load impedance should be 10 kilohms or more.

The analog stereo amplifier following the low-pass filter is another possible source of sound distortion and preferably is a class A output amplifier that isolates voltage control from the current supply. A circuit of this kind avoids the influence of load impedance on voltage amplifier operation. The circuit has two audio outputs: a fixed value of audio for driving an external audio preamplifier and headphone output equipped with a level control.

Fig. 5-41 shows how to connect a compact disc player to a preamplifier or integrated amplifier. These components should have a pair of input terminals marked CD or DAD. If not, then use the aux input terminals. If these are not available, use the tape input jacks.

The line output of the compact disc player is connected to the preamplifier or integrated amplifier by a pair of audio cables ending in phono plugs. On the rear of the compact disc player are a single pair of jacks marked "Line Out." These are the output signal terminals. The audio cables are usually supplied with the compact disc player.

The terminals at the output of the CD and the input of the receiver or integrated amplifier will be marked to identify polarity: either L and R; plus and minus; or a red dot to indicate plus. Or the plugs may be colored red and white. The L-terminal of the disc player should connect to the corresponding L-jack of the receiver or integrated amplifier. Similarly, the R-terminal of the CD should be cable connected to the corresponding R-jack.

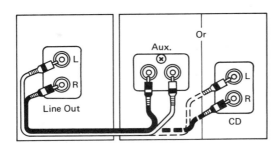

Figure 5-41 Compact disc player can be connected to aux or CD line input of preamplifier or integrated amplifier. Use audio shielded cable equipped with RCA plugs. Watch polarity. Connect left signal output of player to left signal input of amplifier; right output to right input. (Courtesy Akai America, Ltd.)

Connecting a Tape Deck

A pair of input and output audio cables will be needed. While single cables can be used for a total of four individual cables, a simpler arrangement is to use a double (twin or joined) cable as shown in Fig. 5-42. The tape deck has a pair of double jacks, one marked line input, the other line output. Line output means audio signal output and is connected to the tape monitor jacks of the receiver or separate audio amplifier, whichever is used. If the receiver does not have terminals marked tape monitor or tape input, use the aux input instead. The line input of the tape deck is connected to the tape rec (tape recorder) input of the receiver or amplifier. When the tape deck is set to the play mode, the audio signal exits from the tape deck via its line output terminals and is delivered to the tape monitor terminals of the amplifer.

You can expect sound deterioration if you dub the sound from a CD onto audio tape, whether using an audio cassette or open reel. Tape does not have the dynamic range of a compact disc, and it also contributes noise. A CD is an excellent sound source, so you will get better results than in recording AM or FM broadcasts or in dubbing from phono records. But you cannot expect the CD to overcome the inherent deficiencies of tape.

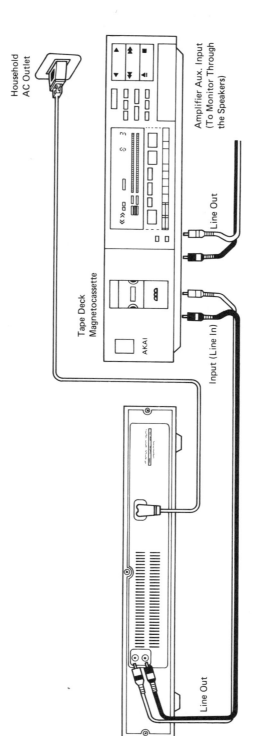

Figure 5-42 Connections for tape deck dubbing. (Courtesy Akai America, Ltd.)

Household
AC Outlet

Amplifier Aux. Input
(To Monitor Through
the Speakers)

Line Out

Tape Deck
Magnetocassette

AKAI

Input (Line In)

Line Out

Dubbing from a compact disc to tape makes little sense. The CD has a longer life expectancy. Phono records are sometimes dubbed onto tape so as to maintain those records in mint condition, something that is unnecessary with the CD. You might want to dub onto cassettes so as to be able to take CD music along with you in your car. However, compact disc players are made for car use, require very little room and can operate from the car's battery. The output sound will be superior to that supplied by a tape dubbed from a CD.

Connecting Headphones

Commonly, compact disc players are also supplied with headphone output with that output having its own signal level control. Customarily, there is just one headphone output, but there may be two, particularly in players in the higher price range. In some units insertion of the headphone jack automatically cuts off signals supplied to the speaker system. If the compact disc player does not have headphone jacks, you will be able to use those that are supplied with the preamplifier or power amplifier. If the compact disc player or the following external amplifier provides for just one set of headphones, you can get an adapter that will let you use two pairs simultaneously.

The headphones can have an impedance of 200 to 600 ohms and can be connected with a 1/4″ (6.3 mm) plug. You can also use standard phone plug-to-stereo mini-jack adapters in the headphone jack. The headphone amplifier in the compact disc player should be able to drive nearly any headphones to concert levels. If you find that the headphone signals are not loud enough, try another pair having a higher input sensitivity. Before doing so, however, make sure the headphone output level control is at its maximum position. Headphone output level can be 100 milliwatts across 32 ohms.

AUDIO AND THE COMPACT DISC PLAYER

Since compact disc players use digital electronics to a substantial degree, they are sometimes incorrectly regarded as a dedicated digital component. The fact is they are not purely digital but are analog from the time the digital-to-analog converter supplies an output to the audio output jacks of the component or to a following filter. Every compact disc player is therefore a hybrid unit, consisting of a combination of digital and analog electronics.

DE-EMPHASIS

Definite values of de-emphasis are built into compact disc players. Using Sony's test disc, YEDS 2, de-emphasis should be -0.37 dB at 1 kHz; -4.53 dB at 5 kHz and -9.04 dB at 10 kHz.

DIGITAL TIME LENS

A digital time lens is an add-on component inserted between the compact disc player and its following preamplifier or integrated power amplifier. The first thing it does is to matrix the L and R signals to form L + R and L − R signals. The L − R signal is then boosted in amplitude relative to the L + R signal and the two signals are rematrixed to produce modified left and right signals. In addition the device inserts an equalization characteristic designed to restore the octave-to-octave balance originally intended by the musicians and the recording engineer.

LIGHT-EMITTING DIODE DISPLAYS

Electroluminescent diodes better known as light-emitting diodes (LEDs) can be used to supply information about the operating status of the compact disc player including track number, elapsed time, remaining operating time, and so on.

LEDs are characterized by color and by construction. Typically, colors are red, green, orange, and yellow. Red is the most widely used color for the in-home player.

The construction of an LED varies from the single type to the seven-segment LED and the dot matrix LED. The single LED, a diode, delivers a narrow wavelength band of light. The voltage drop for the single LED is 1.2 to 2.4 volts with a current range of 2 to 20 milliamperes. LEDs may be grouped and so a seven-segment LED consists of an arrangement of single LEDs. The LEDs can be arranged so the information they supply is numeric only, alphabetic, or alphanumeric.

Alloys of gallium and gallium arsenide (GaAs) produce fairly efficient radiation. The LEDs are packaged in plastic or metal and are made as a diode chip positioned inside a small directional reflector. From a viewpoint of possible downtime, LEDs have a fairly long, useful working life.

LINE VOLTAGE AND POWER

Some CD players are made to operate from a line voltage of either 115 volts or 230 volts AC. If this is the case, set the line voltage selector usually positioned on the rear of the unit to the lower of these two voltages for use in the U.S. No damage will be done to the CD player if the switch is in its 230 volts position but the CD player will probably not function at all. However, if the line voltage selector is set to 115 volts and it is connected to a 230-volt line, the line fuse will most probably open. Damage to the player is possible.

Replacing the Power Fuse

The CD player will be completely inoperative if the line voltage fuse has opened. Replace the fuse only with the size and type recommended by the manufacturer. For a line voltage of 115 a typical fuse would be a slow-blow type rated at 1/2 ampere. Do not replace with one having a higher current carrying capacity. If the replacement fuse opens, check for a short circuit in the plug, the line cord, and the CD player's power supply.

Operating Power

The operating power for a compact disc player ranges from 16 watts to 50 watts. In this respect the power required by a player supplies some indication as to the feature capabilities. Portables, for example, are usually minimum power units and sacrifice functions to keep operating power down so as to extend battery operating life.

DISC LOADING

There are two methods available for loading a compact disc into its player—either top loading or front loading. The front-loading method uses a hinged door that opens so the disc can be inserted.

The advantage of front loading for an in-home player is that other high-fidelity components may possibly be positioned on top of it. Front loading is also the preferred method for compact disc players used in cars.

MULTIPLE CD PLAYERS

At one time record changers were popular but their popularity declined for several reasons. Phono records are played on two sides, a problem that was difficult to overcome. Record changers relied strongly on mechanical contrivances and invariably these became troublesome. Furthermore, the changer did not handle phono records with kindness and so phono record buffs refused to trust their expensive discs to what came to be regarded as mechanical monsters. Changers became used mostly for background music.

Multiple CD changers have eliminated many of the record changer problems of the past. A representative changer is supplied with a magazine that can hold six CD discs. With this arrangement it is possible to access up to 32 tracks on any of the six discs, using random programming. Loading of the discs is handled automatically. The jukebox, probably the most successful of all the phono record changers, is now reappearing as a multiple CD player.

The advantage of the multiple CD player is that it can supply six hours or more of uninterrupted playing. One such unit that can simultaneously store 60 compact discs can randomly access these discs, permitting up to 45 hours of continuous playback. Still another unit intended for commercial use but with possible in-home applications can supply 72 hours of music with random access programming. An optical fiber linkage permits connection to three additional CD players, and playback time is thereby increased to more than several hundred hours.

The multiple CD changer (Fig. 5-43) can be used in the home or car and can play 10 discs. If all 10 discs are played sequentially, a listener can enjoy 10 hours of continuous music from each disc magazine. Direct access permits selection of any track from any disc, from either the player or a remote control. It is possible to play any track randomly from any disc. Additional disc magazines are available.

The disadvantage of multiple CD players is incompatability. A magazine of discs for one multiple CD player will not fit into a comparable unit made by a different manufacturer.

Figure 5-43 Disc magazine holds 10 discs. (Courtesy Sony Corporation of America.)

PROFESSIONAL VERSUS NONPROFESSIONAL CD PLAYERS

CD players for in-home use and those intended for professional work have a number of differences. The output analog signal terminals on the home unit use RCA plugs; the professional type has rear panel Cannon connectors for balanced line outputs. The professional units are designed for rack mounting; those for home use are available in a variety of sizes.

Professional CD players use more effective shielding to make the unit impervious to the RF interference generated in rack-mount installations common to studios. As protection against corrosion, the jacks are gold plated for both fixed and variable outputs. The professional unit may have two audio outputs: one with a fixed 2.0 volts

RMS with the other delivering output that is variable over a 0 to 5-volt range. With the help of the variable output control, it becomes possible to match the output level of the CD player to the input requirements of other components. Still another feature of the professional CD player is a subcode output terminal for the display of still-image graphics.

The inner construction of the professional unit is much more substantial than for those made for in-home use. Since rotating parts and vibrations inside the player can induce microphonics in the high-gain audio circuitry, these models use a special vibration damping assembly. The analog audio circuit board is mounted on a copper-plated solid steel assembly which stabilizes the circuit assembly and effectively damps any internal vibration.

DIFFERENCES IN MUSICAL QUALITY

Not all compact disc players are alike in terms of quality, just as all turntables are not alike. And not all compact discs have the same quality any more than do all phono records. Since the introduction of the first compact disc players, audio manufacturers have worked hard to find ways to design players that would sell on the basis of price rather than on features or quality. With audio components there is always an intense drive toward lower prices, and this is pressured by the gradual increase in the number and variety of discs available. This is augmented by the growing general awareness of the advantages of the CD system versus the analog turntable. There is no question that the CD is much more user friendly and this has tremendous appeal.

There are a large number of different CD players available—different not only in price, but in technology and in quality. The basic technology may be the same and so all CD players can play all CD discs, but it is the sound output that can be and usually is different. CD players can vary not only in the circuitry that is used but can be mechanically dissimilar as well.

There are numerous differences among CD players: the use of oversampling and digital anti-aliasing filters versus direct conversion at the 44.1 kHz data rate followed by "brick-wall" analog filters; if oversampling is used, whether it doubles or quadruples the data rate; the "order" of the filters, that is, how "sharp" they are; whether all 16 bits are converted from digital to analog form or only the 14 most significant ones; and whether a single D/A converter is shared by the left and right channels or separate converters are used for each. Almost everyone would agree that it is preferable to use quadruple oversampling, digital filtering, and to convert all 16 bits using separate D/A converters for each channel. The finest CD players use this approach, yet there are significant differences in sound quality even among them.

In a compact disc player, the serial bit stream is converted into 16-bit parallel "words," which are temporarily stored in a digital buffer (or latch) and then clocked in the D/A converter (Fig. 5-44). Each bit carries a different "weight"; from the most significant bit (MSB) to the least significant bit (LSB). In the converter, each bit generates a current that is summed in a resistor to develop the correct analog output

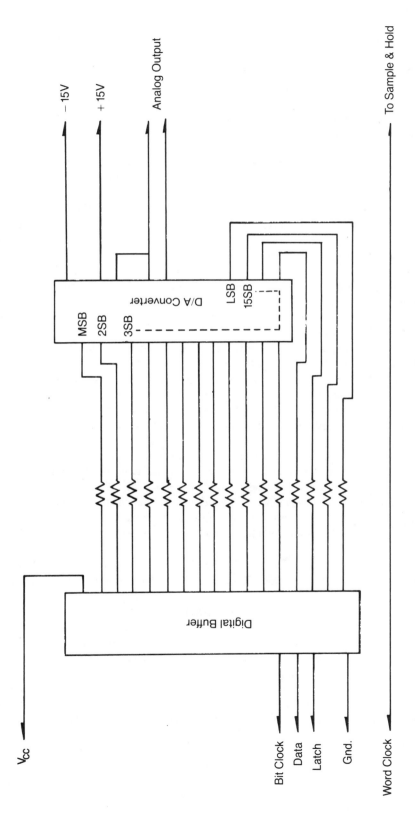

Figure 5-44 Conventional digital-to-analog converter. (Courtesy Nakamichi U.S.A. Corporation.)

voltage. The more significant the bit, the greater the current that bit injects into the summing network. Each successive bit contributes twice as much current, hence generates twice the output voltage, of its nearest less significant neighbor.

The accuracy in the current that is generated by the more significant bits must be much better, in percentage terms, than that needed by the least significant bits to maintain overall accuracy, that is, low distortion. (The most significant bit generates half the total current!) As far as static accuracy is concerned it is possible to find D/A converters that are up for the task. They are expensive and one may have to hand-select the best for a top-of-the-line model, but it is possible.

Dynamically, the situation is quite different. No matter how fast the transistor switches are in the D/A converter and no matter how well its internal circuitry is laid out, some stray capacitance is inevitable and it takes longer to slew a large current change than to slew a small current change.

Thus, it takes a finite time for the converter to "settle down" to the correct output after a digital word is applied. During the settling time, a noise burst or "glitch" is generated. These glitches must be removed to prevent noise in the output and the most common method of deglitching the D/A converter is to use an analog sample-and-hold circuit following conversion (Fig. 5-45).

The actual output of the converter is a series of analog pulses (one for each digital word) whose amplitudes represent the analog values of the signal at the various sample times. The glitches occur at the edges of each pulse. In the sample-and-hold circuit, field-effect transistor (FET) switches are synchronized to the word-clock and used to sample the converter output after it has settled down and to store (or hold) the correct analog values as a charge on a capacitor until the next digital word has been converted and stabilized.

If the FET switches and the storage capacitor were ideal components, there would be no problem with this approach. However, components in the real world aren't ideal. The FET has a finite and nonlinear "on" resistance that distorts the analog signal passing through it. Furthermore, the dielectric in the capacitor has absorption and memory characteristics that prevent the capacitor from accurately responding to small changes in signal level. As a result, the low-level resolution and sound quality of the system is impaired.

The problem occurs in permitting the glitches to be generated and then trying to remove the aftermath in the analog domain. A better technique is to prevent the glitches from occurring in the first place.

In the Nakamichi glitch-free D-to-A converter, the threshold levels of the eight most significant bits are adjusted as they enter the D/A converter so they are in time synchronism with the remaining 8 bits after conversion. Thus, the output pulse reaches its proper value immediately, the conversion is glitch-free and there is no need for a sample-and-hold or other analog deglitcher after the converter.

The threshold levels of the three most significant bits (Fig. 5-46) are adjusted separately from the threshold levels of the next five most significant bits, the former for minimum high-frequency distortion and the latter for minimum low-frequency distortion.

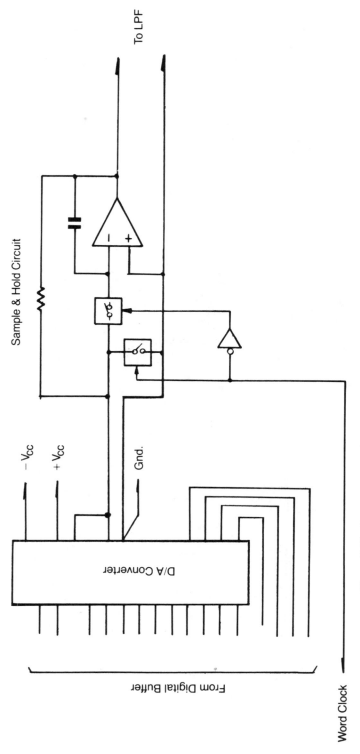

Figure 5-45 Signal processing following the digital-to-analog converter. (Courtesy Nakamichi U.S.A. Corporation.)

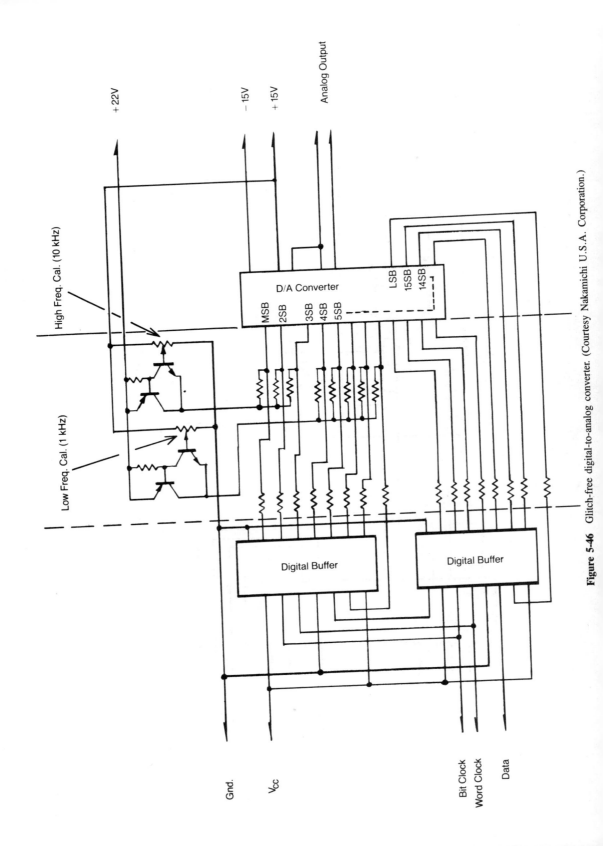

Figure 5-46 Glitch-free digital-to-analog converter. (Courtesy Nakamichi U.S.A. Corporation.)

The glitch-free D/A converter permits the output of the converter (Fig. 5-47) to directly feed the 3rd order Bessel filter (and ultimately the output terminals) without passing through an analog sample-and-hold. Eliminating the sample-and-hold with its distortion prone FETs and low-resolution capacitors greatly improves the sound of the player especially with respect to the transparency and depth of the music, conveyed by how smoothly sound decays into silence.

Many factors contribute to creating differences between players, primarily the way in which they convert the digital signal to analog. Many CD players have only one D/A converter, so after the digital signal is converted to analog, it must be demultiplexed into left- and right-channel signals, a process that adds distortion. A better arrangement is to use two D/A converters so the signal can be demultiplexed while it is still in digital form.

While the emphasis is on digital technology, it is well to remember that every CD player at some point becomes directly involved in analog circuitry. Furthermore, even such prosaic circuitry as the power supply can affect sound quality. The opportunities for differences between CD players are substantial.

There are other factors that can result in variations in musical quality. The audio analog output of the CD player is delivered to high-fidelity components, and since there can be tremendous differences in their quality and capabilities, a compact disc may not sound quite the same when played through various audio systems. Not only is the sound dependent on the quality of the following preamplifier, power amplifier, and speaker systems but also depends on the listening room itself and on outboard components such as an equalizer. As a general rule, the higher the power output rating of the power amplifier, the better the sound.

THE TRIPLE FUNCTION CD PLAYER

Some CD players are not much larger than the compact discs they play and so are small enough and light enough to perform a triple function. They can be used as an in-home unit, a portable, or in an auto. To be able to do so, they must be able to work from a portable battery pack, from the car's battery, and in the home operate from the AC power line, generally via an AC converter. In such units, since they will be subjected to much more vibration and shock than a permanently mounted in-home CD player, two factors are of paramount importance. The first is the method of mounting the laser beam assembly so it is practically shock proof. The other is the design of a hard-working error correction system.

No CD player functions by itself and requires an audio amplifier and accompanying speakers. For in-home use this can be supplied by an existing audio or high-fidelity system. In the car the CD player can deliver its sound to the car's radio receiver. When working as a portable, the CD player can work through the portable's receiver, using the amplifier in that receiver. In all cases, however, no matter how the CD player is used, it must be able to connect to the associated equipment.

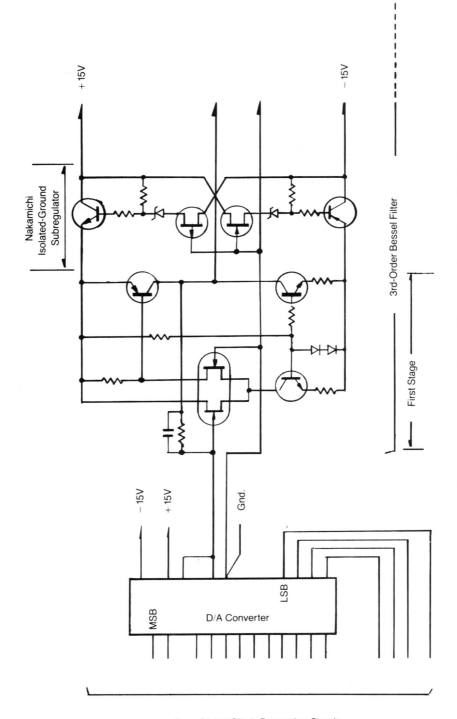

Figure 5-47 Following the D/A converter the signal is processed by a 3rd-order Bessel filter. (Courtesy Nakamichi U.S.A. Corporation.)

From Digital Glitch-Prevention Circuit

COMPILING A PROGRAM

The easiest way to listen to a compact disc is to let it start with the first track and play through without interruption to the last. However, programming is so simple that you can arrange it to suit your own musical tastes. You may prefer doing so for a number of reasons: You may want to change the sequence of the selections; you may want to skip one or more selections; you may want to compare musical passages; or you may want to program prior to dubbing on tape. Programming will not affect the quality of playback. Unlike a VCR there is no tracking control on a compact player nor is one ever needed. The simple act of inserting a disc into the player means that when the door closes, scanning of the disc starts automatically with the number of tracks, time counts, and preliminary data stored in the microprocessor's memory. This means you can program your selections at once.

REMOTE CONTROL

Remote control is now a commonly used adjunct component for compact disc players and like the players, are in a wide range as far as quality and features are concerned. Remote control units are made for specific compact disc players and so are not interchangeable.

Known also as wireless remote control, they operate by using an infrared beam. The number of features is a variable just as is the variety of features of players. A quality remote control device will let you increase or decrease playback volume, speaker muting, and a normalizing button will return all functions to their standard positions.

Other controls include a keypad with digits 0 through 9. These digits address different functions. Thus, depressing digit 9 indicates a selection of track 9. You can also control such functions as pause, play, manual search, repeat programming, and band selection.

For remote control, the compact disc player is equipped with a remote sensor. Not all remote control units have the same operating distance, but with all of them the remote unit must be pointed directly at the remote sensor. Some experimentation will be required to learn the maximum effective distance between the compact disc player and the remote unit.

THE COMPACT DISC
PLAYER:
THE CONTROL PATH

All of the data for the compact disc player is encoded on the compact disc at the time it is manufactured. This includes not only audio information but error control signals, signals for controlling the position of the laser beam, microprocessor signals, and timing signals. At some point in the data flow circuitry of the compact disc player, audio data are separated from all other encoded information and are sent on their own path, ultimately ending in a pair of left and right audio signal output terminals.

Regardless of their ultimate function, the signals obtained by laser pickup from the tracks on the disc are all strengthened by a preamplifier immediately following the laser diodes. It is in this preamp, also called a high-frequency amplifier (HF), that data separation begins. The use of a high-frequency amplifier as a designation for this circuitry is more appropriate than preamplifier, a word commonly used to describe the voltage amplifier in a high-fidelity system. In analog high-fidelity systems the preamplifier requires a bandpass of only about 25 kHz, although these components often are rated at bandpasses of 50 kHz or 100 kHz.

The HF amplifier in the compact disc player must be able to pass a much wider band obtained by multiplying the number of bits (16 in this case) by the sampling frequency, either 44.1 kHz or an even order multiple. As a result the bandpass is close to 1 MHz; hence, HF is a more nearly correct designation.

There are two outputs from the HF amplifier. One of these is the audio signal path described in the preceding chapter. The other lead is to the focusing and tracking control circuitry (Fig. 6-1).

The laser pickup system, generally consisting of four photodiodes (and sometimes six), produces tracking and focusing signals. These signals and those representing audio are strengthened in the HF amplifier. The pits (bumps) and flats are encoded on the

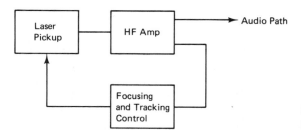

Figure 6-1 Audio and control signals use separate paths following the HF amplifier.

compact disc in a single track running radially from the first track out in the direction of the disc's perimeter. The data for controlling tracking are encoded on the disc at the same time as audio information. This tracking data appear at the output of the photo-diodes and are fed back to a radial tracking coil operated by a tracking servo following amplification. Tracking is handled by a pair of subbeams produced by a glass diffraction grating that is part of the optical system.

While the subbeams are in the same plane as the main tracking beam, they are positioned slightly ahead of and slightly behind that beam. These subbeams produce an error tracking signal if the main beam deviates even slightly from its track. With a left or right tracking deviation an error signal is produced which is fed back to a radial tracking servo which, in turn, moves the objective lens as required to get the main beam back on track.

Not all compact disc players use the same techniques for ensuring correct track-ing. In some players, the entire optical system is moved and in others a mirror is used. This mirror is positioned at right angles to the tracking beam so that the beam is reflected at a right angle. Any error tracking signals are applied to a servo which turns the mirror so that the correct mirror angle always exists. So what we have are three possible tracking error techniques: one in which the objective lens is moved, another in which the entire optical assembly is adjusted and a third in which tracking is controlled by a mirror. All of these methods depend on the return of an error signal to a servo which operates mechanically to return the beam to its correct tracking position.

AUTOMATIC FOCUSING

Both focusing and tracking are handled automatically in the compact disc player and are not subject to user control. The distances involved in tracking and focusing are so small and must be so precise that user control would be impractical.

The objective lens in some optical systems can be moved both horizontally and vertically. It can be adjusted horizontally as one of the techniques previously described for obtaining precise tracking, It can be moved vertically as a method of getting equally precise focusing. To give you some idea of the extremely small distances involved, if the objective lens moves more than one millionth of a meter closer to or farther away from the disc, an amplified error signal is produced and then returned to a servo which acts to put the beam precisely in focus.

THE FRAME

In television all the data to be presented on the screen are arranged in the form of frames. We have a comparable situation in a CD for all the data to be encoded on a disc are also set up as a series of frames. In television, the two fields which constitute a frame not only contain picture information but also data for controlling the line by line sweep that forms the picture.

In the same way a data frame used for a CD contains not only audio information but control data as well. Thus, at the beginning of each frame we have a pattern of 24 bits referred to as a sync pattern and produced by a sync generator at the time the disc is encoded. In the recording process the output of this sync generator (Fig. 6-2) is fed into a channel modulator used to drive the laser disc recording beam. Of course, the channel modulator also receives the audio signals in binary form.

Since the audio data and the sync signals are used sequentially and not simultaneously, they must be time controlled by a clock or timing generator. Because the utmost precision must be maintained, the timing generator is a crystal-controlled oscillator. Since the sync signals are precisely timed, in effect, we encode a clock onto the compact disc when it is cut by the recording laser beam. Consequently, the sync signal pattern located at the beginning of each data frame can be used for supplying timing signals.

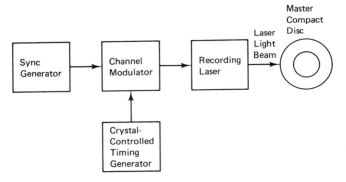

Figure 6-2 Sync pattern of 24 bits is produced by sync generator.

DATA ERRORS

Data errors can be caused by loss of tracking due to mechanical and acoustic vibration. Acoustic feedback and mechanical vibration can trigger the error correction circuits in a player. These circuits are positioned prior to the digital filters whose output is then delivered to the digital-to-analog circuitry.

The error correction may not be audible. You may not hear it as a chirp or interpret it as the result of mistracking. The trouble is that the error correction methods used in a compact disc player can produce sonic roughness or harshness.

In some CD players error correction is handled in fixed-size data blocks. Such players correct errors, whether due to tracking problems or due to data errors on the disc in a fixed-size block of frames. This means that data that are not in error are fixed (even though such fixing is not needed) right along with the data that are in error. The result is harsh, rough sound. If this sound is evidenced on a number of discs, then it is fairly obvious the fault lies in the CD player. A solution to this problem is the use of a variable-size frame window of error correction so that only truly bad data are fixed.

Since the only way the analog signal can be represented digitally is by a series of Os and ls, and since we are talking about billions of such bits on a disc, the chances for digital error are enormous. All it takes is a single change in a bit for the value of the string to become completely different. In an 8-bit group such as 10011001, representing decimal 153, the omission of the most significant bit at the extreme left means the binary value now becomes 00011001 and the decimal equivalent drops from 153 to 25. There is no such thing as a partially correct binary digit. It is either right or it is wrong.

SUBCODING

Audio signals do not occupy the first sections of the first track when a disc is encoded. The first bits of data entered on the disc via the laser cutting beam are the number of musical selections that are available for playback. The number will vary from one disc to the next but numbers such as 9 and 10 are typical for popular music. An opera could be just a single selection.

When a disc has a number of musical selections, there is a pause between them to allow for the insertion of identification codes. Musical selection identification codes are needed when the search function of the compact disc player is used.

Additional nonmusical data are also encoded on the disc to indicate whether de-emphasis should be used or not, since not all discs make use of pre-emphasis. With coding on the disc, de-emphasis is handled automatically and its amount is fixed.

Other data on the disc considered part of the subcode consist of information to be used in the compact disc player as control signals or for front panel display. Unlike the bits used for audio signals, those for subcoding are not audible and are not routed through the audio chain.

Subcoding data are added to the second multiplexer during the encoding process (Fig. 6-3). The second multiplexer serializes the subcoding data that are fed into it. Subcoding data do not occupy a separate track on the compact disc. The positioning of the data is handled on a timing basis by a crystal-controlled oscillator, a timing generator.

In the subcode a binary digit known as a pause bit supplies information to identify the beginning of a musical selection. The pause bit is positioned before each musical band and supplies the microprocessor with a signal that a musical program is about to begin. In turn, the microprocessor reads the subcode to determine if the selection is in accordance with the setting of the controls on the front panel of the compact disc player (Fig. 6-4).

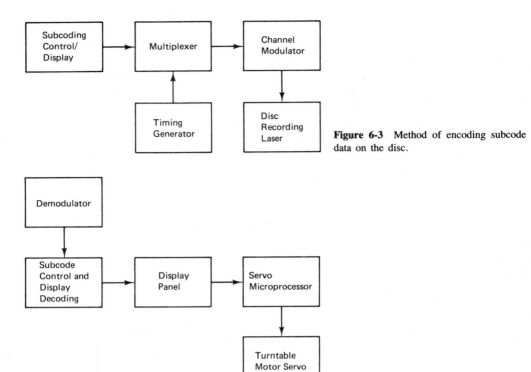

Figure 6-3 Method of encoding subcode data on the disc.

Figure 6-4 Subcode control method.

There is adequate space on the compact disc for existing subcode data. The subcode that is used is contained in every frame but there are also unused subcode bits. Each group of subcode bits is identified by letter beginning with P and ending with W, and so we have P, Q, R, S, T, U, V and W subcodes. Since only the P and Q subcodes are used, the two are sometimes known as the PQ codes. It is the PQ codes that supply band and control data. As mentioned earlier, they carry data about the total number of musical bands, when those bands begin and when they end. They are involved in index points which pinpoint specific musical passages within any selected band. They are also used to turn de-emphasis on as required or to keep it off if the disc being played was not recorded with pre-emphasis, and it supplies information about the final track of the last musical band, when playback of the disc is completed.

The Subcode Block

Unlike the 16-bit arrangement of audio data, subcodes contain only eight bits. The R, S, T, U, V and W subcodes are unused and available for other purposes. Even though these are in different frames, they can be operated as a continuous and sequential data group forming a subcode block, with the subcode blocks measured in the thousands.

There are enough of these to form video pictures, complete with synchronization, data instructions, and parity bits.

There are enough subcode blocks to produce several hundred video images. These are stills and not moving pictures, but they can be used to accompany sound data encoded on the disc. These stills could be musical liner notes along the methods used by analog phono records, pictures of musical bands or composers, pictures of paintings, or pictures intended for specific educational purposes.

To be able to use this subcode information the compact disc player will need to be supplied with subcode data output ports connected to a television monitor. This would avoid the need for modulating an RF carrier. Alternatively, if only a TV set is available, an RF modulator would be needed to interface the compact disc player's still picture output with the antenna input terminals of the TV receiver. The carrier frequency of the modulator would probably be that of either channel 3 or 4. Inevitably in the future, TV sets will be made that are CD ready, just as we now have sets that are cable ready.

MULTIPLEXING

Multiplexing is a technique commonly used in FM broadcasting and is intended for the transmission and separation of stereo signals. It also means the transmission of two channels on a signal carrier so they can be recovered independently in the receiver. To emphasize their ability to handle multiplexed signals, FM receivers are often referred to as MPX, the usual abbreviation for multiplex.

A multiplexing technique is also used as one of the steps in the making of a compact disc. The sampling of an analog waveform, the quantization of a series of instantaneous voltage values of that waveform, and the conversion of their decimal values to binary form are handled separately for the left and right stereo channels. As indicated in Figure 6-5, following the analog-to-digital conversion circuitry, the output is brought into the first of a pair of multiplexers. The multiplexer supplies the input signal to a CIRC error correction coding circuit, immediately followed by the second of the multiplexers. The timing of the data to be encoded is handled by a crystal-controlled clock, a timing generator connected to both multiplexers. Each of the multiplexers handles a single channel of sound with each of the channels handled serially.

A multiplexer can be regarded as a digital switch. It will accept two or more inputs and will then multiplex them into single line output. In the PCM the multiplexer receives the alternate lines of stereo data and then multiplexes them into a single line

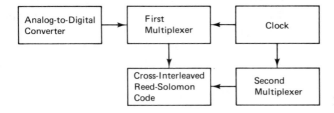

Figure 6-5 Multiplexer connections.

string. An action opposite that of multiplexing can be achieved by a demultiplexer, a unit that accepts a single input, separating that input into two or more lines of data.

MICROPROCESSOR CONTROL

You may read descriptions of compact disc players as being equipped with a microcomputer but this is not entirely correct. The player will have two microprocessors, but a microprocessor and a microcomputer are not identical. A microprocessor has all the circuits necessary to do logic operations; that is, it can control servo motors which will operate laser control circuits, demodulation, error correction, decoding, and the front panel operating display. A microcomputer, on the other hand, can be programmed to do arithmetic functions for which there is no need in the compact disc player. A microcomputer, also called a microcontroller, not only has input and output ports but is also equipped with two types of memory devices: a random-access memory (RAM) and a read-only memory (ROM). The microprocessors incorporated in a compact disc player are equipped with RAM units only. A microcomputer contains a microprocessor, and so a microprocessor can be considered as a part of a computer.

One of the big differences between a ROM and a RAM is that the ROM cannot be changed by the owner of the compact disc player. For the compact disc player, we need a memory that can take instructions and this is done simply by operating the various controls on the front panel of the player.

Basically, the RAM is quite simple. In its elementary form it consists of a capacitor and a transistor. When the capacitor is charged, we have the equivalent of binary 1 and when it is discharged it is the equivalent of binary 0. However, in RAM the charge on the capacitor tends to leak away and, therefore, the capacitor (actually a large number of them) need constant recharging. This process is referred to as capacitor refreshing, or simply, refreshing. A ROM, on the other hand, can retain its data without the need for refreshing.

A microprocessor can be completely stored on a chip, a very small section of semiconductor material. The memory capacity is measured in K units. Usually, the K designation is a multiplier with a value of 1,000. A resistor that measures 5K has a value of 5,000 ohms. In microprocessors K represents 2^{10} or 1,024. This means that a lK memory can store up to 1,024 bits of data. A 64K memory can store 65,536 bits.

Microprocessors are used in compact disc players to perform two basic functions: one to control the various servos, the other is in the audio signal path following demodulation circuitry (Fig. 6-6). The designation for a microprocessor in compact disc block diagrams or circuits is μP. The first letter is the Greek letter mu, representing micro, while the letter P is the abbreviation for processor. Since the units used in compact disc players are microprocessors and not microcomputers, no external software is required. The compact disc player does receive instructions from the user only by means of operating controls on the front of the player. This is a form of programming but it is not the kind of programming used with computers.

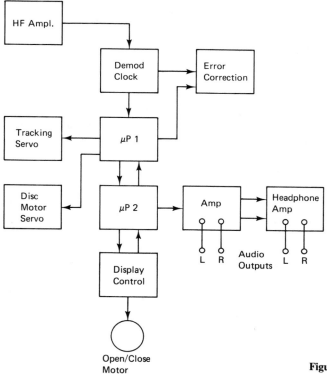

Figure 6-6 Microprocessor control.

COMPARATORS

A comparator is an error measuring system and is used in a CD player as part of the focus error circuitry (Fig. 6-7). The photodiodes in the laser array may also be regarded as a form of comparator for their subbeams supply error signal outputs.

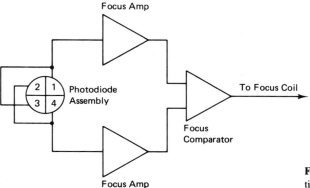

Figure 6-7 Arrangement for determination of focus error.

A comparator circuit (Fig. 6-8) has a pair of inputs and when these are of equal and opposite potential, no current flows through the load as indicated here by resistors *R1* and *R2*. Under these conditions a voltmeter placed across points *A* and *B* would read zero.

If the input potential is upset, that is, if one of the DC voltages becomes larger than the other, a current will flow through the load resistors. If battery *B1* has a larger output voltage point, *A* will become negative with respect to point *B*. If battery *B2* develops a larger potential, the polarity across the load will reverse and point *B* will become negative with respect to point *A*. Consequently, a servo motor connected across output points *A* and *B* will rotate in one direction or the other, depending on the polarity of the potential across its input points. This potential is known as an error voltage.

The servo motor will result in a feedback voltage to source voltages *B1* or *B2* in such a manner that these two voltages will once again have the same potential. When this happens the voltage across points *A* and *B* will decrease to zero and the servo motor will stop functioning.

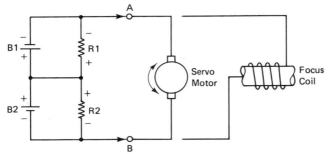

Figure 6-8 Basic comparator circuit.

The photodiodes are also comparators. As long as each photodiode receives an equal amount of reflected light from the bottom surface of the compact disc, their voltage outputs are equal and opposite. Although there are four photodiodes, they are wired as shunted pairs.

If the tracking beam should deviate, one pair of photodiodes will receive more light than the other pair. The resulting voltage difference can be applied to a pair of focus voltage amplifiers with their outputs supplied to the input of the focus comparator. As long as the laser beam is in focus, the voltages applied to the two inputs of the focus comparator are equal in potential but opposite in polarity. When an out-of-focus condition occurs, this balanced input voltage is upset and the focus comparator sends an error current to a focus coil. The coil moves to focus the beam on the track. This, in turn, means that the photodiodes will now receive equal amounts of reflected laser light and their voltage outputs will become equal but opposite in potential. As a result the comparator will have no output and the focusing coil will remain in position.

Note that in this example a focusing coil is used instead of a servo. A focusing coil works somewhat like the voice coil in a loudspeaker. A voice coil can be considered as a motor having limited or restricted movement. When a current flows through the focusing coil, it will move in one direction or the other depending on the direction of the current through it.

A comparator can be used not only to obtain an optimum operating condition, as in the case of laser beam tracking, but also to make certain that components function in an optimum manner. As an example, the laser diodes must produce a certain amount of light output. Obviously, an inadequate amount of light could mean complete loss of audio signal output. However, an excessive amount of light could also result in an inability to focus the beam. A comparator (Fig. 6-9) is used to make sure that the light output from the laser diode assembly remains adequate at all times.

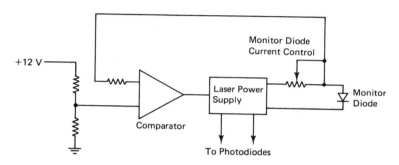

Figure 6-9 Control arrangement for laser beam current.

The laser diode emits two beams of light. One of these is the scanning beam which is focused on the disc. The other beam, moving in a direction opposite that of the scanning beam, is allowed to fall on a monitor diode behind the laser. The monitor diode develops a voltage that is proportional to the amount of light falling on it. This voltage working as a control is fed back to the laser power supply, increasing its output when the beam is weak and decreasing it when the beam is stronger. The control works to maintain a constant light output from the laser beam photodiodes.

The comparator receives two input voltages. One of these is a DC reference voltage. The other is a signal fed back from the monitor diode. When the voltage that is fed back is equal to the reference voltage, there is no output from the comparator and the power supply delivers its rated voltage to the monitor diode. The variable resistor between the monitor diode and the laser supply is used to make the initial adjustment for producing the correct amount of monitor diode current. If that current should increase or decrease, the result would be a change in the voltage drop across the variable resistor with the voltage change fed back to the comparator. As a result the output from the comparator would drive the laser power supply to have a higher operating voltage output which, in turn, would increase the voltage to the photodiodes, raising their output current. With photodiodes, the problem is not usually excessive current output but rather a decrease, since the resistance of the photodiodes increases with time.

INTEGRATED CIRCUITS

Integrated circuits (IC) are used throughout compact disc players and without them, it is doubtful that the compact disc player could exist. It is also known as a chip or microchip and it is made of a very small section of silicon, a semiconductor material, usually 1/4-inch square. This area is sometimes referred to as real estate.

Prior to the development of the IC, radio parts were discrete units as individual items which were wired one to the other. They consisted of resistors, capacitors, coils, vacuum tubes and somewhat later, transistors. Point-to-point wiring continued to be used even following the invention of the transistor. Not only was this method of building electronic devices slow and costly, miniaturization using discrete parts was difficult. However, with the invention of the IC we went rapidly from miniaturization to subminiaturization and then to microminiaturization.

A complete circuit can be constructed on a chip with not hundreds, or thousands, but hundreds of thousands of transistors. Not only are ICs better than point-to-point wired components, but they are more reliable, they cost less, and they can work faster. Furthermore, they are capable of handling digital signals without degrading them. As far as reliability is concerned, the IC is one of the least likely components in a compact disc player to become defective.

To give you some idea of how many ICs are used in a compact disc player, an error detection circuit used to control radial tracking could have as many as eight ICs, forward and reverse circuits as many as eleven. A motor control circuit could have as many as three ICs, the power supply five, the laser control circuit two, the focus control circuit three, the turntable motor amplifier two, decoder circuitry two, and the signal processing circuitry ten. Some compact disc players use more, others less. This does not mean individual transistors are not used but they are outnumbered by the ICs.

IC Structure

The IC is housed in a plastic or ceramic enclosure with plastic used more often because of its economy. The connecting leads (Fig. 6-10) may extend horizontally or more often downward. They are often (but not always) numbered in a counterclockwise manner starting on the left side from a top view (Fig. 6-11).

While the pins can be arranged on all four sides of the package, they are usually arranged on only two sides. ICs of this kind are referred to as dual in-line packages or DIPs. The number of pins is often 14, 16 or 24 but DIPs having fewer or more pins are also available. Generally, with more than 24 pins you will find these on all four sides. In one four-sided IC the unit has a total of 80 pins. This is done in the case of compact disc players to be used as portables or in cars to economize on space.

There is no standardization in making connections to ICs. Pin 7 is sometimes connected to ground while pin 14 is the plus voltage lead. However, do not assume this is always the case. Do not substitute an IC for one that is defective unless the replacement is identical with the original. The fact that a pair of ICs have the same number of pins is no assurance they are duplicates. If an IC used in a compact disc

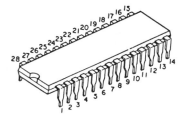

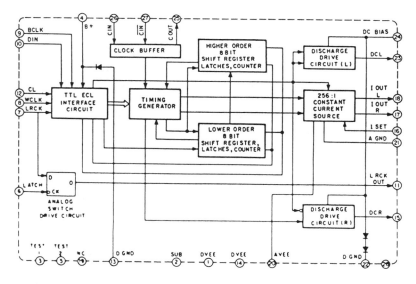

Figure 6-10 Dual in-line package (DIP) and the circuitry it contains. (Courtesy Alpine Electronics of America, Inc.)

player has one or more unused pins, let them remain that way. Do not ground them, connect them to a plus voltage line, and do not use them as tie points. Unless abused in some way, ICs have a low failure rate, something to keep in mind when servicing compact disc players.

Logic Circuitry

Logic circuits used in compact disc players can also be mounted on chips. A logic circuit has inputs and outputs which are both digital. Logic consists of one or more operating conditions that may exclude each other or that may be essential to each other. Logic circuitry consists of gates or electronic switches which may block signals or which may allow them to pass through under certain operating conditions.

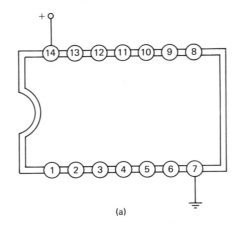

(a)

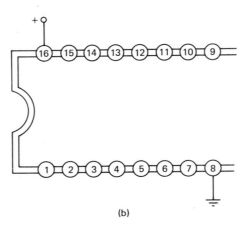

(b)

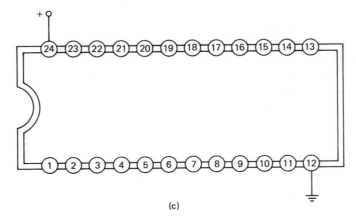

(c)

Figure 6-11 Pin numbering systems.

The most commonly used gates are AND (Fig. 6-12) and OR (Fig. 6-13). Gates are switches and a pair of these in series is called AND logic circuitry. With a pair of switches in series, both must be closed for a signal pulse to pass through; that is, switch 1 AND switch 2 must be closed, and it is from this behavior that we obtain the name AND circuit. An OR circuit consists of a pair of switches in parallel. Either one OR the other of the switches must be closed for a signal to pass through. The switches could be mechanical types but in electronics, diodes and transistors are used instead. Special symbols are used for AND and OR gates (Fig. 6-14).

The opposite of an AND circuit is a NAND or negative AND. A NAND circuit can be regarded as two or more switches in series (just like an AND circuit). A NAND circuit will function if any one or all of its switches are open.

A NOR circuit is the opposite of an OR. The two or more parallel switches are still used but for a NOR logic circuit the switches must be open to produce a desired result. The symbols for NAND and NOR logic circuits are almost the same as those for AND and OR but have a small circle on the output terminal (Fig. 6-15). The track detector circuitry used in a compact disc player uses three NOR logic circuits. The advantage of such switching is that the NOR switches work completely automatically and extremely rapidly. The NOR IC can have one, two, or three inputs but has only one output.

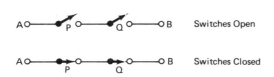

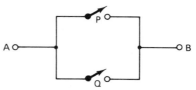

Figure 6-12 AND circuit consists of two or more switches in series. In this arrangement switch *P* AND switch *Q* must both be closed for a signal pulse to travel from *A* to *B*.

Figure 6-13 OR logic circuit. Either switch *P* OR switch *Q* must be closed for a pulse to travel from *A* to *B*.

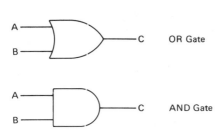

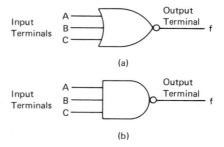

Figure 6-14 Symbols for OR gate and AND gate.

Figure 6-15 Symbol for NOR circuit (a). It can have two or more input terminals identified here as *A*, *B* and *C*, and one output terminal, *f*. Drawing (b) is for a NAND circuit.

7

FEATURES, FUNCTIONS, AND SPECS

There are four ways of learning about any specific compact disc player. Read a detailed list of its specs, gather whatever information you can acquire about its features, become familiar with its functions, and finally, get hands-on experience. Some of the written information can be acquired from magazines which make detailed test reports and which sometimes make a comparative analysis of the features of a number of compact disc players, supplemented by information supplied by the manufacturer.

Features and functions are not static, for a manufacturer will not only produce new models but each succeeding generation will contain improvements and additional features as well. That is why it is risky to purchase first-generation compact disc players. Manufacturers as well as users learn from experience, and while the earliest compact disc players may be attractive from a price viewpoint, they are not always the best buy.

A feature of a compact disc player is a description of its electrical or physical attributes. A feature may be top loading or front loading. It could be a small detail such as the size and kind of feet supplied with the compact disc player to minimize vibration, or it could be the type of operating controls used or the kind of readouts.

A function is a specific kind of operation. It could include programmable random playback, index search, repeat play, fast scanning, and track skipping. However, the terms "features" and "functions" are often used interchangeably.

Information concerning features and functions is supplied in a number of different ways. It is included in the manufacturer's instruction manual shipped with the product. You will find them partially listed and emphasized in the manufacturer's advertising and sometimes in point-of-purchase counter literature in a dealer's store. A good source of information are technical magazines which supply test reports and sometimes a comparative analysis of a number of different players.

The best test of a compact disc and its player is to make that player go through all of the functions claimed for it. Even brand new discs are not always perfect and some, including top name brands, can manage to get past quality control.

A listing of features, sometimes called bells and whistles, is also essential. The price range of CD players varies from less than $200 to more than $1200. It would be unreasonable to expect players in all categories to be equally functional. But if you are to get the most for your money when buying a CD player, it is essential to make a comparison of features before deciding whether it is worth paying for those you may never use.

The various functions of a CD player are frequently included with the specs (specifications) but a problem may arise because the same function may be identified in different ways. Furthermore, controls on CD players may be dual function types carrying a pair of unfamiliar names. Specs are a listing of the electrical and electronic characteristics of a compact disc player. While specs can be verified by independent testing agencies, and while the data are often accompanied by impressive looking graphs, what you may read in a spec is often determined by the way in which a test is done and the kind of equipment used in conducting the test. Tests are sometimes conducted at frequencies which make the results much better than they would be at other frequencies. The trouble with specs is that some manufacturers play a numbers game, although this is less true of those who have a reputation to maintain.

CD PLAYER VERSUS TURNTABLE

The CD player and the phono turntable are different in every respect, electrically, electronically and physically. However, we make comparisons between these two since they both deliver sound from a disc (Table 7-1). The best analysis of a CD player is to compare it with another CD player rather than a turntable.

FEATURES

Output Terminals

The output terminals of a compact disc player represent a minor feature but do supply a significant clue to component quality. Terminals made of a standard alloy can and do corrode depending on location. The only difference is that in some areas the effect is more rapid than in others. Corrosion produces increased contact resistance and can result in poor or intermittent sound output. Commercial cleaners are available for removing rust or delaying its inevitable return.

Higher quality compact disc players are equipped with gold-plated output terminals. Furthermore, there may be two pairs of such terminals, with one pair supplying a fixed output level, often 2 volts, enough to drive following audio equipment. The other pair of terminals will supply a variable output via front panel controls ranging from 0

TABLE 7-1 COMPARATIVE ANALYSIS OF CD SYSTEM VERSUS LP PLAYER.

	CD System	Conventional LP Player
Specifications		
Frequency response	20 Hz - 20 kHz ± 0.5dB	30 Hz - 20 kHz ± 3dB
Dynamic range	More than 90dB	70dB (at 1 kHz)
S/N	90dB (with-MSB)	60dB
Harmonic distortion	Less than 0.01%	1 - 2%
Separation	More than 90dB	25 - 30dB
Wow & flutter	Quartz precision	0.03%
Dimensions		
Disc	12 cm (dia.)	30 cm (dia.)
Playing time (on one side)	60 minutes (max. 74 minutes)	20 - 25 minutes
Operation/Reliability		
Durability Disc	Semi-permanent	High-frequency response is degraded after being played several tens of times
Stylus	Over 5,000 hours	500 - 600 hours
Operation	• Quick and easy access due to micro-computer control • A variety of programmed play possible • Increased resistivity to external vibration	• Needs stylus pressure adjustment • Easily affected by external vibration
Maintenance	Dust, scratches, and fingerprints are made almost insignificant	Dust and scratches cause noise

(Courtesy Sony Corporation of America)

volt to 5 volts. This will let you match the output level of the compact disc player to that of other components in your audio system, so a constant output volume will be maintained without the need for amplifier volume control adjustments when switching between other sources and CD playback.

Some compact disc players have the output level control mounted on the rear panel for two reasons. The first is that the level control is a one-time adjustment; the other is that it makes the front panel less complicated and appears to be more user friendly. However, having the output level control on the front panel is a definite convenience.

A compact disc player may also have an illuminated front-panel readout indicating the amount of output voltage. There is no guesswork about the signal output. A display of output volume level is indicated with a multisegmented two-color level display on the front panel. When fixed output level connections are made, the display remains fixed at the 0 dB reference mark which corresponds to a 2-volt output level. When the output volume is raised above this point, the display segments appear in red.

This setup is not only a useful operating feature but is an aid in servicing. In the event of a no-sound condition, the display of output level (or its absence) is an indication of whether the trouble is in the compact disc player or in the following amplifier.

Sampling

Also known as the sampling rate, the standard basic frequency for sampling the instantaneous values of an analog sound waveform is 44.1 kHz. Double frequency sampling is commonly used, while a few compact disc players use quadruple frequency sampling. For double frequency sampling, the frequency is 88.2 kHz and for quadruple sampling the rate is 176.4 kHz. Double and quadruple sampling, sometimes called oversampling, usually implies a rate of 88.2 kHz. If quadruple sampling is used, it should be specified as such.

Automatic Load and Start

Positioning of the laser pickup beam is handled automatically. Just press the open/close button, put the disc on the platter support, and press the start button. No manual cueing is required or possible.

Headphone Output

Headphone output is equipped with a level control that permits sound adjustment independently of the speakers. Insertion of the headphone plug may or may not cut off speaker sound. If not, the speaker volume control can be positioned for any sound output wanted.

Subcode Output Terminals

Compact discs may be made in the future with video still pictures encoded plus accompanying text material displayed on a television monitor. This could also be fed into a television receiver via a radio-frequency modulator. The added visual and audio data are referred to as a subcode and do not displace existing encoded music but supplement it, thus taking advantage of the additional track coding space available on the compact disc. The use of subcode terminals also means the compact disc player is equipped with circuitry to handle the additional data. You will find subcode terminals only on higher quality level compact disc players.

Vibration Damping

One of the serious problems with analog turntables is high susceptibility to vibration. For best reproduction these units need to be mounted on a substantial support that is literally shake proof. Furthermore, such players must be positioned so they are absolutely horizontal.

These two operating characteristics, vibration and horizontal operation, have either been eliminated or diminished in the compact disc player. The player can operate in any position ranging from horizontal to vertical. While for an in-home installation, horizontal positioning is esthetically satisfying, it is not a playback necessity. Compact disc players in cars and portables are often used when horizontal positioning is purely accidental.

The compact disc player is much less sensitive to vibration than transcription turntables but there is no question that the less the vibration the better. Vibration does present a potential sound reproduction problem since it can modulate the music signal. Compact disc players are full of potential sources of mechanical vibration: the disc rotation mechanism, the pickup head feed mechanism and head servo mechanisms. Even the power transformer in the power supply is capable of transmitting some vibration through its mounting assembly. While the sum of all these vibrations is admittedly small, it can be transmitted to the digital-to-analog converter and the analog audio circuitry. One technique for overcoming this problem is mounting the entire disc rotation mechanism, the disc tray and loading assembly as isolated units within the player itself, supported by a floating suspension.

The problem of vibration-induced sound modulation is greater in units in which the size of the component is an important factor. This would apply especially to portable units or to those designed for car use in which space is at a premium. Vibration generated in close proximity to a component's audio circuitry can modulate the audio signal, introducing distortion components into the music signal.

If the vibration is produced by the unit's power transformer, the result could be hum-induced modulation. This is not a problem that corrects itself but in time becomes worse. It could also become a difficult servicing problem since the repair could not only be replacement of the transformer but some method for damping its mounting.

CD Player Feet

One of the differences between a top quality compact disc player and one that is a low cost mass-market item can be seen in the attention paid to what may appear to be small details. Thus, the compact disc player is mounted on rubber feet or some synthetic substitute. The best arrangement is one in which the feet are large. They support the weight of the player and are capable of absorbing any form of external vibration.

Not only is the material for the feet carefully selected but in the manufacturing process it should be treated with antiaging and antioxidant compounds. As feet made for a compact disc player get older, they change their composition and become friable unless they are so treated.

Error Correction

There are a number of different techniques that can be used for correcting disc scanning errors. When a commonly used error correction system senses an error, it blanks the incorrect information and inserts an estimated signal in its place. The error correction window or the actual amount of signal replaced has a fixed length, so each time the error correction circuit is triggered a specific amount of signal is removed and replaced. This is a crude method and could be compared to cutting off a finger when just a fingernail needs to be trimmed. The result, of course, is that what you hear does not correspond to the true digital form of the encoded signal.

A better technique is one which utilizes a continuously variable window. When an error caused by a scratched or dirty disc is detected, the signal is blanked and estimated only for the length of the actual error. Therefore, error correction is more accurate and smoother in operation.

Handshake Microprocessing

All compact disc players contain a microprocessor to handle control and error adjustment functions. However, a player might contain two high speed 8-bit microprocessors, sometimes referred to as a computer on a chip (although as indicated earlier, there is a difference between a computer and a microprocessor). These double microprocessors work in a "handshake" mode which means that if one microprocessor reaches its functional limit, it passes the excess work load to the second processor. By using this design, the compact disc player can process more information and can do so faster. This results in better error correction and better linearity, permitting the manufacturer to equip the compact disc players with highly sophisticated control functions.

Digital Filters

The compact disc player may be equipped with double resolution digital filters to effectively separate the sampling frequency noise band from the audio spectrum (Fig. 7-1). These minimize interference in the audio band and permit the use of a fifth-order low-pass filter so that phase distortion at the higher audio frequencies is avoided. With

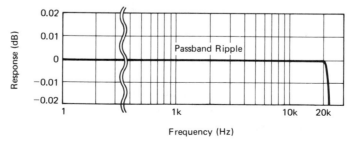

Figure 7-1 Digital filter characteristics.

the sampling frequency set at twice the standard 44.1 kHz (88.2 kHz), the filters suppress unwanted ripple to less than $\pm$ 0.0025 dB, while ensuring that the noise level is kept to at least 90 dB below the audio signal.

Tracking Error Distortion

Data are not supplied in a manufacturer's spec sheets on tracking error distortion. The compact disc player is equipped with a three-beam laser pickup head with the three beams focused on the disc surface. The center beam picks up the digital audio signal while the two outer beams provide real-time tracking information for the servo control circuitry. A well-designed optical system should be able to detect deviations in tracking as small as 0.2 micron. Its ability to do so effectively eliminates tracking error-induced distortion.

Digital Brick Wall Filtering

Some of the early adverse comments about compact disc sound were attributed to phase shift in the high audio frequencies. However, by utilizing double oversampling, an extremely steep digital filter system, plus a phase-corrected analog filter, phase shift has been lowered to 2 degrees at the extreme top end of the audio spectrum at 20 kHz. It is not uncommon, however, in compact disc players that do not pay as much attention to filtering to have phase shifts ranging from 80 degrees to 180 degrees. The manufacturers of such compact disc players rely on the fact that few people have a listening range that extends that high and that they may not be able to aurally detect large amounts of phase shift.

Digital-to-Analog Conversion

A compact disc player will commonly use a 14-bit digital-to-analog converter. These 14-bit units must quadruple (that is, multiply the basic 44.1 kHz sampling rate by 4), to approximate the last 2 digits in the 16-bit word recorded on the disc. What this means is that this kind of a setup reads an actual 14-bit word and then must average the signal to resolve the last two digits. However, by using 16-bit decode chips with double oversampling, all 16 bits in each digital word are read. The advantage of this system is improved linearity and as much as a 6 dB increase in the signal-to-noise ratio.

The Power Supply

Every compact disc player is equipped with at least one power supply, and some compact disc players may have as many as five. A quality power supply will be one that is regulated; that is, its output voltage will remain constant regardless of any fluctuations in the load. The power supplies must be well filtered to prevent any hum modulation. The power transformer should be physically located as far as possible from the pickup and low level stages and should be completely shielded, preferably with heavy gauge steel.

When a manufacturer claims to have multiple power supplies, it is difficult to determine without a schematic diagram exactly what this means. It implies separate power supplies each with its own power transformer, rectifiers and filters. But it could also mean a single power transformer having multiple secondary windings and separate rectifiers and filters. Furthermore, a power supply is not a regulated type unless it is specifically identified as such.

The Preamplifier

The stereo audio output of the digital-to-analog converter is not delivered directly to the output terminals but to the input of a built-in preamplifier which is a voltage amplifier stage. Amplifier design is such today that the unit should be able to have a bandpass much wider than the audio spectrum and virtually unmeasurable distortion. Again, what is actually available in the way of audio output is directly related to the attention paid to quality elsewhere in the compact disc player.

Readouts

Compact disc players vary in the number of readouts and in their color, size and location. If the compact disc player is to be mounted at eye level, a moderately-sized readout is satisfactory. If not, then larger readouts are preferable. Typical readouts would include the track or index number, the remaining time on the disc or the elapsed time of each cut, and 1 to 30 programmed track or index numbers (Fig. 7-2).

Figure 7-2 Track and time display.

FUNCTIONS

By correctly using the various keys on the front panel of the compact disc player, it is possible to have the compact disc player perform many desired functions. The functions that are available depend on the design and construction of the player and cannot be added at some later date; that is, the compact disc player does not lend itself to upgrading. For that reason it is essential when selecting a compact disc player to be sure it has all the desired features. At the same time there is not much point in buying a player that has interesting features which you will never use. All of this is a matter of personal preference.

The CD player offers a number of convenience features. Though manual access to a piece of music on the disc is simply impossible since the track pitch is 1.6 μm, the CD player enables total electronic control using the built-in central processing unit (CPU) and the eight control bits inserted after the sync bits on the disc. The control bits are equivalent to approximately 2.7% of the total digital codes recorded on the disc.

Lead-in and Lead-out Signals

The lead-in signal is located just in front of where the signal area starts, while the lead-out signal appears right after the end of the signal area. These two signals are used to control the movement of the optical pickup.

Table of Contents

Written in the lead-in area is the time information on control codes including the start time of each selection as well as the total number and playing time of selections. These can be read out before performance starts for the convenience of program search. Such information can also be displayed.

Control Codes

These codes distinguish between 2-channel recording and 4-channel recording. They can also detect whether pre-emphasis is given to a particular recording.

Direct Access

Direct access means the ability to reach any track on the compact disc using an entry keyboard. All you need to do is to enter the number of the desired selection and the player will locate it automatically.

Random Playback

When you want to listen to a number of selections in a specific sequence, you can use the programmable random playback capability of the player. The number of random selections you can choose will vary with each compact disc player but a good feature is to be able to pick 12 selections for playback in any desired order. To be able to remember which musical tracks you have selected, the choices you have made can be confirmed by the display panel, assuming the player has this feature.

Index Search

On long pieces of music such as symphonies or operas, index marks supply access within what is otherwise one piece of music. Index search means you can select particular sections of a musical composition. The beginning and end of each selection of an otherwise long composition can have index points. These points can easily be reached with the fast forward and reverse search keys when the disc is in its stop mode or with direct access keys.

To search index numbers, the disc must have these numbers encoded at the time the disc is made. An index number is also known as a track number and indexing is sometimes referred to as search/index. Index search allows the listener to locate specially coded index points and commence play automatically. Search/index does not mean forward movement only, for it lets you cue either forward or reverse audibly and at high speed.

Music Search

You can access the music on a disc in different ways. You can use the skip control keys, marked + and − so that you can move sequentially to the beginning of each track, in forward and reverse. You can also use the search control keys to scan the disc at slow to high speeds, with partial muting if the search function is accessed from the play mode or with total muting when accessed from the pause mode. Two speed music search lets you listen to music at normal pitch or search through the disc at high speed.

Space Insert

Frequently the selections on a compact disc follow each other almost immediately. In many professional applications it is necessary to have a few seconds of silence between selections. It is also important to have a space between selections when recording on a cassette deck that offers a music search capability where the deck senses the silence between selections.

If the compact disc player is equipped with a space insert control, a three-second blank interval is automatically inserted between playback of each track for appropriate spacing of musical selections.

Repeat Play

Use the repeat play function when you want continuous background music. All you need to do is press the repeat key and this will enable you to get playback of the entire disc in its normal recorded sequence. If you have entered a random playback program, the programmed sequence will be repeated rather than the normal sequence. It is even possible to select a specific segment of the disc, from one point to another, for repeated playback.

Treble De-Emphasis

De-emphasis is automatic and is keyed into the compact disc at the time it is encoded. But the way in which the de-emphasis circuitry is constructed can cause some difference in the quality of the playback when the same disc is used on two different compact disc players. At the time the compact disc is encoded the treble range is supplied with a 10 dB boost. To be able to listen to the audio signal as it existed originally the compact disc player must supply a complementary 10 dB drop. However, because of component tolerances it is possible for one CD player to decrease the treble by more or less than 10 dB. With an increase of more than 10 dB the high-frequency end of the audio will sound somewhat duller than it should, but with a de-emphasis of less than 10 dB the sound will acquire a greater amount of brilliance. The variations in these two characteristics will depend on the amount of excess boost or the extent to which it is inadequate. Since de-emphasis covers a range of about 2-1/2 octaves, any overboost or underboost may be quite noticeable, particularly if the composition being played is well known. The difficulty here is that the fault may be incorrectly attributed to the disc instead of to the player.

Disc Loading and Handling

Compact discs can be loaded from the top or from the front depending on the type used by the compact disc player. The top-loading type is convenient if you do not plan to stack any components above it. Another advantage is that top loading is spring loaded and does not require a separate motor so its operating mechanism is simpler, possibly leading to a lower purchase price.

Front-loading units can be manually or motor controlled, although the latter type is more common. The front-loading player can be rack mounted and put in any convenient, practical position in a high-fidelity system. With motorized units a tray is used to accept and hold the disc and is controlled from the front panel by a pushbutton.

Disc handling is still another consideration. The disc must not only be loaded into the player but it must also be removed. You should be able to load and unload without putting your fingers on the disc surface. The best arrangement would seem to be motorized front-door loading. At the touch of a button, the motorized drawer slides out to accept the CD and with another touch of the button it slides back to load the disc.

There is also a form of loading known as double drawer. This involves the use of a pair of adjacent compact disc players both contained within the same housing but otherwise independent of each other. Each player can be operated individually, but can be used to double the memory capacity. As a result the combination can be used to supply two hours of uninterrupted music.

Since the laser beam assembly is so close to where the disc is placed, the laser will not function as long as the door covering the disc entryway is open. Manufacturers supply printed instruction sheets with the compact disc players warning against putting fingers inside the disc drawer, but when servicing make sure this does not happen by cutting off both disc motor drive and laser beam operating voltages.

A/B Repeat

Also known as automatic music search, A/B repeat is a variation of random access and permits the repeated playback of any section of the compact disc between any two preprogrammed designated points. Playback will continue until the programming is defeated. With A/B repeat it is not necessary to play back an entire band on the disc but just a portion of it. Alternatively, it is also possible to play back two or more bands, but not necessarily between the start of the first band and the end of the last one.

Forward and Backward Jump for Tracks and Indexes

With this function you can have a jump capability for indexes as well as tracks. Being able to locate indexes in this manner is useful when listening to classical music, operas, and other long selections in which indexes are used to mark the beginnings of specific sections within a track.

Rollover

Problems are created with some compact disc players when more than one key is depressed simutaneously. The difficulty is that contrary instructions may be issued. Rollover, then, comes under the classification of errors.

Various techniques are used for rollover correction. One, known as two-key rollover, is that the control signals issued by the closing of two keys simultaneously are ignored until the user removes his fingers from both keys and then touches just one of them. In another approach, if the two keys are not touched simultaneously, the second of the two keys will be the one to generate the instructional signals. While it is somewhat unlikely that more than two keys will ever be depressed, it is still possible to provide rollover protection. In this instance the last of the keys to be touched will be the one that is operative.

The force with which a key is struck has no effect on the way it performs and does not affect the instructions. A compact disc player is a precision instrument and should be treated as such. Depressing keys in extremely rapid succession can cause operating problems and it is advisable to allow a few seconds between each key operation.

Delete Play Programming

If you have programmed a number of musical selections, you need not eliminate all of them if you want to remove only one or more. All that is necessary is to depress the musical selection button corresponding to the track that is to be removed from programming and then to depress the cancel button. You can follow this procedure even while the compact disc player is in its play mode, and you can also eliminate more than one preprogrammed musical selection.

Musical Selection Sampling: Auto Scan or Index Scan

The total amount of playback time on a compact disc is one hour, with the selections indicated on the disc label. Not all discs will have the same number of musical choices. A typical amount is about ten, but it can be more or less than this.

If you have just bought a disc and want to sample each of the musical selections, you can do so with each selection played for ten seconds (Fig.7-3). Following the completion of each ten-second playback time, the laser beam automatically moves to the next track and plays the next musical selection for another ten seconds. This short-time scanning of each musical band will continue until reading the last musical band by the laser beam has been completed. During this entire time the music number will be displayed.

Following the ten-second playback time of each band, the compact disc player will automatically move into its fast scanning mode. Some CD players have an auto music scan control; others use an index scan button. Just touch the index button to hear the first ten seconds of each band. If you then touch the play button it will stop the scanning process and will play the entire selection.

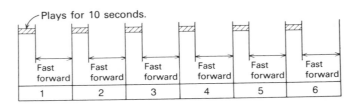

Figure 7-3 Musical selection sampling.

Access Time

CD players are made to permit the selection of any recorded band of music. Access time is typically 2.0 seconds and is the amount of time required from the moment the access choice is entered until the music is played back. Access time does not necessarily mean the time needed to reach the first band, but to any chosen band. Access time is so short it may seem instantaneous.

Ambience Control

The purpose of stereo is to simulate the reproduction of sound from the approximate center of an orchestra or other sound group to the left, subsequently called left-channnel sound (L) and from the center to the right or right-channel sound (R).

The problem with this concept is that it arbitrarily groups sounds produced by a small number of artists recording in a limited area as well as concert hall sounds. To control the various differences between left and right sound channels one CD player (dbx Model DX3) is equipped with an ambience control. It helps simulate the spaciousness of a concert hall by enlarging the difference between channels or by reducing it giving the closeup sonic image of a small group. The ambience control on the CD player adds or subtracts L-R (difference) information in the midrange and treble, increasing or decreasing the spaciousness of the sound field (Fig. 7-4).

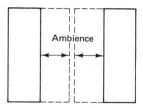

Figure 7-4 Ambience control is used to bring left- and right-channel sound closer or farther apart. (Courtesy dbx, div. BSR North America Ltd.)

The Disc Directory

When a compact disc is made the encoding of musical information is not started immediately. Instead, data are encoded preceding each musical band, supplying information about the length of the band in time units. A code is also included that specifies the location of the band. This code known as the disc directory enables accessing of each musical composition by the compact disc player's microprocessor. While you can program the compact disc player to supply desired selections, it will play the entire disc through one musical band after the other to the end of the disc unless otherwise instructed.

Track Display

Compact disc players supply an illuminated readout indicating the number of the track being played. Using a segmented bar display, a few may also indicate the maximum number of tracks available. However, you can always get this information from the label on the disc. After a track has been played there is a short pause so that one musical composition does not run into the next. While all the bands have the same dynamic range you may need to readjust the volume control on your high-fidelity system for particular selections. Track or index numbers up to 99 are available, although many CD players do not go this high.

Display of Elapsed Time

Many compact disc players have an illuminated readout indicating the amount of elapsed time. This is the amount of time from the moment the first track of the first musical selection is played. Elapsed time, also called play or playing time, is supplied as four digits consisting of two digits followed by a colon which is followed by another two digits. Thus, 4 minutes and 37 seconds is shown as 04:37, and 21 minutes, 5 seconds as 21:05. Although the maximum playing time of a disc is an hour, a compact disc player may have an indicator showing elapsed or remaining time up to 99 minutes: 59 seconds.

Many compact disc players also have a display indicating remaining playing time. While remaining playing time can be calculated by subtracting elapsed time from 60, it is certainly more convenient to have a remaining time readout. It also has the advantage of alerting the user that it may be time to select the next disc for playback.

Skip

There are two types of skip: forward and back. These are separate functions and the fact that a compact disc player has a forward skip function does not automatically mean it also has an automatic skip backward capability. Usually, however, skip forward and skip backward accompany each other. Skip may mean moving to a selected time on a disc or it may mean skipping over tracks.

Repeat Any One Track

With some compact disc players you can select any track and have that track (a single complete musical selection) play over and over again. This is a programming function, but is quite different from programming in which several musical bands are chosen to be played in succession.

Skip/Search

Some CD players are equipped with a skip/search control. Depressing this key means the laser scanning beam will jump forward or backward to the beginning of each track. You can use this control by depressing it and listening to the cueing sound.

Track Skip

With this feature a track that is being scanned can be terminated and the next track in the sequence can be read, with the selection of that next track handled automatically.

Repeat

A compact disc player may be equipped with a repeat control that lets you repeat a whole program, the whole disc, or just a small part of the disc.

Repeat Any Segment

If you have a very long selection encoded on a disc, such as an opera or a concert, you might want to listen to just a selected portion, not just once but repeatedly.

Clear Program

When you select and program a substantial number of musical bands to be played, it is not necessary to clear each one individually if you no longer have an interest in the program. A single control will let you erase the program. This is something you should do if you want to set up a new replacement program or if you want to have the disc play through all of the encoded musical compositions.

On/Off Pause

In a high-fidelity system you will find a mute control that will weaken the sound output considerably but will not turn it off. Compact disc players are not equipped with a mute control which is a helpful feature if you want to answer a telephone or do not want to interrupt a conversation. However, many compact disc players have a pause control which can be turned on or off. The advantage of the pause control is that it stops sound output but lets you pick up at the exact playback point once again.

Of course you could turn the volume control down but then you would miss hearing some of the music because the disc would continue its rotation. Furthermore, you might not turn the volume control to its previous setting. The pause control, on the other hand, is an on/off device and can be reset easily to continue previous operating conditions.

If your compact disc player is supplying its output to a high-fidelity system, and this is quite likely for an in-home entertainment setup, you can still use the mute control on the hi/fi to cut down on sound volume, but the compact disc will continue rotating. Hi/fi mute controls generally supply a sound attenuation of 20 dB.

Universal Functions

It must be fairly obvious that not all compact disc players have the same features and the same functions. However, there are some functions that are fairly common to most players and these include: disc repeat (the player can repeat all of the selections on a disc until stopped); play, pause and stop controls; a track selection capability; open and close functions; and track display. Many also have a segmented bar-graph display and also individual number displays. Some compact disc players also illuminate the spinning disc during play.

Arrangement of Operating Controls

There is no standardization concerning the way in which operating controls appear on the front panel of a compact disc player. With some units only the more widely used controls are exposed with those less likely to be called into action hidden beneath a hinged panel. The theory is that the fewer controls that are visible the more user friendly the player will appear to be. Another method is to group the more widely used controls in one part of the panel with those used less often elsewhere on the panel.

Audible Fast Search

While you may know the numbers and titles of the different bands of music on a disc, you may only be able to recognize them by hearing them. In that case you may have the option of using audible fast search. This feature will let you use the fast forward or reverse functions and you will hear the music played at an increased speed. With a turntable an increase in speed results in a change in pitch but with audible fast search of a CD player the pitch will remain the same as in regular play.

Audible fast search does not mean you must listen to all the bands on the disc. You can start at any band you wish and move either forward or reverse, although forward is better since the music is more recognizable.

Automatic Pause

When playing a compact disc, ordinarily there will be a short pause between musical bands. However, if you are dubbing from the compact disc to cassette tape or open reel, you may want more control by stopping after each musical selection. If the CD player is equipped with an automatic pause (also called auto-pause) feature playback will stop following each band. If the CD player is not provided with this feature you will need to use the pause control manually.

Cueing

This is the method used for finding the beginning of any track on the compact disc and not necessarily the first track of the first band. The track may be the first one of any band or any other track in that band.

D/A Filtering

D/A filtering refers to the digital/analog filters used in a compact disc player. At the time the signal is converted from its digital format to analog, filters are used to remove unwanted ultrasonic frequencies from the audio signal. These filters may be analog or digital types or a combination of the two. The disadvantage of the analog filter is that it may result in a small amount of phase shift. Claims have been made that this degrades the signal, something that can only be determined subjectively by a listening test.

Delete Programming

Any selection can be skipped automatically by using the delete programming function. Subsequent to random access to a number of bands and their playback, you can eliminate certain bands and then continue playback. Another technique would be to erase all programming by using the clear control and then to program, skipping unwanted bands. Both techniques produce the same results but delete programming is faster.

Disc Data

Each compact disc contains miscellaneous information in addition to bands for music. These data include selection of numbers, the length of each selection, and so on. This information is scanned to provide the various functions detailed in the features section of a CD player's specification sheet.

Displays

Also called an illumination pattern or music calendar, displays supply the user with information about what the CD player is doing at any time. The most commonly used types of display are fluorescent and light-emitting diode (LED).

Some CD players are quite limited in this respect and simply supply a fluorescent display of the disc track number and the total playing time. More elaborate players may have a number of illuminated displays indicating the various functions including the track number (the track being played), playing time in minutes and seconds, total number of tracks available, remaining playing time, next program number, and for portable units a battery charge indicator. Displays can be single or dual and illumination patterns can be in several colors such as orange, green, red and blue, or may be only a single color. Some displays are more elaborate and are multifunction types which indicate the track number, the elapsed time of the disc being played, the total available playing time of the remaining bands, the number of the selected track being played, the end of the disc (last track of the final band), and open and closed disc tray.

With some CD players there is no control over the illumination patterns which turn on automatically depending on the function being used. Some players are equipped with display buttons and each push of the button will display the operational status of the player. These include the track number (the display will show the track number of the musical selection presently playing), lap time (the display will indicate how much time has elapsed since the start of the track being played), and remain time (the display shows how much time is left until the end of the final band).

Four-Way Repeat

Repeat is not necessarily a single function. Thus, with a capability known as four-way repeat you can listen to a single track played repeatedly or to an entire disc played over and over again. Other forms of repeat play include repeating selections you have programmed or any part of any band on the disc. Some four-way repeat functions also let you touch a button to bypass the next selection, either forward or reverse.

Full

Assigning tracks on a compact disc to memory is limited by the memory capability of the CD player and this varies from player to player. If, for example, a player has a 15-band limitation, you will not be able to force it to accept 20 bands. The word "full" will be displayed when all the available bands, or portions of bands, are in the memory.

Graphics Subcode Port

This is a special output port designed for future CD graphic applications such as song title, lyrics and program notes.

Auto Space

This feature delays playback of any given music selection for three seconds. It is suitable for CD broadcast and recording applications.

Positioning

Unlike a transcription turntable, some CD players can be operated in any position and the position can be changed while the unit is in use. They tolerate vibration and therefore can be used for disc playback in a car. An attempt was made a number of decades ago to use turntables in vehicles but the effort was unsuccessful.

Not all CD players can tolerate changes in position when the player is active. Some players such as portables or those used in cars are specifically designed to withstand vibration and/or position changes. Those intended for in-home use will quite possibly be less immune. You can wallop the sides of some CD players without affecting disc tracking by the laser beam; others may not have this ability.

Some portable music systems are now combined with other audio components. You can find a horizontal-loading digital disc player combined with an AM/FM/MPX receiver, a seven-band graphic equalizer and detachable speakers.

Portable CD players have many of the features characteristic of fixed position, in-home units. They may be equipped with automatic search, a display showing elapsed time and remaining time on the disc, an automatic open/close disc tray, and soft touch logic controls.

Programmability

Compact disc players use microprocessors so all major functions are automatic. Thus, all you need do is to push a button to audition samples of all the recordings on a disc. The microprocessor handles the details of finding each one, playing short passages, and moving on to another until you press a control to defeat the action.

With programmed play you can choose a number of selections from the disc and in a representative player this can be 16 bands played automatically in any order you select. If you wish, the same band can be selected more than once.

Depending on the compact disc player, programmability lets you repeat all the bands or just the programmed ones, using skip and search modes for not using certain bands and moving to desired selections. With a feature known as index search, you can start playback at any index point on an indexed disc. Thus, you need not listen to an entire selection but just to any desired portion of it. If the CD player has automatic random selection you can skip to any track on the disc at the touch of a button. With manual search you can press "fast forward" or "fast back" to monitor two-second samples across the disc and find the selection you want. With repeat playback you can repeat the entire disc or just the programmed selections. The amount of access time required to cue and play a selection can be as little as 2.6 seconds, or less.

Random Access

With this feature it is possible to direct the laser beam to read any part of the disc. Bands of music can be skipped, but this skipping action need not be in direct numerical sequence. Bands can be played in any order. With some CD players it is also possible to make a selection of portions of one or more musical bands.

Random access should indicate the number of musical bands that can be reached. A representative spec would state: "random access programmability to 15 bands." With some CD players it is possible to access any of up to 99 tracks on a disc and to program up to 30 of these to play in any order. If index numbers, a guide to musical program highlights, are present on a CD, these can be accessed. There may be a repeat A-B function that can isolate the material between any two points on a CD and automatically play that section as many times as desired.

If the random access function is not used, the CD player will be in its all play mode. This means that all musical selections will be played with none skipped in the order in which they appear on the disc.

With multiband random access programmability, program repeat, start, stop, and scan features permit the listener to have full and independent control of all the musical bands on a disc. It is not necessary to memorize or write the choices since at the start of playback a display will show the total number of tracks and the total amount of playback time. At the time of playback, the display will indicate the track being played and also the amount of elapsed time.

Time Access

Playback of a disc is a linear function of time. All musical passages of the same length will take the same amount of playback time. Some compact disc players take advantage of this playback characteristic by letting the user punch in the precise number of minutes and seconds at which a desired musical selection will begin.

With the time code function, you can tell the time lapse from the beginning of each selection in minutes, seconds, and 1/75 of a second. During the blank space between selections, time is counted down.

The control bits can be used in a variety of ways. They not only let you locate any portion of music exactly and quickly, but also allow random playback in any order you set. And despite the long playing time of an hour on one side, access to the desired point can be achieved almost instantly. This is one of the greatest advantages of the CD system and cannot be found in any other system.

Subcode Access

Classical compositions recorded on compact discs, especially operas, may have arias of special interest for listeners. These can be accessed quickly by using special subcode indexing numbers. Subcode indexing consists of index numbers within an existing pair of index numbers, somewhat like a quotation within a quotation. Thus, the user may not only find a particular musical passage quickly, but may also access a special part of that musical passage. The CD player may also be equipped with a subcode output terminal for future applications.

Repeat

With this feature the CD player repeats playback of the entire disc or those selected tracks that have been stored in the memory. Continuous playback of the entire disc means the compact disc player lends itself nicely to supplying background music for as long as required without demanding special attention.

Scanning Velocity

The speed with which the pits (bumps) and flats on the compact disc are scanned is at the rate of 1.2 to 1.4 meters per second. This velocity is contant and remains the same no matter where on the disc the laser beams strikes. It is the same at the beginning of the disc and at its end.

Search Time

During a random access function search time is the amount of time required for the CD player to find the start of a selected band or a particular part of a band. A representative value is between two and three seconds and when used in a spec sheet is the maximum amount of time. Actually, some random searches require less than two seconds.

Shuffle Play

One manufacturer of compact disc players has designed an unusual feature consisting of a variable random sequence for all the bands on a disc. It could be referred to as a random surprise since with the variable feature the listener does not know what the musical arrangement will be.

Calibration Tone

Some of the higher quality compact disc players are equipped with a calibration tone. It is operated by a control marked CAL TONE that connects a 1,000 Hz calibrating tone to the output so that the recording level of a connected tape deck can be accurately adjusted. The calibration tone corresponds to the maximum output level. This maximum level is system dependent and will not be exceeded even by short peak pulses. In certain applications it may be useful to signal the end of a program or of a sequence within the program. This can be done by using the calibration tone as an alarm.

CONTROLS AND THEIR FUNCTIONS

CD players do not all have the same functions nor do they have the same controls. This not only applies to units made by different manufacturers but also to different models made by the same manufacturer. Furthermore, various names may be applied to controls even though they have the same or similar functions. The following list is a general one; a particular CD player may have more controls or less.

Drawer Open/Close Button

Press this control when loading or unloading a disc.

Drawer Open/Close Indicator

This is an indicator light which flashes when you open or close the disc drawer. It will remain lighted when the drawer is fully open but will extinguish when the drawer is fully closed.

Fast Back Button

You can identify this button by a pair of adjacent arrows pointing to the left. Press this button to reverse playback. Fast back indicates a search that moves toward the beginning of the musical bands.

Fast Forward Button

Like the fast back button, this uses a pair of adjacent arrows. However, these point to the right. Fast forward indicates a search that moves toward the end of the musical bands.

Index Indicator

Indexing is a method of locating bands by number. The index indicator displays the index number.

Memory

Press this button when memorizing programs for random memory track search. CD players vary in their memory capabilities. The player may be equipped with an illuminated readout to indicate the number of bands which have been stored in memory. It will not store in excess of its capacity.

Output Jacks

These are usually located on the rear apron of the CD player. Use them for connecting the player to the input terminals of a receiver, preamplifier, or integrated amplifier. Not all of these components have input jacks for a CD player. If they do, the jacks will be marked CD. If not, then make the connections to the AUX or tape play terminals. Do not connect to terminals marked phono.

Pause Button

If you press this button during playback, the play will come to a temporary pause and the pause indicator will light. To defeat the pause control, depress the play button, This will release the player from its pause mode and it will once again begin playback. You can identify the pause button by two black squares arranged horizontally near the button.

Pause Indicator

This illuminated indicator will light during a temporary pause. It will also light after flashing, if the temporary pause button is pressed when loading a disc or operating direct play.

Play Button

The identification for this control is a single arrow pointing to the right. Press this button to begin disc playback. During playback the play indicator will light.

Play Indicator

This illuminated indicator will flash during access, a high speed movement. It will also remain lighted during play.

Program Number Buttons

The number of program buttons will vary, depending on the CD player. These are used for program play with random memory track search function or for track number selection.

Repeat Button

Press this button if you want repeat play.

Repeat Indicator

This indicator lights during normal repeat play and blinks during repeat play between two designated points.

Stop/Clear Button

Press this button to stop playback or to clear the program. The control is identified by a single black square placed near it.

Time Counter

This display shows the amount of elapsed playing time in minutes and seconds. In the display, minutes are abbreviated as MIN and seconds are abbreviated as SEC.

Track Number Indicator

This displays the track number being played or the track numbers of programmed selections.

TEST SPECIFICATIONS

As in the case of other high-fidelity components, manufacturers of CD players release test specifications (specs). Not all manufacturers supply the same specs and may omit some or include others they consider important. Furthermore, the information in a spec may be more detailed in one listing than in another. Thus, a spec as simple as signal-to-noise ratio may be made with or without de-emphasis, nor is there any indication as to whether the data is weighted or unweighted.

Spec Comparative Analysis

Reading a set of specs by itself is generally futile unless you are familiar with the electronic characteristics of CD players and know what to look for. The best way is to compare the specs of one player with those of one or more (preferably more) players, Such information is supplied by high-fidelity sound magazines, usually on a semiannual or annual basis. Another technique is to read test reports, collect sales literature, and to read manufacturers' promotional material.

Impedance

The output impedance of a CD player across the terminals to be connected to a following preamplifier is fairly low. For some players it is 22 ohms, with others it is 300 ohms, 600 ohms, or 1,000 ohms. The input impedance of the load across the input terminals of the preamplifier to which the player is connected is much higher than the output impedance of the CD player, and can range from 5K ohms to 10K.

Channel Separation

All compact discs are recorded in stereo and supply two channels of sound. Channel separation ranges from 85 dB to 90 dB compared to 25 dB to 30 dB for a conventional analog LP phono record. The balance between two channels, a number you will rarely see in a spec sheet, is less than ± 1/4 dB.

Data on channel separation are often given at a specific frequency, generally 1 kHz. It is not safe to assume the channel separation supplied at this frequency is the same as that throughout the audio band. Often the separation specified at 1 kHz is optimum with the separation at other frequencies not as good.

Stereo channel separation (Fig. 7-5) is closely associated with crosstalk, a condition in which the sound of one channel leaks into the other channel. Signal leakage is

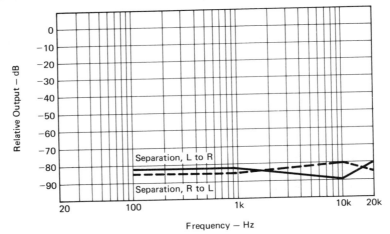

Figure 7-5   Stereo separation.

used as a test for channel separation. Test tones at 0 dB are supplied to one channel and the amount of signal crossing to the other channel is measured. The signal that has crossed over is attenuated. It tends to get poorer with an increase in audio frequency and is not as good at 20 kHz as it is at 1 kHz. A better method of presenting stereo separation in a spec sheet would be to show it in graph form from 20 Hz to 20 kHz or, alternatively, at a number of spot frequencies, possibly 20 Hz, 1 kHz, 5 kHz, 10 kHz and 20 kHz.

Dynamic Range

Dynamic range is the sonic distance between the softest sound and the loudest. It is not the same for music played live versus music that is recorded. In a live situation there is no practical limitation because sound can range from 0 dB, the point at which sound is barely heard, to 130 dB, with the sound at the threshhold of pain. No in-home electronic apparatus reproduces sound with such an extensive dynamic range.

One of the highly touted advantages of a compact disc is its dynamic range, usually 90 dB compared to about 60 dB (or less) for the usual phono record (Fig. 7-6). During CD playback an unexpectedly loud sonic passage can have a level that is practically ear shattering, particularly disturbing when using the CD for background music or when dubbing from the CD to tape. You can use your volume control to keep the level of these loud passages down but in doing so soft musical passages will not be heard. The dilemma is that if you want to hear pianissimo passages you must accept the loud volume of fortissimo. If the CD player is being used in a car, the unexpectedly loud sound can be a hazard to driving. One cure that can be used with in-home CD playing is to listen to music with one hand on the system's volume control, but this is an unsatisfactory solution.

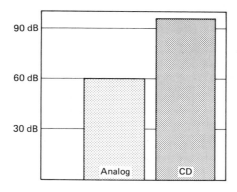

Figure 7-6 Dynamic range of compact disc versus typical analog source, measured at 1 kHz. (Courtesy Marantz Company, Inc.)

In some instances a compact disc may be made from an analog disc or from a digital master with these sound sources subjected to limiting, in effect reducing the dynamic range of the music on the compact disc. The result of this technique is that certain instruments that are percussion types (such as the piano), brass instruments, loud instrumental group sounds, musical transients, and the crashing of cymbals will sound damped.

To obtain control over dynamic range one manufacturer has equipped the CD player (dbx Model DX3) with a control labeled "Dynamics." Using just a single knob you get complete control of the dynamic range of any compact disc. When turned counterclockwise dynamic range is achieved by sound compression. The music compressor circuitry operated by this control boosts the level of soft musical passages and reduces the level of loud sounds. But by rotating the control clockwise to its DAIR (digital audio impact recovery) position, the sound limiting action is eliminated. The dynamic range limiting circuitry does not work only on extremes but can supply a wide range of dynamic control (Fig. 7-7). Thus the use of the dynamic range control permits a variation of sound level from 60 dB (full compression) to 96 db, with the control

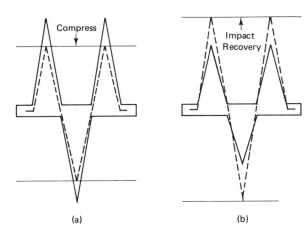

Figure 7-7 Effect of dynamic range compression (a) and impact recovery (b). The dashed lines represent dynamic range. (Courtesy dbx, div. BSR North America Ltd.)

knob in its center position to 106 dB, with the control at its maximum clockwise setting.

Dynamic Range Problems

While a dynamic range of 90 dB for a CD player is impressive, it does raise problems. The output of the player must ultimately be delivered to a power amplifier and it may be that the typical high-fidelity power amp may not have the signal handling capability called for by such a wide dynamic range. If it cannot cope with the signal, the result will be clipping, particularly on peaks, resulting in distortion. One solution would be to use amplifiers having a greater power capability but this in turn would mean the need to use speakers also having a higher power handling rating.

Dynamic range in a spec sheet does not indicate whether the figures are weighted or not. Typical figures could be 94 dB unweighted; 99 dB A-weighted. However with such very high figures for this characteristic, it does not appear to make much difference whether the numbers supplied are weighted or not.

Frequency Response

This is a measure of the range of audio frequencies that can be handled by a component and for CD players is usually 5 Hz to 20 kHz. However, this response is more meaningful if it is accompanied by the deviation, ordinarily ± 0.5 dB. This deviation is most often due to the digital/analog output converter in the CD player.

Frequency response in a test spec should be considered as a generalized statement and not one which is specific. Thus, the deviation in frequency response is not uniform over the entire audio frequency band but is more usually present at the high frequency end (Fig. 7-8). In some instances a manufacturer will show a graph of the frequency response indicated as a ruler flat line from 5 Hz to 20 kHz. It will be flat if each horizontal line on that graph represents a deviation of 10 dB or more, but the deviation will be apparent if those horizontal lines are 0.1 dB.

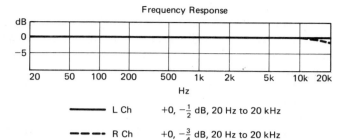

Figure 7-8 Right-channel frequency response has slight dip at the high-frequency end.

L Ch $+0, -\frac{1}{2}$ dB, 20 Hz to 20 kHz

R Ch $+0, -\frac{3}{4}$ dB, 20 Hz to 20 kHz

Because compact disc players operate in stereo, the frequency response of each sound channel is tested separately, using an audio sweep generator with the sound output indicated on a level meter. Spec sheets do not list the frequency response of the left and right sound channels separately. Since just a single graph is shown or just a single frequency response is indicated, the presumption is that the response of both channels is identical in terms of frequency and frequency deviation (Fig. 7-9).

Frequency response is the frequency range not only of the compact disc but of its associated player as well. While the spec for this is usually 20 Hz to 20 kHz, ± 0.5 dB, its excellence is better appreciated by comparing it with that of a typical analog LP phono record, often 30 Hz to 20 kHz, ± 3 dB. The deviation is as important as the frequency range, if not more so. For CD players the deviation in frequency response is attributable to the de-emphasis network and the low-pass output smoothing filter.

In terms of frequency response and deviation, the CD system is equal to or superior to some of its associated components. Since the basic sound source is a microphone, consider that most microphones have a much more limited response. There are some that do have a response from 20 Hz to 20 kHz with a variation of no more than 1 dB. The problem is that such microphones are more sensitive to hum and also to rumble from studio devices such as air conditioners or other mechanical equipment. Consequently, some microphones are deliberately designed to have a low-frequency rolloff as much as 5 dB around 100 Hz. Microphones must also contend with proximity effect, a form of vocal distortion when used too close to the mouth. In some instances proximity effect is deliberately sought since it introduces bass boost, with the most pronounced low-frequency gain below 100 Hz.

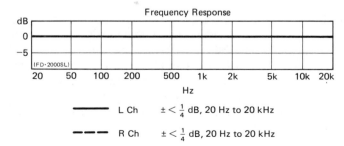

L Ch $\pm < \frac{1}{4}$ dB, 20 Hz to 20 kHz

R Ch $\pm < \frac{1}{4}$ dB, 20 Hz to 20 kHz

Figure 7-9 Frequency response for left and right channels is identical over the entire audio range.

The fact that the frequency response of a CD player will extend from 20 Hz to 20 kHz does not mean that is what you will hear. All that these numbers supply is the response capability of the CD player. What you will actually hear will depend on the response of the following preamplifier and power amplifier, the speaker system, the acoustics of the listening room and your hearing response.

The range of 20 Hz to 20 kHz is one that was selected arbitrarily. It is doubtful if any human being has such a hearing spectrum. What we can hear depends on age, sex, musical training and the condition of the physiology of the ear. At the low-frequency end what we consider to be 60 Hz hum is probably the second harmonic at 120 Hz. At the high-frequency end there are few of us who do not have a sound response rolloff at about 15 kHz, or even lower.

For portable CD players the frequency response deviation may not be as good as the fixed-position in-home types. While the response is over the same range, 20 Hz to 20 kHz, the deviation can be as much as plus or minus 3 dB.

Signal-to-Noise Ratio

Abbreviated as S/N this measurement is a comparison of the signal level to the amount of electrical noise present and is measured in dB. The S/N can be measured at any selected point in a component but is tested most often at the output. The output S/N is generally understood unless otherwise indicated. All active components produce some amount of noise. S/N is an important spec since it indicates how quiet the background will be in comparison to the signal.

If the S/N is large enough, noise will not be heard even though present, a condition known as masking effect. The signal-to-noise ratio does not remain constant since the level of the signal voltage varies. For very quiet musical passages, electrical noise levels not ordinarily heard can become evident. A signal-to-noise ratio of 60 dB is an indication that the signal is 1,000 times stronger than any electrical noise that is present. The higher the signal-to-noise ratio, the better. A representative value for the S/N of a compact disc player is about 90 dB, indicating that the signal is 31,620 times as great as the electrical noise. A better quality compact disc player will have an S/N as high as 95 dB.

While the S/N can be measured with reference to a tone having a fixed amplitude, an arbitrary reference such as 0 dB is generally selected. A test disc is used that has flats only with these representing binary zeros. Since there are no pits on such a disc, the output theoretically should be complete silence. Any noise that is produced is measured with respect to 0 dB.

The human ear does not have a linear response and is more or less sensitive to various sound frequencies. To take this physical characteristic into consideration test results can be weighted or changed. The S/N of a CD player is generally supplied unweighted; that is, the frequency characteristics of the human ear are ignored. The difference between the two figures, A-weighted and unweighted, is approximately 3 or 4 dB. In either case the signal-to-noise ratio of a CD player can be considered excellent.

Sometimes the signal-to-noise figure is indicated in another way and is simply listed as output noise. A representative spec would be shown as: 100 dB below 2 volts. S/N figures are sometimes supplied with or without active de-emphasis and may be A-weighted, referenced to 0 dB. A representative S/N spec could then be: "without de-emphasis, 101 dB; with de-emphasis 105 dB."

The S/N ratio of a CD player is much better than that of a turntable using an analog record. Here the S/N is about 60 dB or higher. The much higher S/N of the CD player means the unit is extraordinarily quiet. There should be no speaker sound from an active CD player until the laser scanning beam impinges on the first string of bits and that sound output should be clear of any extraneous signals.

The S/N ratio can be improved at the high-frequency end of the signal by passing it through a pre-emphasis circuit, boosting higher frequency tones. To return to the original sound output the signal must be sent through a de-emphasis network.

Wow and Flutter

Wow is a variation in reproduced sound and is caused by a low speed change. Flutter is also due to a speed change but is a rapid wavering in pitch. For a top quality turntable playing an analog phono record, wow and flutter (the two are generally associated) could be about 0.03 percent. For a compact disc player wow and flutter would be about 30 times less, but is actually below 0.001 percent, a figure so low that it is far below audible levels and its magnitude is insufficient to permit accurate measurements.

Total Harmonic Distortion

A musical tone is a composite consisting of a fundamental tone and a number of harmonics, all of which are multiples of the fundamental. If new harmonics are generated or if the amplitudes of the original harmonics are increased or decreased, the resultant wave would no longer be an identical replica of the original sound.

Abbreviated as THD, total harmonic distortion is measured at 1 kHz and for a representative CD player will be about 0.004 percent to about 0.008 percent. Note the percentage. Decimally the amount of THD when specified in this range could be 0.00006, defying the sensitivity of the average human ear to detect it.

THD is a ratio measuring the total amount of unwanted harmonic content compared to the original signal. This does not mean this is the amount of THD present at the speakers' output for some will be contributed by the amplifiers following the CD player. However, the CD player will not be an important factor in supplying the distortion and any distortion that is heard will be principally due to the use of other components in the hi/fi chain.

As a form of distortion, THD is not as obnoxious as intermodulation distortion (IM) since its distortion products are harmonically related to the fundamental. However, it is still distortion since the composite wave formed by the fundamental and its harmonics do not completely resemble the original sound waveform.

While a value for THD may be supplied in a manufacturer's specs for a CD player, the distortion is not a fixed quantity but varies depending on frequency (Fig. 7-10). Test instruments are available for measuring THD but there is no standardization on how the tests should be conducted. Attempting to make an evaluation by a listening test is difficult unless the composition is very well known, if you have musical training, and if the THD is in excess of at least 1 percent. This latter figure is unlikely for the CD player. If a figure for THD is supplied in a spec sheet, this should be under the worst operating condition, supplying the highest percentage. Since manufacturers are not in agreement on how the test should be conducted, it is safe to assume that figures appearing in a spec sheet are the result of the best test and operating conditions from the manufacturer's viewpoint. Still, compared to analog components (Fig. 7-11), THD figures for a CD player are gratifyingly low.

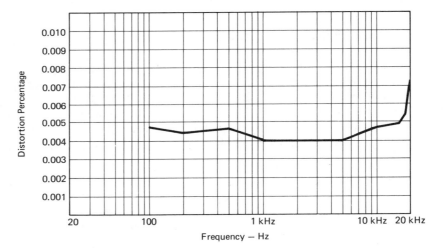

Figure 7-10   Percentage of total harmonic distortion versus frequency.

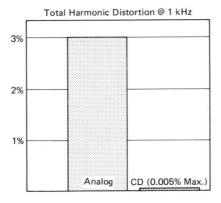

Figure 7-11   Total harmonic distortion of CD player versus typical analog source, measured at 1 kHz. (Courtesy Marantz Company, Inc.)

Intermodulation Distortion

Abbreviated as IM, this is a condition produced in a nonlinear active analog circuit. When more than one audio frequency is fed into such a circuit, the output not only contains the original input signal frequencies but their sum and difference frequencies as well. If, for example, two audio frequencies such as 800 Hz and 1,500 Hz are present at the input, the output will contain the original frequencies (800 Hz and 1,500 Hz) and their sum (800 Hz + 1,500 Hz = 2,300 Hz) and also their difference (1,500 Hz - 800 Hz = 700 Hz). The sum and difference frequencies, 2,300 Hz and 700 Hz in this case, are not harmonically related to the original frequencies and so result in reproduced tones which are unpleasant.

Intermodulation distortion may not be included in various manufacturers' specs for CD players and if supplied at a single frequency is not too meaningful unless the selected frequency is one in which the IM figure is highest. IM can be measured by supplying a pair of sine wave voltages to the CD player, using a 4 to 1 voltage ratio, a figure that more nearly approximates actual working conditions. Rated intermodulation distortion figures are supplied as a percentage and a value of 0.0025 percent could be considered good. A figure such as this is much lower than IM figures for audio power amplifiers, with values of 0.1 percent to 0.5 percent being quite common.

PORTABLE AND CAR COMPACT DISC PLAYERS

Because a compact disc player can be made not much larger than a compact disc, 4-23/32 inches (120 mm) in diameter, it lends itself quite well to portable use and also as an add-on component for car sound systems. The compact disc is well named and just a half dozen of them, requiring very little room, will supply six hours of musical entertainment. Furthermore, the compact discs that are used with an in-home player are suitable for either portable or car players.

As a portable or installed in a car, the compact disc player is subject to grueling working conditions. It was for this reason that the analog record player was never adopted for car use, although at least one manufacturer tried to promote a model for this application. Portable record players were a little more successful but because a number of phono records made a sizable package and because the portable phono player could only be used in a fixed location, the success of such units could only be called modest.

In terms of being vibration proof the compact disc player does much better in this respect than any portable phono player. It can be played in any position, approximately horizontal when placed on a bench or table or almost vertical when carried with a shoulder strap (Fig. 8-1).

Despite the stringent tracking demands of the compact disc player, it is being used in both portable and auto environments. The reason for its adoption is due to two factors: The laser beam assembly is designed to tolerate vibration and the player has a number of error correction systems available. This combination is such that the compact disc player is astonishingly capable of tolerating shock. A blow that would send the needle of a phono cartridge on a turntable skittering across and scratching the surface of a record will not disturb the playback of a compact disc. And yet the dimensions of the track and the diameter of the focused laser scanning beam are so minute they make the groove and stylus of a transcription turntable gross by comparison.

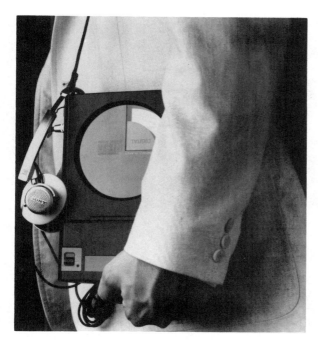

Figure 8-1 Portable CD player with carrying case, battery pack and headphones. (Courtesy Sony Corporation of America.)

THE PORTABLE CD PLAYER

The compact disc player is a sound source in the same way that cassette or open reel tape decks, transcription turntables and microphones are sound sources. The player can be included in portables either as a supplement to a cassette deck or as a sound source replacing the cassette. Typically, a portable (Fig. 8-2) consists of a disc player, a cassette deck, an AM/FM mono/FM stereo radio. Some units also include a seven-band graphic equalizer and detachable speakers.

Portables are battery operated but depending on design can be used in the home or in a car. In the home some units can be operated from the AC power line with the help of an AC adapter. If rechargeable batteries are used such as NiCads, these can be put on charge at the time the CD player is being operated from the AC line.

The portable compact disc player has one great advantage: It can be used anywhere. It is independent of static, no tuning is required, there are no advertising commercials, no pickup of unwanted stations, and no interference from power lines. However, there is a price to be paid. The musical quality capabilities of the compact disc are far superior to the amplifiers and speakers used by the portable. These can only degrade compact disc sound, but if the portable is used purely for entertainment purposes, possibly to supply background music, then it is superior to radio broadcast reception and produces better results than recorded cassette tape since there is no hiss. The length of play is a decided advantage. The compact disc supplies a full hour of uninterrupted music. Even a C-60 audio cassette tape must be flipped to give an equal

Figure 8-2 Portable compact disc player combined with cassette deck, AM/FM/MPX radio and a pair of speakers. (Courtesy Sanyo Electric, Inc.)

amount of musical time unless you use a deck with automatic return. The output amplifier has a limited power capability, a concession to the need for a reasonable length of battery life. The speaker system is equally poor, and even if the speakers are detachable types, the sound is like mono rather than stereo from the two speakers. Furthermore, if the portable is placed outdoors the lack of an enclosed listening space means almost a complete absence of reverberant sound, a characteristic that adds depth to music.

Types of Portables

There are two basic types of portables: stand alone and combination. A stand-alone is not equipped for speaker operation but depends on headphones. The compact disc player contains a small stereo amplifier with enough signal output to satisfy the input signal requirements of a headset. For this kind of use a pair of quality headphones will supply excellent high-fidelity sound. This would be characteristic of the unit in Figure 8-1. The combination unit of Figure 8-2 supplies the convenience of speaker sound, has detachable speakers, and other sound sources such as a cassette player and a radio receiver but the compact disc supplies sound quality over and beyond the capabilities of the speakers and amplifier.

Portable Compact Disc Player Features

Portable compact disc players have some of the features and functions that characterize in-home units. An automatic music search system quickly finds a favorite sound track on a disc. The user can also monitor the program number, elapsed time and remaining time on the disc through a multifunction LED display. Other features could include an automatic open/close disc tray and soft touch logic controls. The component may have a detachable carry handle.

Portable Combination Disc Player Features

In addition to the features specified for portable CDs, the combination unit would also have features such as a battery strength LED, a built-in condenser microphone, detachable speakers containing 4-inch woofers and piezo tweeters, loudness control, a three-digit tape counter, and an auxiliary magnetic phono input jack. The unit may also be equipped with a five-band graphic equalizer. Not all combination portables have these features, but generally the higher the cost, the greater the number of features available.

Accessories for the Portable Compact Disc Player

Various accessories are available for the portable player. One of these is a shockproof strap-equipped carrying case (Fig. 8-3), an AC converter, lightweight headphones, and a power adapter that permits the portable player to get operating DC voltage from the cigarette lighter in a car.

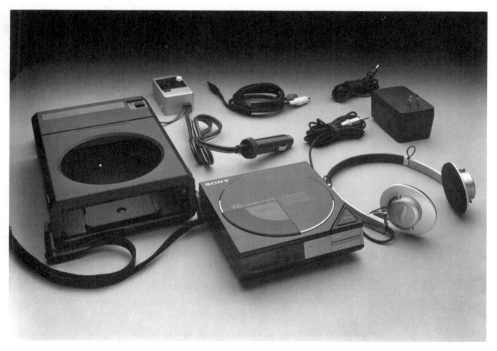

Figure 8-3 Portable CD player and its accessories. (Courtesy Sony Corporation of America.)

Compact Disc Player Sizes

Compact disc players are available in three basic sizes. The smallest is the portable shown at the top right in Figure 8-4. It is also the lightest since weight is an important factor. The next larger size is the player used in a vehicle and is shown at the upper left in the photo. The largest is the in-home player and, as you can see, is substantially bigger. However, in all three the disc-holding compartment accommodates discs of the same size.

Figure 8-4 Three types of CD players. In-home unit (bottom); car player (upper left); portable (upper right). (Courtesy Sony Corporation of America.)

COMPACT DISC PLAYERS FOR CARS

There are two types of compact disc players that can be used in cars: the portable player and the car player. The advantage of the portable player is that no external connections are necessary, as the unit is completely independent. The portable can also be removed from the car and either stored in the trunk or carried away, making it more theft proof. The disadvantage of using the combination portable in the car is that it does not take advantage of the power amplifier(s) or of the speakers in the car's high-fidelity system and some of these are very impressive.

Although compact disc players made specifically for cars and those used as portables are alike in the sense that both are subject to vibration and to mishandling with neither operated in a fixed location, they are different in certain respects. The compact disc player made for car use has a tremendous advantage in its power supply, the car battery. The electrical energy contained in such a battery is said to be sufficient to lift one ton one mile into the sky. This advantage is needed not so much by the compact disc player whose operating needs are quite modest (generally less than 50 watts), but by the power amplifier(s). And unlike portable units, the car compact disc player can take advantage of the car's speaker system. Typically, a car may have a pair of speakers mounted left/right in the front doors and another pair positioned under the rear deck. Furthermore, some car sound systems are equipped with a subwoofer, a bass tone speaker, which is highly desirable yet not often used in home high-fidelity systems.

Problems of the Car Compact Disc Player

The car compact disc player is a component that must·be adapted to the special limitations of an auto. There are two essential difficulties: installation and the connection to the existing sound system.

Compact disc players can be installed in cars in three ways: in dash (Fig. 8-5), under dash (Fig. 8-6), and in the console. In-dash installation is convenient but this means getting a compact disc player that is integrated with a radio receiver. The advantage is not only in saving space but no special wiring is needed from the compact disc player to the power amplifiers (also called the main amplifiers) already in position in the car. Furthermore, a control on the front of the radio set/compact disc player

Figure 8-5 In-dash combination CD player and car radio. (Courtesy Sony Corporation of America.)

Figure 8-6   Under-dash compact disc player. (Courtesy Sony Corporation of America.)

permits quick selection of the compact disc player as the sound source. The disadvantage of this arrangement is that you must accept the features and functions supplied by the compact disc player and these may not include all the ones you want.

Disc Loading

Compact disc players for cars (Fig. 8-7) are commonly add-on devices and most often are mounted under dash or in a console. If the player is such that it can be mounted on

Figure 8-7   CD player mounted in car's console. (Courtesy Philips Auto Audio/ Amperex.)

a pair of slides, (Fig. 8-8) the unit can be top loading. The advantage of this arrangement is that putting the disc in for play is somewhat easier than by front loading.

Front loading is most often used for the car compact disc player. To load the disc hold it by the edge (Fig. 8-9) with the label side up. Press the drawer open/close button if you find your fingers or any objects are stuck or wedged in the drawer and the drawer will open.

While the compact disc player is not being used keep the drawer closed to prevent the entry of dust and dirt, especially if you are driving your car with the windows open, or if there are smokers in the car with the windows open or closed. If you press the drawer open/close button while the drawer is in the process of opening the drawer will not close.

Figure 8-8 Compact disc player mounted on slides. (Courtesy Philips Auto Audio/ Amperex.)

— Place with label side up.

Figure 8-9 Correct method of inserting disc in player.

Noise Suppression

The electrical system of a car's engine is possibly one of the best of the world's collection of electrical noise generators. This electrical noise can reach electronic components in two ways: by radiation and through the DC power line. The fact that the compact disc player does not use an antenna does not mean it cannot pick up radiated noise. It can do so through connecting wires and via internal wiring. It can also pick up electrical noise through its connection to the car's battery.

Compact disc players for cars come equipped with a noise suppressor. The noise suppressor can be mounted using mounting hardware (Fig. 8-10). If the compact disc player is to be installed inside the dashboard or console and there is space available behind it, the noise suppressor can be mounted there as shown. The compact disc player may also have some provision for mounting the noise suppressor on its rear panel (Fig.8-11).

If a car battery is new or in good condition and is well charged, its impedance is usually very low. Electrical noise is shunted via this low impedance to ground, in this case the car frame. But for older batteries that can no longer hold a full charge, the impedance of the battery becomes higher. The noise voltage developed across the battery's impedance can then be fed into the compact disc player by the power line. One method of ensuring a battery's low impedance is to shunt a high value of capaci-

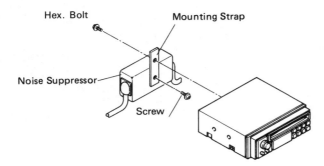

Hex. Bolt   Mounting Strap

Noise Suppressor—

Screw

Figure 8-10 Noise suppressor mounting. (Courtesy Alpine Electronics of America, Inc.)

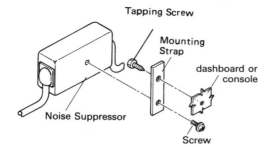

Figure 8-11 Alternate method of mounting noise suppressor. (Courtesy Alpine Electronics of America, Inc.)

tance directly across the battery's output terminals. Use an electrolytic capacitor of 1,000 microfarads or higher. Since the electrolytic is polarized, connect the plus and minus terminals of the capacitor to the corresponding plus and minus terminals of the battery. The capacitor will also help cut down on noise picked up by the car's radio receiver.

Checking the Car Battery

The car's battery is the DC power source for the compact disc player. That voltage is 14.4 volts DC and is the amount of voltage across the positive and negative terminals with the battery working under load. A good check is to measure the voltage with the car's high beams turned on but with the engine turned off. A voltage check of the battery with no car electrical components operating is meaningless because even a practically dead battery will read the full amount of battery voltage without a load.

MOUNTING THE COMPACT DISC CAR PLAYER

If the compact disc player is an add-on unit, mount it as close to the existing in-dash radio as possible. There are three commonly used mounting techniques for these players. The first uses a pair of individual side brackets (Fig. 8-12). The second is similar

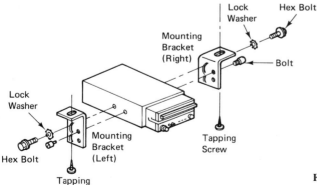

Figure 8-12 Individual side brackets for CD player support.

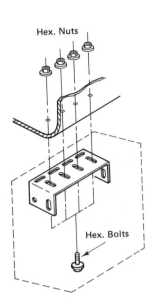

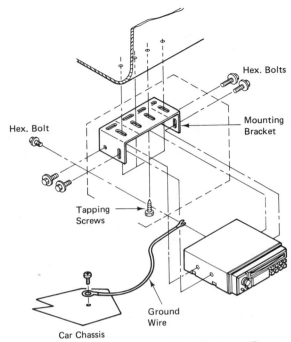

Figure 8-13 Single bracket for CD player installation. (Courtesy Alpine Electronics of America, Inc.)

Figure 8-14 Installation details for CD player. (Courtesy Alpine Electronics of America, Inc.)

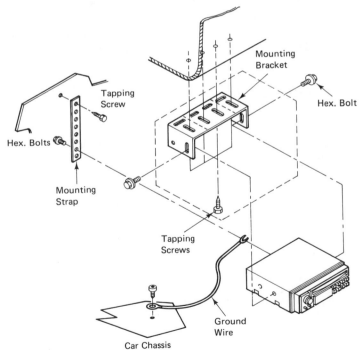

Figure 8-15 Rear mounting strap adds support and helps prevent theft. (Courtesy Alpine Electronics of America, Inc.)

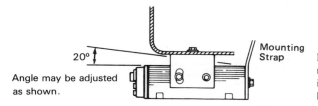

Figure 8-16 Tilting player upward will make it easier to insert disc and to read illuminated displays. (Courtesy Alpine Electronics of America, Inc.)

but supplies a third bracket to support the compact disc player from the rear. The final method uses a bracket that supplies support from the sides and the top (Fig. 8-13).

Mounting the compact disc player is easy, assuming there is enough room under the dash (Fig. 8-14). If the player has mounting holes for a rear strap as well, be sure to use it because this will not only supply additional support but will also make the disc player less susceptible to theft (Fig. 8-15). Some players have mounting holes drilled so the player can be mounted at some desired angle (Fig. 8-16). The adjustment angle can be as much as 20 degrees.

In-Dash or In-Console Mounting

For an in-dash mounting the opening to be cut depends on the size of the player. Most cars have a 180 mm x 50 mm cut-out provision in the dashboard.

For a console mounting it will be necessary to cut an opening 172 mm x 49 mm (Fig. 8-17) for the average compact disc player. Mount the player using a mounting bracket (Fig. 8-18). When the mounting is completed put the front trimplate on and around the front end of the unit.

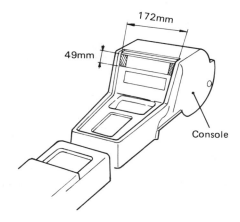

Figure 8-17 Console mounting for CD player. (Courtesy Alpine Electronics of America, Inc.)

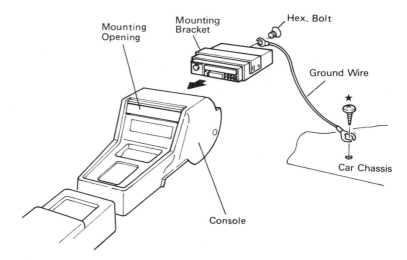

Figure 8-18   Installation details for console mounting. (Courtesy Alpine Electronics of America, Inc.)

DC-TO-DC CONVERTER

The compact disc player used in a car may require as much as 30 volts DC for some of its circuitry. Since the battery as the power source in the car can supply only 12.6 volts, some means must be used for stepping up this voltage to the required amount. This can be done by a DC-to-DC converter. The input to the converter is the battery voltage and in the converter this is used to drive a power oscillator whose output is AC. This is delivered to a step-up transformer followed by a rectifier and filter. The DC-to-DC converter (Fig. 8-19) is a separate unit held in place in any convenient behind-the-dash location by a pair of Velcro strips, one on each end of the unit.

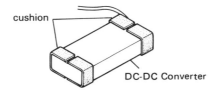

Figure 8-19   DC-to-DC converter. (Courtesy Alpine Electronics of America, Inc.)

THE GROUND CONNECTION

Compact disc players for car use have a ground wire. Attach this wire to the frame of the car. The connection is usually to a self-tapping screw already fixed into the frame and you can select any convenient screw for this purpose. If no screw is available drill a suitable hole and mount a screw. In either case scrape away any paint or rust beneath the screw head. The metal surface should be clean and shiny to assure good contact. The ground wire must be fastened securely.

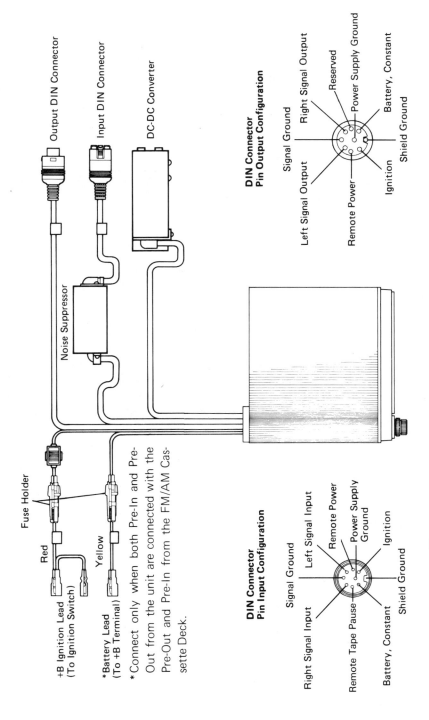

Output DIN Connector

Input DIN Connector

DC-DC Converter

Noise Suppressor

Fuse Holder

Red

+B Ignition Lead
(To Ignition Switch)

Yellow

*Battery Lead
(To +B Terminal)

*Connect only when both Pre-In and Pre-
Out from the unit are connected with the
Pre-Out and Pre-In from the FM/AM Cas-
sette Deck.

**DIN Connector
Pin Input Configuration**

Signal Ground

Left Signal Input

Remote Power

Power Supply
Ground

Right Signal Input

Remote Tape Pause

Battery, Constant

Ignition

Shield Ground

**DIN Connector
Pin Output Configuration**

Signal Ground

Right Signal Output

Reserved

Power Supply Ground

Battery, Constant

Left Signal Output

Remote Power

Ignition

Shield Ground

Figure 8-20 Connections for CD player. (Courtesy Alpine Electronics of America, Inc.)

The wiring diagram (Fig. 8-20) shows two battery connections but only one of these should be used. The DC input can be obtained from either the plus terminal on the ignition switch or the plus terminal directly on the battery. No minus connection is required since that is obtained through the ground wire fastened to the frame of the car.

While you do have a choice of two battery connections, there are certain advantages to each. If the power lead is wired to the ignition switch, turning off the ignition will also automatically turn off power input to the compact disc player. This has the advantage that you will not forget to turn off the player when you leave the car. If you connect to the battery plus terminal you will now be independent of the ignition switch and will be able to use the player at any time. However, you will need to remember to turn off the player when it is not in use or when you leave the car.

FEATURES AND FUNCTIONS

The compact disc player for car use may have some features not found in in-home units but a number of them, of course, will be the same.

Scan

The player may have a scan system that plays ten seconds from the start of each selection. Upon completing this short time scan, it will automatically proceed to scanning the next. If you like the musical introduction, a control lets you defeat this function and the band is played completely. If you take no further action, the following musical band will be played completely unless you push the scan button again.

Automatic Track Selection

You can hear any selection desired by depressing a front panel track control. The number of the track will be illuminated on the panel. The panel will also have a logic control marked "track" and a pair of arrows indicating forward or reverse. When the desired track number is displayed, depress the track control and the track number indicated will be played.

Repeat

Touch this control and a musical selection will be repeated. It will continue repeating until you defeat the control.

Play Data

The panel will have illuminated readouts to supply information as to the status of the disc being played. You will know the track number, playing time, the remaining time in minutes and seconds, and the total amount of remaining playing time for the entire disc. This is for a typical player, but they are not all alike and the operating information will vary from one player to the next.

Logic Controls

These are sometimes known as soft-touch controls. Instead of depressing a pushbutton, a light touch is all that is needed. Soft-touch controls are flush with the front panel of the player. The lettering of the controls should be large enough to let you read the data without difficulty and without the need for bending your head for better visibility.

Accidental Skipping

If part of a selection should be skipped accidentally due to car vibration, play will return at once to the point where the skip began. If the fault is due to car vibration and the disc is in good condition, you will then be able to listen to the entire disc. But if the disc is the source of the trouble, the sound will continuously skip and repeat. If that should be the case you can use the front panel controls to move ahead to the next selection. When you have the opportunity, clean the disc and then try it again. If cleaning does not remove the problem you can still use the disc, either pressing the skip control when that selection is reached or by programming playing to skip the defective band automatically.

Electronic Specs

As far as these specifications are concerned, they are as good for the car player as they are for any other type. The frequency response is from 4 or 5 Hz to 20 kHz with a variation of ± 1 dB; wow and flutter are below measurable limits; stereo separation is 85 dB or better; signal-to-noise ratio when measured at 1 kHz is 90 dB or better and harmonic distortion is 0.005 percent referenced to 0 dB at 1 kHz.

If the compact disc player is associated with a tuner, the arrangement could be as in Figure 8-21. Here two different sound sources are used: a CD player and a tuner for

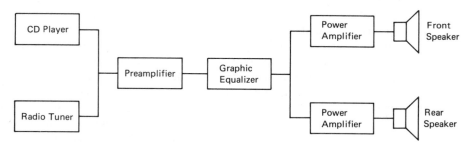

Figure 8-21 Auto sound system using CD player and radio tuner.

AM/FM/FM MPX. Either sound source can be switched into a graphic equalizer whose audio output is used to drive a pair of power amplifiers which, in turn, operate front and rear speakers.

COMPACT DISC PLAYER CONNECTIONS

In the integrated AM/FM tuner and CD player (Fig. 8-22), the output is audio with the signal source selected by a control on the front panel of the unit. The signal is supplied to a power amplifier, often called a main amplifier, via cable using a DIN (Deutsche

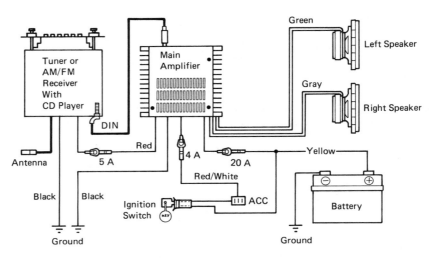

Figure 8-22   Connections for combined tuner or AM/FM receiver with CD player.

Industrie Normen) connector at one end. Some car-integrated CD players use a DIN socket but others have all the connecting wires emerging directly from the unit.

The output of the main amplifier consists of a double pair of wires which is connected to the speakers by a force-fit slide-on tab. These are the connections to the voice coils of the speakers with the left speaker for left-channel sound; the right speaker for right-channel sound.

The integrated tuner/CD gets its DC operating power from the main amp via a five-ampere fuse. The main amplifier gets its power via a connection to the ignition switch. The color coding for the speakers is identified as green and gray, although other colors are used. The input impedance of the speakers is usually 4 ohms and should match the output impedance of the main amplifier. If the sound output from the tuner/CD player is inadequate when the CD player is active, adjust the output level control for the player. Since the tuner and the player share a volume control, you can turn the CD output level to maximum. Because the player has a wide dynamic range, usually about 90 dB, a better procedure is to adjust the CD level output control for an output of no more than one volt.

THE CD MAIN AMPLIFIER

Other than an on/off switch the main amplifier used in a car CD sound system is not equipped with operating controls. This means the amplifier can be more conveniently located in the car trunk if there is some provision for turning it on or off from the driver's seat.

This can be done if the integrated CD player/AM/FM receiver is equipped with a remote relay. The relay is DC operated and is switch controlled from the front panel. In other installations power is supplied automatically to the remote relay when the integrated CD player/receiver is turned on (Fig. 8-23). The system shown in this diagram uses four speakers, with two mounted in the front of the car, usually in the car doors; the other two are in the rear, using the rear deck as the speaker suspension. The high power main amplifier is protected by a 20-ampere fuse.

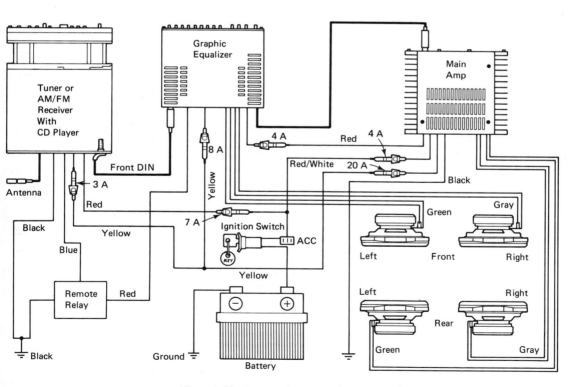

Figure 8-23 Car sound system using remote relay.

THE INDEPENDENT CD PLAYER

If the CD player is not integrated with the car's receiver but is an add-on component, it will need to be supplied with DC power independently. This can be done by running the DC wire line supplied with the player to the ignition switch. The advantage of doing this instead of running the line right to the battery is that closing the ignition switch automatically turns off the CD player. With a separate line to the battery it is possible to forget to turn off the power switch on the CD player.

Not only must the independent CD player be supplied with DC power but its audio output must somehow be connected to the input terminals of the main amplifier. The CD unit does have a small stereo amplifier but the output of this amplifier is not enough to drive a speaker system directly.

There are several ways of using the compact disc player to drive the main amplifier(s) in the car's sound system. If the main amplifier has an input jack for accepting the audio output of the CD player, all that is necessary is to use an audio cable equipped with a suitable plug. If the main amplifier is equipped with a single jack for audio input, a switch could be used to supply a choice of sound from the car's receiver or the compact disc player's audio output. Still another method is to connect the compact disc player to the car's receiver.

THE CD PLAYER/ADAPTER

Most car radios do not have auxiliary audio input jacks for add-on components. However, it is possible to access the audio system of the car radio by transmitting an FM stereo signal directly through the antenna of the radio. The radio receiver is tuned to the transmission frequency of the adapter in the same way as any other station is tuned in. The adapter emits a strong signal making the radio receiver capable of supplying its following main amplifier with a substantial input voltage.

The adapter (Fig. 8-24a) is connected in series between the car antenna and the car's radio receiver. The adapter is equipped with a switch that disconnects the external antenna so the only signal to reach the car's antenna will be that of the CD player via the adapter.

The adapter gets its operating power from the car's battery via a lead (marked red) which is wired to the battery plus terminal on the car's fuse block mounted right behind the dash. Alternatively, the adapter can be connected to get its DC voltage from the car's cigarette lighter.

The adapter can also be used with a portable CD player. While the DC input to the adapter is 14 volts, a resistive network in the player drops this to the nine volts needed by the portable CD player. The advantage is that the portable need not use its battery supply when working in the car.

The circuitry of an adapter is simple. It consists of an oscillator tuned to a frequency on the FM band, such as 90.1 MHz. The oscillator is modulated by the audio signal from the CD player which is fed into the antenna input terminal of the receiver.

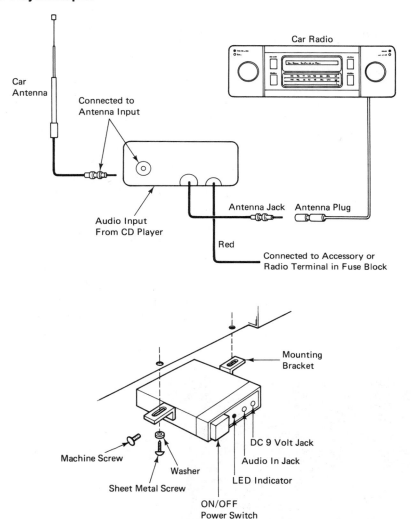

Figure 8-24(a)   Method of using adapter to supply car radio with audio signal from CD player and mounting arrangement. (Courtesy Sparkomatic Corporation.)

A switch on the front panel of the adapter can be used to select FM broadcast band reception or the modulated signal from the adapter. When the CD signal is being used the antenna is disconnected automatically; hence, no signal is radiated into space from the adapter when the CD player is being used.

The adapter can also be used with a CD player designed for permanent installation in the car. The connections are the same as for the portable CD player. The CD player and the adapter will both get their DC working voltage from the DC terminal on the ignition switch or via the car's cigarette lighter.

Figure 8-24b shows another wireless adapter that enables you to play your CD player through your car's FM radio speaker system. The attachment is merely plugged into the car's lighter outlet, thus supplying DC power to the unit. No other wiring is needed.

If a portable CD player is used, there is no need to be concerned about making a permanent mount. The player should not be subjected to any excessive vibration. Best operation from the player is obtained by putting the player on the car seat and the connecting cords supplied with the adapter are usually long enough to permit this. Bouncing may cause the player to become mute temporarily but sound will be restored as soon as the heavy vibrations stop.

It is advisable to restrain the CD player to keep it from moving freely, otherwise during quick stops or if someone inadvertently pulls on the cables, the player may fall off the car seat and become damaged.

The best arrangement, of course, is to mount a CD player intended for car use with the adapter securely under the dash. Fortunately such CD players are about the same size as the discs they play and require very little space, as does the adapter. The overall dimensions of the adapter are 3-1/4″ x 1″ x 3-1/2″ and so is actually smaller than the in-dash CD player.

The mounting of the adapter is along the same lines as the procedure used for CD players. Mounting brackets are supplied with the unit and only one pair are required. The brackets are fastened to the sides of the adapter by machine screws and once the brackets are in place, the unit is held in position by a pair of sheet metal screws.

Figure 8-24(b)   CD player adapter. (Courtesy Dynasound Organizer, Div. Hartzell Manufacturing, Inc.)

Mounting the adapter is not as difficult as finding space for it. One method would be to loosen the screws for the CD player so the adapter can be sandwiched in between the lower end of the dash and the CD player. The thickness of the adapter is only one inch and so this should be possible.

The most convenient way of having a CD player in your car is by having a unit that is integrated with an AM/FM/MPX receiver. This can be a permanent installation or one that is mounted on slides so it can be removed, leaving only a conspicuous hole to discourage thieves. The connections at the rear can be via a multiconductor DIN cable supplying DC voltage and speaker connections. If the DIN and antenna connectors are slide-on instead of screw-on types, the connections and disconnections take just a few moments. The slide-out supports are sufficiently long so that reaching the rear of the receiver is easy. The unit can then be stored in the car's trunk when the car is to be parked.

As a further deterrent to theft, it is possible to get a fake front that substitutes as a panel when the receiver/CD player is removed. The artificial front is that of a cheap radio receiver, discouraging a thief looking for a high-priced car sound component.

CAR COMPACT DISC PLAYER REQUIREMENTS

Disc handling, vibration, and size represent three major problem areas for the successful installation of a CD player in a car. A fourth difficulty is connecting the audio output of the player into the car's audio sound system.

Size Reduction

A major factor in the reduction of compact disc player size to make it suitable for car installation has been the use of large-scale integrated (LSI) circuits. The LSI is a chip with one of these designed for servo control, laser focus and tracking location, while the other handles D/A conversion, error correction and filtering. Thus, with these LSIs it becomes possible to reduce the size of the player by diminishing the size and number of components.

At the same time these new LSIs add reliability by combining discrete functions and circuits on each chip. While the triple laser scanning beam approach has been kept, the laser head, mounting and servo systems to conserve space and maintain proper tracking have all been downsized.

Changes in CD Insertion

The standard method of inserting a disc into a CD player would in a car's environment expose the disc to contamination by road dust, high heat, scratches and fingerprints, and possibly provide a distraction for the driver as well. One solution to these problems is a cartridge carrier that holds the disc and slips into the unit's loading slot. Similar to the standard CD jewel box case, the carrier is a lightweight plastic cartridge into which any compact disc can be inserted.

When the cartridge and disc are inserted into the player, a shutter built into the cartridge opens to permit tracking by the player's laser pickup. Upon ejection, the shutter closes prior to the release of the cartridge. The cartridge carrier protects the disc and the player and its ease of handling allows a driver to load a disc while maintaining driving concentration.

Floating Suspension

Road shocks and vibration present another significant problem for car audio compact disc players. The manufacturer of one such unit has developed a floating suspension for it. The disc transport system, drive mechanism and laser pickup are isolated in a separate section within the CD player itself. The effect of external vibration on one element or another is cancelled since tracking and disc rotation are treated as one self-contained system.

The use of a high-density VLSI (very large-scale integrated circuit) chip for primary digital functions was created to both simplify and stabilize player operation. This plus the development of the miniaturized laser optic assembly have made the miniaturized CD player possible.

THREE-IN-ONE CD PLAYERS

While CD players are available as three distinct types (the in-home player, the portable, and the car player), it is possible to get one that consists of the equivalent of three stand-alone units. It consists of a player that will work as an in-dash unit, as a battery pack portable, or as part of a home stereo system. It can be used for permanent installation and is also sized for standard DIN openings in a car's dashboard. The unit can be installed in a car, truck or boat through the use of a special DIN-sized support tray automatically connected to the vehicle's power supply. A preamplifier is built into the tray. By installing support trays in several vehicles, it is possible to transfer the CD player anytime at the owner's convenience. A battery pack converts the CD player to a walkabout set and a clip-on AC converter allows connection to a home audio system.

The fact that a unit is a portable or designed for use in a car or in a combination of both does not mean the elimination of features or lower grade specs. You can expect a frequency response of 20 Hz to 20 kHz, auto repeat play, auto start-restart, forward or reverse track skipping, programmable music search and illuminated function display.

CAR AMPLIFIERS AND SPEAKERS

The compact disc player imposes a heavier demand on the power amplifiers used in the car's sound system than an AM/FM tuner or cassette deck. Since the dynamic range of the CD player is so much greater than these other two components, a main amplifier that might have been suitable up to the time of the inclusion of the CD player now may be inadequate. This is testimony to the fact that a substantial improvement in any component of a sound system, or the inclusion of a new, highly advanced component (as in the case of the CD player) can necessitate an upgrading of other components in that system. In this case those other components consist of the power (main) amplifier(s) and the speakers.

Improvements in the main amplifier section can include adding more speakers in series or in shunt with the existing speaker system. But simply adding more speakers does not automatically mean greater power output, just a greater capability of handling the power output of the main amplifiers. Upgrading, then, means replacing the existing main amplifiers with those that have a higher output, plus the addition of speakers capable of handling that increased output.

This is not a "must" situation. You can add a CD player of any type, in-dash or portable, to an existing car audio sound system. The only problem in doing so is that you may not be taking advantage of the full sound output capabilities of the player.

The Subwoofer

Most car sound systems and in-home sound systems are not equipped with a subwoofer, a speaker specifically designed to reproduce sounds below the frequency reproducing capabilities of the typical woofer. This involves three problems:. the first is that of placement, the second is that of driving power, and finally there is the need for a suitable crossover network.

Since the subwoofer is not a directional type, it can be mounted in almost any convenient place. In some installations it has been placed beneath the driver's seat. As far as driving power is concerned, the subwoofer typically requires more signal driving power than a woofer, midrange or tweeter. A crossover is required to separate deep bass tones from the rest of the sound spectrum and to route these tones to the subwoofer. Unless an electronic crossover is used, this is built into the speaker enclosure. In some auto-sound installations a separate main amplifier is used solely for driving the subwoofer. This is not necessary if the existing main amplifiers have a high enough power rating to be able to drive the subwoofer in addition to the other speakers.

The easiest way to add a subwoofer is to connect it in parallel with an existing woofer or woofer/midrange speaker. Generally, such speakers have a voice coil impedance of four ohms and if this is also the impedance of the subwoofer, then the total impedance drops to two ohms, dangerously close to a short circuit. If the woofer/midrange has an impedance rated at eight ohms, and if the subwoofer is also eight ohms, the resulting impedance will be four ohms when these units are wired in parallel which can be tolerated.

The best arrangement, however, for installing a subwoofer is to use a separate main amplifier for driving this speaker, particularly since the subwoofer will most likely have a voice coil impedance of four ohms. This low impedance is required since the subwoofer voice coil requires a substantial amount of audio driving power.

THE TRANSIT SCREW

In-home entertainment components such as a video cassette recorder, a turntable or a cassette deck are characterized by moving parts and are often shipped with a transit screw in place. The CD car player is also so equipped. This screw located on the back panel or on the subsurface of the unit is there to keep any movable internal mechanism in place for protection against possible damage in transit. No unit will work with this screw in position and it must be loosened or removed prior to operating the component. Make sure you loosen the transit screw and not any other screw used to hold parts or the cover in place. Some CD car players have a label attached to the transit screw for identification.

There are two types of transit screws. One is known as a captive and all it requires is loosening. Do not try to force it out completely since this can damage the screw. If the screw is not a captive type, remove it completely but save it in the event the CD player must be shipped. When shipping the player, possibly to be serviced, be sure to put the transit screw back in its original position. Any damage in transit caused by not using this screw will possibly be at your expense. Be sure to attach a tag to the screw prior to shipping calling attention to the fact that the screw is used for transit only. You can expect more servicing needs with the car CD player than one used in the home. (Not all CD players are equipped with transit screws.)

INHOSPITABLE ENVIRONMENT PROBLEMS

As far as the CD player is concerned, a car or other vehicle can only be regarded as a hostile environment. To give the CD player an optimum opportunity to work well, make sure it is not exposed to direct sun and heat, high humidity, excessive dust or vibration. Some of these precautions will apply more to a portable player than to a fixed-position unit. Do not keep a portable on the car's rear deck where it will be baked by the sun.

CD players for cars sometimes have a built-in self-protection circuit. When the ambient temperature is over 120° F (50° C) the self-protection circuit functions and disables the player. The operating temperature range for a compact disc player is from 10° C to 50° C. (15° F to 120° F). Also keep a portable on a seat rather than on the car floor. Not only will it be more removed from the source of vibration but the seat will supply a cushioning effect.

The car CD player may have a built-in shock absorber or you may add your own in the form of rubber grommets or a small section of rubber sheet, or you may try to have both. Use these when installing the player and position them between the support brackets and the CD player. Extremely severe driving conditions could possibly interfere with playback. If so, turn the CD player off until driving conditions improve.

DYNAMIC RANGE

One characteristic of all compact disc players is wide dynamic range. If you are only accustomed to the playback of analog phono records, you may be surprised at sudden blasts of sound when using a CD. Before you play a disc turn the volume control down to a low level. Get some experience with the musical characteristics of the disc. Play it through and adjust the volume control to give you satisfactory sound for the loudest sound the disc will produce.

The human ear has a dynamic listening range of about 130 dB. At zero dB there is complete silence; at 130 dB the sound is so loud it is not only painful but can cause physiological damage. The car's compact disc player supplies a sound output with a dynamic range of 0 to 90 dB. While this is a tremendous range especially when compared to an analog phono record or audio cassettes, it does mean the units are more susceptible to environmental acoustics.

Music can get down to zero dB and its beauty is in the fact that it can use silence as a technique between musical passages, or with some of the tones having a sound level of just a few dB. This assumes, of course, that the listening environment is such that these silent periods can be appreciated.

An auto is inherently a noisy listening setup. There is noise from the car engine, from the movement of the tires, squeaks in the car body, from the wind, from passing vehicles and from passengers. Even if the passengers are quiet there is sound from their movements. However, if the car windows are kept closed, concentration on low musical sound levels can lead to dangerous driving.

In the home the extraneous sound level can be more strictly controlled. Still, the usual in-home sounds may make it impossible to listen to music that is not much above zero dB. The telephone, the movement of people, and conversation mean there is a constant level of noise. The ideal arrangement is to use headphones. These can also be used in the car, but not by the driver.

SOUND COMPRESSION

The compact disc player may have a built-in sound compressor. This means you can listen to compact discs for background music without the loss of quiet passages. Also, you can make cassettes of CDs for car stereos and personal portables.

It may seem strange to have a compressor in a CD player but in a noisy environment such as a car, pianissimo passages must compete with wind, car operating noises and passengers' conversation. This combination can often reach as high as 70 dB. Compressor circuitry helps keep the music being played back in a range that is more practical for a car. It also makes it unnecessary to ride gain on the volume control.

The best arrangement is to have a sound compressor that can be controlled by a switch positioned on the front panel, giving the user an option.

CAR HI-FI SYSTEMS

Just as in the case of home high-fidelity systems, a setup used for the car or any other vehicle can be simple or elaborate. A car hi-fi system is not a home hi-fi system put into a vehicle but is a system of its own with its own requirements. If anything, a car hi-fi system requires more attention to installation and because of the nature of its environment, demands components that can tolerate adverse operating conditions.

Receiver with Built-in CD Player

The simplest CD system (Fig. 8-25) and the easiest to install and connect consists of an AM/FM receiver with a built-in CD player, driving a left/right pair of speakers. The CD player is internally connected to the power amplifier built into the receiver. A control on the front panel of the receiver selects the sound source, in this case that supplied by the receiver or by the CD player.

The disadvantage of such a system is that while the built-in amplifier might be satisfactory for radio signals it could well be inadequate for a CD player. The use of just a pair of speakers would also seem to be an indication of the limited power output

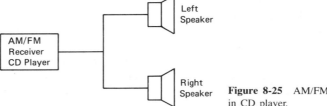

Figure 8-25 AM/FM receiver with built-in CD player.

of the amplifier in the receiver. In the absence of any other indication, we can assume the speakers are single drivers covering entire audio range and certainly incapable of doing justice to the CD player. An improvement is the use of separate speakers for bass/midrange tones and another pair of speakers working as a tweeter (Fig. 8-26).

CD Player with Graphic Equalizer

The fact that a compact disc player can have a flat frequency response from 5 Hz to 20 kHz, does not mean there is no need for equalization. The acoustics of the car's interior are such that treble tones are readily absorbed by the extensive use of padding and carpeting. Treble tones having a weaker energy content than midrange and bass tones also need reinforcement.

Some car hi-fi systems can be far more elaborate than those used in the home. Car systems have numerous disadvantages, notably a high external noise level and vibration, but there is one favorable point: The listening "room" is small and is completely enclosed, supplying in effect a cocoon-like listening environment.

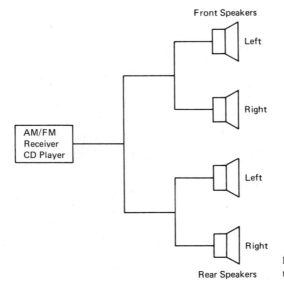

Figure 8-26 Improved system using additional speakers.

When you consider the limited mounting space, it is astonishing that some hi-fi systems in the car are as elaborate as they are. The diagram in Figure 8-27 uses a pair of main amplifiers, a graphic equalizer, and a digital time delay. The digital time delay is adjustable and supplies a sound delay between the front and rear speakers. In this way it can supply a moderately good imitation of the sound reverberation in a concert hall, a chamber, or an auditorium.

The dividing networks can be passive types mounted inside the speaker enclosures or can be electronic crossovers positioned externally to the speakers. Although not indicated in the illustration, both main amplifiers are probably mounted in the trunk and are relay controlled from the driver's seat.

THE COMPACT DISC CHANGER

When a component hi-fi system is used in a car the main amplifier(s) is frequently mounted in the trunk. The main amplifier has no operating controls and can be turned on and off by a relay positioned inside the car's receiver.

Because the sound output of the compact disc player can be connected to the main amplifier, it would also be logical to put the player inside the car's trunk as well, except for the fact that discs must be inserted into the player manually. This problem is overcome by the use of a ten-disc magazine changer designed for easy installation in a vehicle's trunk or rear compartment. (Some systems have fewer or more than 10 discs.) Playback is controlled by a small device positioned near the driver. It can rapidly access any disc selection. The in-trunk player can also send up to six different messages to the control panel regarding the operational status of the player (Fig. 8-28).

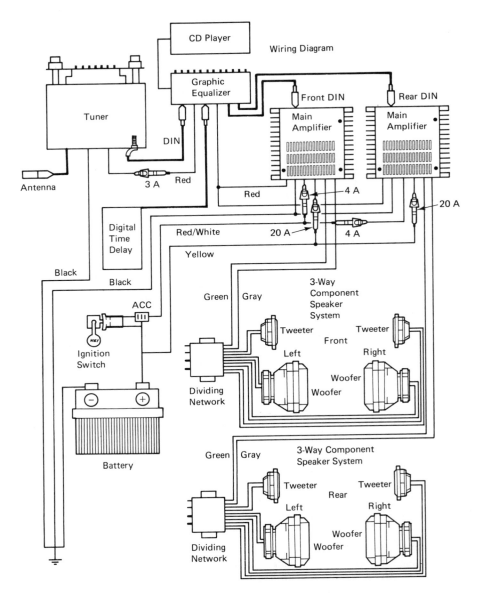

Figure 8-27 Sound system for car. Wiring is simplified if tuner has built-in CD player.

The control unit is connected by cable to the changer mechanism and is a small design that can be installed in the dash of most domestic or foreign cars. Alternatively, the control pad can also be left unmounted to allow for passenger operation.

When the unit is first turned on, playback starts automatically from the beginning of the first disc. If all ten discs are utilized sequentially, a listener can enjoy ten hours of continuous music pleasure without having to replace the magazine in the CD changer.

A random music sensor lets you repeat or randomly select up to five selections from any of up to ten discs. A program play feature makes it possible to program into memory up to ten selections from any of up to ten discs, with memory status being maintained even if you change listening sources during operation.

Other options include direct selection by disc and track number, an automatic music sensor that lets the user skip from song to song in either direction, and music search for sampling the music at ten times normal speed in either forward or reverse direction.

Figure 8-28   Compact disc changer for car shown with remote control, ten-disc magazine and AM/FM tuner pack. (Courtesy Sony Corporation of America.)

COMPACT DISC PLAYER
HIGH-FIDELITY SYSTEMS

The compact disc player used in the home in a high-fidelity system has a number of advantages over players used in vehicles. There are no space restrictions and the player can be the same size as other high-fidelity components, permitting a more esthetic appearance. The front panel can also be larger and so the operating controls are easier to adjust.

The inclusion of a compact disc player in a high-fidelity system possibly leads to an upgrading in that system, usually of the power amplifiers and speakers. This is necessary to take full advantage of the type of audio signal output supplied by the CD player.

CONNECTING THE COMPACT DISC PLAYER

The compact disc player may be supplied with an independent pair of shielded audio cables with RCA plugs at both ends (Fig. 9-1). With some players the cables are internally connected to the compact disc player; all that is needed is to plug the connectors into the aux input of a receiver or preamplifier. Use the tape or monitor input

Figure 9-1 Audio cable with RCA plugs at both ends.

jacks if these are the only spares. Do not use the phono input ports since these are wired to equalization circuits in the receiver and are not needed for the CD player.

The jacks on the rear of the compact disc player may be identified as "line out," "audio out," or simply "out" but since the player has only one set of output terminals, there is no possibility of confusion. The terminals will also be marked "left" and "right"; these should be wired to the corresponding left and right ports on the receiver or amplifier. The cables will be color coded as an aid in observing polarity, generally red and black, although other colors are used. The cables can be twinned; that is, they may consist of a pair of individual cables joined for most of their length but separate cables are also used. The best cables are those that have gold-plated plugs, an effective deterrent to corrosion.

The Basic CD Player System

A basic system can consist of nothing more than an AM/FM/MPX receiver plus an outboard compact disc player (Fig. 9-2). But even with an elementary arrangement of

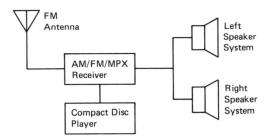

Figure 9-2 Basic high-fidelity system using outboard compact disc player.

this kind the system has three signal sound sources: AM broadcast, FM broadcast, and compact disc. The receiver should be equipped with a signal source selector. With older receivers it may be necessary to put in an add-on signal switcher. Newer receivers will have a separate port for CD player input and so this will be indicated on the signal source selector.

It is difficult to upgrade a system of this kind. The power amplifier in the receiver cannot be changed and installing a new set of speakers having a higher power capability will not be helpful. Possibly the chief advantage of this system is its economy.

Multiple Speaker System

The next CD high-fidelity system (Fig. 9-3) looks somewhat different from the one preceding it, but the only change is in the speaker arrangement. The speakers are now two-way types, using a tweeter and a midrange/woofer. It might seem as though the headphones are an addition but nearly all receivers as well as compact disc players have a jack for headphone use. Consequently, the system in Figure 9-2 is also equipped with headphones even though the diagram does not indicate this.

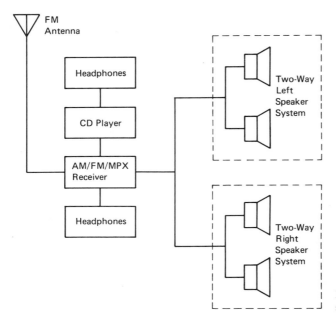

Figure 9-3 CD system using two-way speakers.

With some systems inserting headphones into the receiver automatically cuts off the speakers. The headphone connection to the compact disc player may not have this facility. For best headphone sound, however, it is better to use headphones with the CD player rather than the receiver. To cut off speaker sound simply turn down the volume control on the receiver.

USING A CD PLAYER AND A TURNTABLE

A CD player and a phono turntable have two basic similarities. Both are audio sound sources and neither has a recording facility and can be used for playback only. It might seem that using a turntable and a CD player is an unnecessary duplication but the turntable has far more software available. Furthermore, phono records cost less than compact discs.

With the arrangement in Figure 9-4, the turntable is connected to the phono input of the receiver and the CD player to the aux input. The cables used are the same. In the case of the turntable, the cables are usually wired directly into the component; with the CD player they can be wired in or supplied separately. Both the turntable and the CD player have a ground wire and these should both be connected to the same ground point. Connecting the ground leads to separate ground points, even though this may be more convenient, can lead to the formation of troublesome ground loops, resulting in hum which is often difficult to trace.

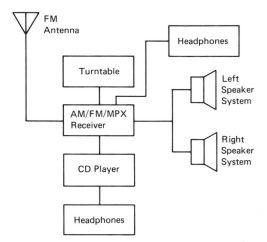

Figure 9-4 High-fidelity system using turntable and CD player.

System with a Cassette Deck

The inclusion of a cassette deck (Fig. 9-5) makes the high-fidelity system more flexible because another sound source has been added. The cassette deck has a recording facility which is something not possible with either the turntable or the CD player.

Although this system has become more elaborate, it still has the disadvantage of having the power amplifier integrated into the receiver. The only way to upgrade would be to replace the receiver with one having a power amplifer with a more substantial power output, or changing the system by substituting a separate preamplifier and power amplifier in place of the receiver.

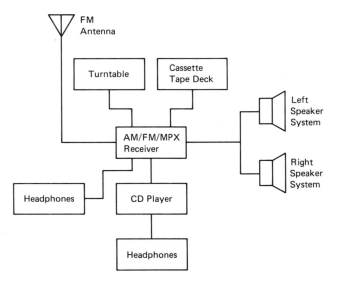

Figure 9-5 CD high-fidelity system using turntable, cassette deck and stereo FM receiver.

Upgrading an existing high-fidelity system by installing an outboard compact disc player may not be as simple as the diagram in Figure 9-5 indicates. This modification presents two problems. The first is the question of how to connect the CD player to the receiver. This is not difficult if the receiver is equipped with an aux input, but generally older sets do not have this facility. The next problem is one of signal source switching. The receiver may be able to switch from radio to phono to tape deck but has no additional switching position to accommodate the CD player.

Of these two difficulties, switching is the easier, since an outboard switcher can be used. The switcher should be a type that is equipped with RCA jacks that will accept RCA plugs.

If the receiver does not have an aux input, it may be possible to open it and make the connections across the terminals of the volume control. This will let you take advantage of the audio amplifier system in the receiver.

System Connections

The block diagrams in all of the illustrations to this point are overall views and do not show actual connections. These are easy enough to make (Fig. 9-6) since the same kind of cables and connectors are used for the compact disc player, the turntable, and the cassette deck.

The central component is the receiver which is equipped with input ports for a cassette deck, an open reel deck, a turntable and a compact disc player. While four separate antennas are shown these represent possible options. The AM outdoor antenna can be eliminated and the built-in loopstick used in its place. The three FM antennas are shown simply to indicate connections to the antenna terminal board and only one would actually be used.

The speakers, marked A and B, can be installed front and rear or one pair can be placed in another room. Generally there is a control on the front panel marked A, B, A + B. .With this control you can listen to speaker pair A, speaker pair B, or all the speakers at the same time.

When connecting all the components, the cassette deck, the compact disc player, the turntable, and the speakers it is necessary to observe polarity. Polarity on the components may be indicated by plus (+) and minus (−) symbols or plus on the speakers may be color coded with a red dot. The speaker wires and the cables connecting the components to the receiver are usually color coded to represent polarity. Red is often used for plus; black for minus, although any other color scheme can be used. If a color mix is used it is helpful to put tags on the wires to call attention to polarity.

CD Integrated Amplifier System

A receiver is an integrated unit and consists of individual components mounted on the same chassis. These include a tuner, a preamplifier (voltage amplifier), and a power amplifier. The receiver can be divided into two or three components.

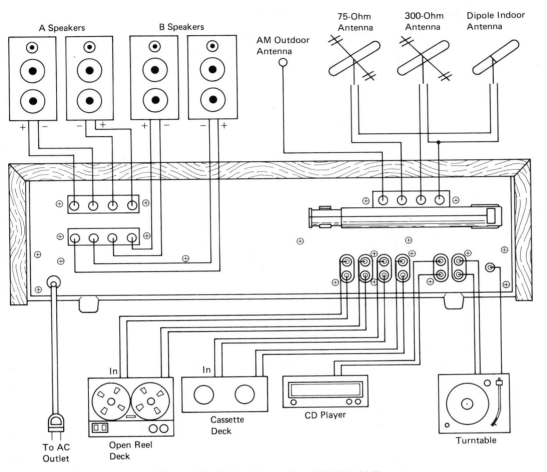

Figure 9-6 Wiring diagram for a CD high-fidelity system.

An integrated amplifier consists of a preamplifier and a power amplifier mounted on the same chassis and in a single housing (Fig. 9-7). This system is superior to those shown earlier for several reasons. The integrated amplifier is usually equipped with stereo power amplifiers having a higher power capability than those used in a receiver. If this amplifier becomes inadequate because of the inclusion of a compact disc player, it can be replaced without any need for changing the tuner. The integrated amplifier is generally equipped with more input ports, permitting the installation of additional components at some future time.

Although the drawing shows just a single pair of speakers used left/right in front of the listener, this system could possibly include another pair for left/right rear positioning or as a B speaker setup in another room.

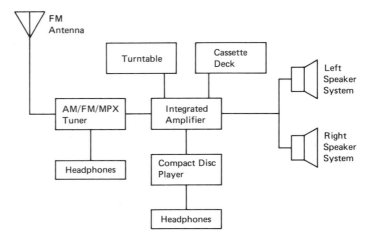

Figure 9-7 The receiver is separated into two components—a tuner and an integrated amplifier. An advantage is that the integrated amplifier is more likely to have sound input ports than a receiver or tuner.

System with an Equalizer

In any high-fidelity system regardless of the number and quality of the components, the listening room gets first choice of the sound frequencies. It may absorb some frequencies or be highly reflective of others and the listener gets only what remains. The result can be some frequencies which are excessively brilliant and others which sound muted or muffled. The fact that a compact disc has a frequency response capability of 5 Hz to 20 kHz and even if this full gamut of frequencies is recorded on the disc, it does not mean this is what you will hear. Even if you could possibly hear all these frequencies, it does not mean you will hear them equally well with both ears. Between the effect the listening room will have on various sound frequencies, your limited hearing range, and the hearing discrepancy between your left and right ears, what you will ultimately hear is not what is recorded on the compact disc. An equalizer will help compensate to a limited degree.

In its crudest form an equalizer is a tone control. The difficulty with a tone control is that its frequency coverage is too broad. The poorest of these is the single control that covers the entire audio band. Separate controls for bass and treble are better and individual controls for bass, midrange and treble are best. An equalizer divides the audio spectrum into narrower slices and even the most limited of these is superior to a receiver's or an amplifier's tone controls.

In Figure 9-8 the audio output of the compact disc player is fed into the input ports of the equalizer and the output of this component is delivered to the CD or aux inputs of the integrated amplifier. While headphones are shown connected to the integrated amplifier, another pair could be plugged into the compact disc player. This would precede the equalizer, enabling you to evaluate the effectiveness of the equalizer by comparing the two kinds of headphone sound and also with speaker sound.

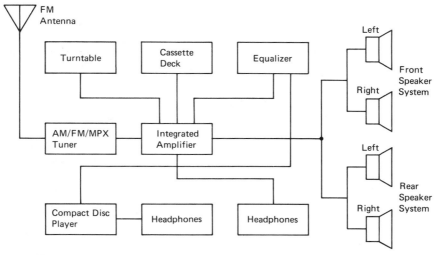

Figure 9-8 CD high-fidelity system using an equalizer. Assuming identical headphones, this setup lets you make an A/B comparison between CD player sound and integrated amplifier sound.

System with a Sound Processor

The new component added to the growing high-fidelity system is a sound processor (Fig. 9-9). This could be a dynamic range expander or a noise reduction unit. It is not needed for the compact disc player because its dynamic range is more than adequate and its noise level is remarkably low. However, it is essential for components such as the turntable and the cassette deck. With the compact disc working, keep the sound processor turned off.

Separate Pre- and Power Amplifiers

The integrated power amplifier illustrated in the preceding hookups can be separated into individual units consisting of a pre- and power amplifier, an arrangement that has a number of advantages. Preamps are generally designed to accommodate a fairly large number of components and so the preamp is often used as a control center. With this kind of hookup and installing a compact disc player for the first time, the power amplifier can be upgraded without disturbing the preamp or the tuner. The power amp may also have outputs for more than the single pair of speakers (Fig. 9-10).

Another new component indicated in this illustration is a pair of microphones. These can be used for those who enjoy a "sing along" or who may want to make an instrumental recording or use the hi-fi system as an in-home public address system. With this arrangement it is possible to dub from the compact disc to tape with or without microphone sound.

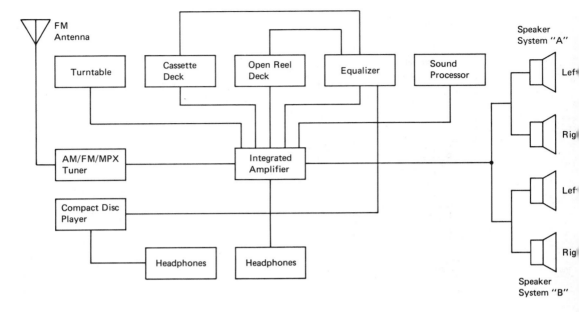

Figure 9-9 CD high-fidelity system using a sound processor.

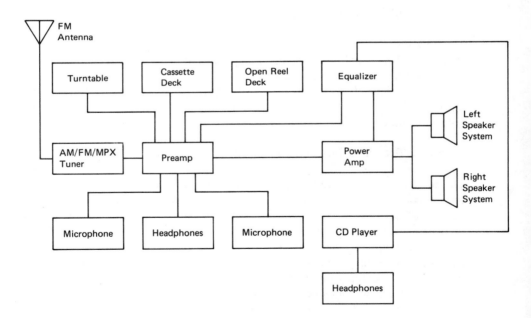

Figure 9-10 Separation of the integrated amplifier into a preamplifier and a power amplifier.

214

The Multiamp System

To accommodate the compact disc's audio output there is often a need for upgrading the hi-fi system by replacing the power amplifier with one having a higher output rating. This does not necessarily mean the old power amplifier must be discarded, for it can be used in a multiamp system (Fig. 9-11).

This hi-fi system hookup uses not one but two power amplifiers. Although shown as two separate components, they can be integrated on one chassis. The integrated form may be more economical but the use of separate amps makes it easier and less costly if it should become necessary to upgrade the system further by installing a still higher power amplifier.

One of the power amplifiers is used to drive a pair of separate tweeters, mounted front left and right. Although not indicated in the diagram an additional pair of tweeters could be installed in the rear, also left/right.

One of the features of this installation is the use of an electronic crossover instead of the usual passive crossover built into the speaker enclosure. The crossover separates the audio range into treble tones which are then routed to the tweeters, and bass/midrange tones for delivery to the midrange/woofer drivers.

The two power amplifiers need not have the same output ratings. The one used for the tweeters can be smaller since treble tones do not require as much energy.

The hookup in Figure 9-11 is a stripped-down version and is shown in this way to emphasize the inclusion of an electronic crossover. All of the add-on components previously used can be included (Fig. 9-12). The power amps can drive more speaker systems than those shown in this drawing, depending on the power capabilities of these amplifiers. For example, it could be an A, B, C speaker system in which left-right

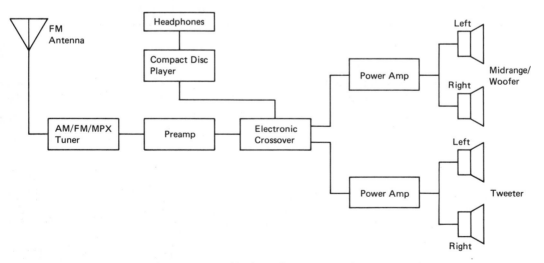

Figure 9-11 CD system with electronic crossover and a pair of power amplifiers.

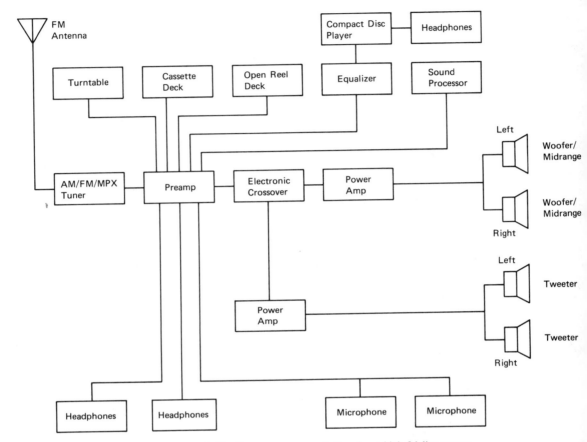

Figure 9-12   Component compact disc player high-fidelity system.

speakers (A) are mounted in front; left-right speakers (B) are positioned in the rear; and a third set of left-right speakers (C) are placed in another room. Using a control on the preamp, various speaker combinations can be selected.

CD Player Triamp System

An unusual arrangement for getting the most out of a compact disc player would be to use a triamp system (Fig. 9-13). This hookup has three separate power amplifiers instead of single or dual integrated units. The power amps do not have the same ratings. The amp for the woofers supplies more audio power output, that for the midrange somewhat less while the power amp for the tweeters has the lowest power rating.

Although a subwoofer is not shown in this illustration, it could be included. It could have its own built-in crossover and driven by the power amp servicing the woofers or its own power amp connected to the electronic crossover. While all the other

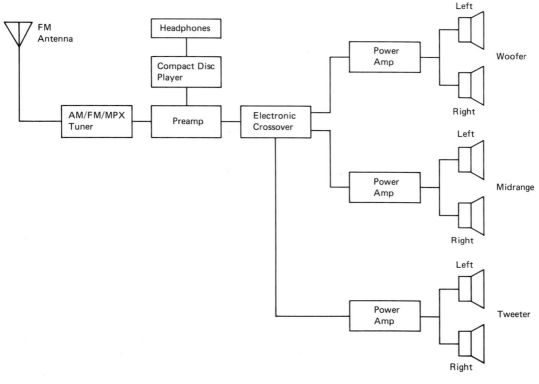

Figure 9-13 Compact disc player triamp system. Other components such as a turntable, tape decks, equalizer and sound processor could be included.

speakers are shown as left-right pairs, a single subwoofer could be used since there is very little stereo separation at subwoofer frequencies.

Wiring the Compact Disc Player Systems

While the block diagrams shown previously supply an overall view of various high-fidelity systems, they do not indicate the actual connections to be made. This information can be supplied by a wiring diagram (Fig. 9-14). Although this does show a fairly elaborate arrangement, it can be simplified by omitting one or more components. For the sake of clarity, some of the connections are indicated by single lines. These represent a pair of wires or cables and before the connections are made are split into wire pairs.

Power Outlets

One of the complications in using a large number of components in a high-fidelity system is that each of these, with the exception of the speakers, requires a connection to

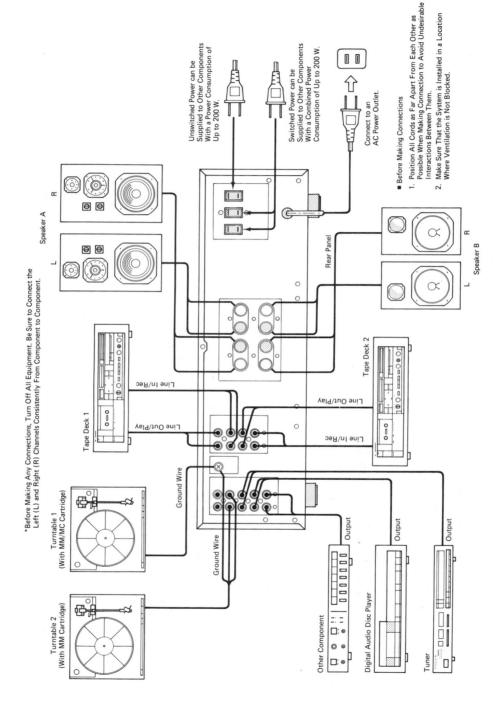

Figure 9-14 Wiring arrangement for a compact-disc player high-fidelity system.

*Before Making Any Connections, Turn Off All Equipment. Be Sure to Connect the Left (L) and Right (R) Channels Consistently From Component to Component.

Speaker A

R

L

Unswitched Power can be Supplied to Other Components With a Power Consumption of Up to 200 W.

Switched Power can be Supplied to Other Components With a Combined Power Consumption of Up to 200 W.

Connect to an AC Power Outlet.

■ Before Making Connections
1. Position All Cords as Far Apart From Each Other as Possible When Making Connection to Avoid Undesirable Interactions Between Them.
2. Make Sure That the System is Installed in a Location Where Ventilation is Not Blocked.

Rear Panel

Speaker B

R

L

Tape Deck 1

Line In/Rec

Line Out/Play

Tape Deck 2

Line Out/Play

Line In/Rec

Ground Wire

Turntable 1
(With MM/MC Cartridge)

Ground Wire

Turntable 2
(With MM Cartridge)

Other Component

Output

Digital Audio Disc Player

Output

Tuner

Output

218

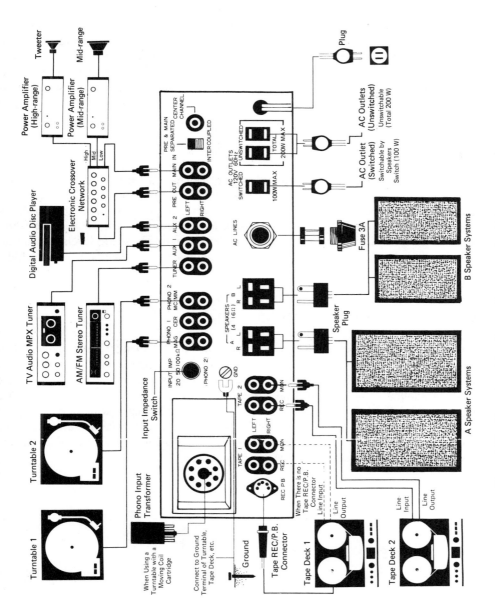

Figure 9-15 Alternative wiring diagram for compact disc high-fidelity system.

a power outlet. However, some of these components are equipped with convenience outlets positioned on the rear panel. These are switched and unswitched types. The unswitched outlets are comparable to regular wall outlets; the component using them must be able to switch power on and off. With switched outlets the power switch on one component can turn a number of components on or off.

The crossover networks of this system are contained within the speaker enclosures but a different arrangement (Fig. 9-15) uses an electronic crossover plus a pair of amplifiers: one for the tweeters, another for the midrange/woofers.

OUTPUT SIGNAL LEVEL

The CD player should be equipped with a pair of output jacks: fixed and variable. The fixed output jacks will provide the correct signal levels to the inputs of the receiver or amplifier. If the output sound level of the compact disc player is noticeably louder or softer than that of the FM tuner, tape deck or analog turntable, use the variable output jacks of the compact disc player to adjust its level control for sound levels that are the same as the other sources. Since music varies significantly in loudness, it is a good idea to play the same type of music when making this adjustment.

PLACEMENT OF THE COMPACT DISC PLAYER

Since the line power required by the player is generally less than 50 watts, the unit does not have the heat disposal problems of other units such as power amplifiers. If the area across the top of the player is adequate and if the unit is a front-loading type, you can position another component such as a turntable on top of it. Since the turntable dust cover is rear hinged, it needs ample vertical space. The CD player will not be harmed if you put the turntable on it. The turntable, however, should have as substantial and vibration-proof support as possible and for this reason should at least be put on the top shelf of your high-fidelity sound system rack.

10

MAINTENANCE AND TESTING

The purchase of a quality compact disc player and a personal library of compact discs can represent a substantial investment. It makes economic sense to observe easy-to-follow precautions in the way the player and discs are used plus the enjoyment to be obtained from optimum performance. When you consider the precision required to make discs and their players which are truly state-of-the-art devices, it is evident that they need owners who are user friendly.

THE INDESTRUCTIBLE COMPACT DISC

During the early days of compact discs extravagant claims were made including the statement that dust and dirt had no effect on the disc's playback capabilities. Some enthusiasts claimed that the surface of the disc could be smeared with peanut butter and that the disc would ignore such treatment. Furthermore, since the disc was coated with a layer of plastic, much was made of the apparent ability of the compact disc to ignore fingerprints. It seemed as though the disc could be handled in any way and remain immune to electrical interference, heat, humidity, cigarette smoke, and mishandling. Comparisons were made to the phono record with the analog disc always a poor second. In short, it was no contest.

A lot of that, of course, was complete nonsense. Compact discs can become scratched. They can become dirty and while they may not require as much tender loving care as phono records, they can suffer from mishandling and misuse. When this occurs, the effects will be evident in playback.

Discs should be kept clean and handled with care. It is true that some compact discs will play well despite fingerprints and some will ignore disc scratches. However, that is an unqualified statement and needs some reservations. Whether a scratch will be significant will depend on whether the scratch is across the disc or runs parallel to the bumps. If it runs across the disc it may damage just a few bits of each frame, which could possibly be handled by error correction circuitry. If it runs parallel to the tracks it could wipe out or damage a large series of sequential bits beyond the capacity of error correction circuitry to handle.

Whether a fingerprint will interfere with playback depends on the chemical composition, and thickness of the fingerprint. In some instances, depending on the compact disc player, it may be impossible to avoid fingerprinting the disc. If the fingerprint is due to natural skin oils and perspiration, it may be difficult to be aware of the possible damage being done. The load/unload mechanism of the player may be such that the only way to handle the compact disc is by its surface.

Are Compact Discs Indestructible?

Compact discs should outlast analog phono records by far, assuming equal amounts of playback times. A phono record has grooves which can collect dust; a compact disc has bumps and although these are covered with plastic, its surface area (the flats) can become dirty. It is essential for the laser beam to be able to reach both bumps and flats in an unobstructed manner.

Basic Precautions

The tracks of a compact disc are micron sized. There may be as many as 15 billion bits (only 1/16,000 of an inch wide) of information recorded on the underside of the disc, the playback surface, and excessive dust can result in intermittent interruptions of sound. While it is advisable to use available commercial cleaners for disc cleaning, some compact disc users remove ordinary dust and fingerprints by breathing on the disc and wiping it gently with a clean cotton handkerchief or gauze. Consider this as a temporary method since the handkerchief may possibly put more dust and lint on the disc than it removes. If you use this technique always wipe the disc along its radius, from the center to the outer edge.

As a preliminary guide to disc protection, keep them out of direct sunlight or heat. While this is unlikely to happen inside a room, it can happen if the discs are kept on a window sill or on the dashboard or rear deck of an auto. If the sunlight or heat is strong enough, the plastic covering on the disc can be affected. Keep the discs out of areas where there is a high concentration of dust by making sure the discs are put back in their protective cases when not in use.

Another cleaning technique is to use a clean, lint-free, soft, dry cloth and ethyl alcohol as a solvent for the oil contained in a fingerprint. Again, move the cloth from the center of the disc to the edge, using straight strokes. Do not clean the disc by following a circular pattern around the its surface. Pay particular attention to the undersurface of the disc, for that is the playback area.

Do not use solvents whose chemical composition is unknown and never experiment with such solvents unless you are willing to sacrifice the disc. Stay away from any cleaning liquid that contains abrasives.

Commercial Cleaning Methods

A common technique for cleaning an analog phono record is to blow across it. This method, when used for compact discs, will be equally useless. There are a number of commercial cleaning systems which are advisable for maintaining the disc in pristine condition. The automatic compact disc radial cleaning system (Fig. 10-1) occupies barely more horizontal space than a compact disc. The system rotates the disc at the touch of a button while cleaning it with a chamois-topped pad.

The operation of a compact disc player's error correction circuitry which interpolates (or fills in) the missing data caused by laser mistracking is kept at a minimum by providing a clean disc surface. Two C cells operate the unit. The soft, dry chamois which performs the cleaning operation rests atop a ring that rotates gently against the turning disc.

Figure 10-1 Automatic compact disc cleaning system. (Courtesy Signet.)

The Label Problem

Some of the inks used for printing labels on compact discs are alcohol based. When they come in contact with alcohol-based cleaning fluids they will either dissolve or smear.

Some cleaning fluids not only spoil the label but also do an inadequate job of cleaning, leaving a residue on the surface. Not only domestic do-it-yourself cleaners but some commercial cleaners as well are guilty of this. Avoid using soap or detergents for they can leave an invisible film on the disc's surface.

Although information is stored on a compact disc beneath a plastic-coated surface, contaminants can cause the laser to miss some of the information on the tracks. The result can be audio dropouts or distortion, despite the sophisticated error correction circuitry in many of today's compact disc players. The easiest way to detect surface residue is by holding the disc up to the light to examine the surface scanned by the laser beam.

Likewise, the eye and the ear can detect scratches on the surface that are caused by a cleaning mechanism. A properly made cleaning mechanism can do an excellent job, but some brands can lack even pressure with particle abrasion if the pad is not cleaned properly.

Manufacturers of compact discs recommend cleaning discs in a straight line from the center of the disc to the edge, that is, at 90 degrees to the circular pattern. These radial strokes move contaminants crosswise to the direction of recorded material, not along the same path or in a parallel direction. Radial strokes thus minimize the blocking or scratching of the micron-sized, sequentially coded bumps and flats that contain the encoded information. One way of checking a disc for cleanliness is to compare it with one that is brand new and has just been removed from its container (Fig. 10-2).

Commercial cleaning systems are often wet types that depend on the use of a solvent. There is also a dry system designed to keep compact discs in clean playing condition while preventing accidental damage to the surfaces. The disc to be cleaned is placed, label side down, on the system turntable. A hinged transparent dust cover is then closed and a slide lever on top is moved back and forth (Fig. 10-3). Each movement pushes the disc around 30 degrees. The motion is repeated until the disc makes a complete revolution. As it revolves it makes gentle contact with a soft, specially constructed pad. A fine-bristle brush is used to remove dust and dirt from the pad which should be replaced when it becomes soiled. Although the system is used dry, a special cleaning fluid and cleaning paper are included for careful hand treatment of especially obstinate dirt and spots.

A third cleaning method features premoistened cleaning pads (Fig. 10-4). This compact disc cleaner is the same size as the jewel box housing the compact disc. To use, begin by simply putting the compact disc into the holder on one side of the unit. Remove one of the premoistened cleaning pads on the other side, wipe the disc, and then put the used pad back in its original place. A soft foam burnisher is also included to dry off any residual cleaning solution. Each cleaning pad contains a special liquid

Figure 10-2 Dirty disc (above) compared to one that is brand new (below). (Courtesy Discwasher, Div. International Jensen Inc.)

cleaner. The pad is attached to a plastic holder that lets the user clean to the edge of the disc while holding it securely in place.

DISC STORAGE

When a compact disc is not being used, store it in its original plastic box. This will not only help keep the disc clean but will protect it against accidental damage.

Figure 10-3 Compact disc dry cleaning method. (Courtesy Audio-Technica U.S. Inc.)

Figure 10-4 Disc cleaner uses premoistened pads. (Courtesy Geneva Group of Companies, Nortronics.)

Figure 10-5(a)　Compact disc storage system holds four CDs and uses same space as phono record albums. (Courtesy Geneva Group of Companies, Nortronics.)

Just as there are a number of different ways of cleaning compact discs, so too are there various ways of storing them. One method is the use of paper sleeves in which you can store or carry the discs. Paper gives the impression that it does not have strength but we now have paper that cannot be torn manually. These paper sleeves are made of a spunbound olefin that does not yield readily to tearing or moisture. It also has a clear front panel so you can easily see the compact disc label. These sleeves are not intended to replace the jewel boxes in which compact discs are sold and are simply used to supply protection when the jewel box is not immediately available.

Another idea in compact disc storage consists of a holder which is the same size as a record album. The advantage is that many users of compact discs are also phono record buffs. The holder made of clear plastic (Fig. 10-5a) will hold and display four compact disc jewel boxes, the standard case in which compact discs are purchased. The advantage is that it does not force the compact disc purchaser to find a storage unit for this new medium. These storage albums are designed with a handle, making them easy to carry. Each jewel box opens completely in the storage unit so there is no need to remove it to play the CD.

Still another storage unit is designed to hold ten compact discs in their jewel boxes (also called library cases) for quick selection. The storage system is equipped with a touch release mechanism to hold the compact disc in position so it cannot slide out accidently but at the same time can be removed at the touch of a finger.

CAUSES OF TROUBLE

There are five possible causes of trouble that can involve compact disc systems. These are (1) the compact disc, (2) the compact disc player, (3) the associated high-fidelity system, (4) the external power supply consisting either of batteries or power supplied by the AC line, and (5) the user of the compact disc player. Compact disc player systems are user friendly and considering the state-of-the-art electronic sophistication of both the compact disc and its player are remarkably easy to use. They are easier to set up and operate than an analog phono record and turntable, particularly since no compact disc player adjustments are required.

Is It the Disc or Player That Is Defective?

Often enough a customer will bring a compact disc player into a service facility with the complaint that the player does not track properly. The audio will have constant dropouts. Although this could be due to a bad laser beam optic assembly or misalignment, the trouble can also be a defective disc.

The obvious solution is to play a disc known to be in good working order. Every user of a compact disc system should set aside one disc for this purpose and regard it as a test disc. This method can be used to determine if it is a disc or its player that is at fault. However, as a final check, examine the disc that is troublesome. Hold the disc up to the light and check for pinholes and check the surface. The light from the reflective surface should be uniform.

Aural Test of a Compact Disc

It may seem strange to say, but it is better for a compact disc to have a definite defect. In some instances it may be difficult to know if a disc is defective. The playback may sound good but you may have a suspicion that it is not quite as good as it should be.

An aural test of a compact disc that may have a defect is purely subjective. There are several methods of checking but none are definitive. You can buy a replacement disc and check one against the other, but you may end up with a pair of discs that are identical. You can examine the disc carefully to see if you can find any physical defects. You can assume the disc is defective and return it to the store where you purchased it.

Phase Test

A phase test can be made of the CD player using test tones of 2 kHz and 20 kHz. The two signals should have simultaneous zero-axis crossing in the same direction. (Fig. 10-5b) This would indicate an ideal phase response. Such phase accuracy results in superior stereo imaging.

The test is done by using a twin test tone signal with 2 kHz in the left channel and 20 kHz in the right. Their zero-crossings at center show almost perfect coincidence.

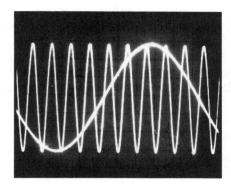

Figure 10-5(b) Phase response using 2 kHz and 20 kHz test frequencies. (Courtesy Analog & Digital Systems, Inc.)

Proper Care of Compact Discs

The proper care of a compact disc not only involves cleanliness but handling as well. Both are related since improper handling can result in a dirty disc.

Improper disc handling can shorten its life. Hold the disc so that you do not leave fingerprints on it (Fig. 10-6). Open the jewel box by its edges. Remove the disc by

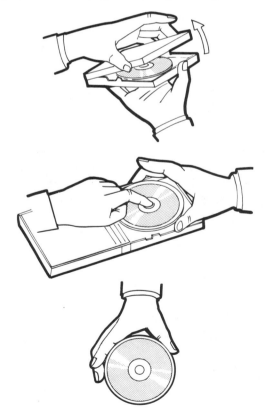

Figure 10-6 Proper method of removing compact disc from its jewel box.

holding its edge, supporting it with a finger through the center hole. That center hole is sufficiently large to enable you to get a good grip on the disc. After you remove the disc you can hold it by gripping it around its circumference.

Imperfections on the surface of a disc can best be detected by ear. Often when an audio dropout occurs, either on a compact disc but particularly on conventional vinyl discs, the listener may not always hear it because of the acoustic properties of the listening room. If you want to make sure, listen to the compact disc through headphones. The intermittent dropout is unmistakable and often a listener will think there is something wrong with the system or wiring when the only problem can be due to the disc.

COMPACT DISC PLAYER PROBLEMS

Cleanliness is as important to the compact disc player as it is to discs if only for the reason that dust and dirt can be transferred from the player to the disc. Clean off dirt on the surfaces with a clean, soft, dry cloth. Never use thinners, benzene or alcohol since these will damage the finish.

Radio-Frequency Interference

The compact disc player can cause interference to television reception, to radio receiver reception and to the proper operation of an in-home computer. Compact disc players generate and use radio-frequency energy and if not installed and used properly in strict accordance with the manufacturer's instructions, it can cause radio-frequency interference (RFI).

A compact disc player must be type tested and found to comply with the limits for a Class B computing device in accordance with the specifications in Subpart J of Part 15 of FCC Rules which are designed to provide reasonable protection against such interference when the compact disc player is installed in any residence. However, there is no guarantee that interference will not occur in a particular installation. If, however, the compact disc player does cause interference to radio or television reception, or if it does cause erratic operation of a computer, there are certain steps to follow which may possibly cure the problem.

The first step to take is to make sure that it is indeed the compact disc player that is the source of the interference. Turn on the radio receiver, television set or the computer and get the device to operate but with the compact disc player turned off. Then, turn the player on and note if interference manifests itself. The result can be horizontal wavy lines across the television or computer screen, noise in a radio receiver, or incorrect results out of the computer.

Televison Interference

Television interference can be caused in two ways: by feedback through the AC power line and by broadcast interference, in which the compact disc player radiates a signal. To check on interference via the power line, turn on both the TV set and the CD player. As a first step try reversing the TV set's power line plug. Sometimes this simple expedient will produce a cure. If this does not work, try connecting the TV set to a different outlet. If the power line cord of the set is not long enough, use a 25-foot or a 50-foot extension cord. Keep trying different outlets until you find one whose use will eliminate the interference. If this does remove the RFI and you want to continue using the same outlet, you can do so by installing a line noise filter.

It is possible that changing TV set outlets will not eliminate the interference but will only reduce it slightly. In that case the interference stems from the power line and also by pickup of the TV antenna, its transmission line (the download), or both.

The download of the TV antenna will be either 300-ohm transmission line or 75-ohm coaxial cable. If it is coaxial cable you can eliminate it immediately as a possible interference signal pickup source since all such line is shielded with metallic braid which is automatically grounded when connected to the TV set's antenna signal input terminals. If the download is 300-ohm transmission line, also known as two-wire line or twin lead, it is possible that this line is unshielded. If so, replace it with shielded 300-ohm line.

You can also substitute 75-ohm coaxial cable for the 300-ohm twin lead but this will mean installing an impedance matching transformer at the antenna and also at the antenna input terminals on the TV set. Installing shielded twin lead is easier.

It is also possible that the TV antenna is picking up the interfering signal. If the antenna is equipped with a rotator, try turning the antenna to see if changing its orientation will eliminate the interference. If your antenna does not have a rotator, you can experiment with a rabbit-ear indoor type. Connect it in place of your regular lead in, and then rotate the antenna for a minimum interference pickup point. That is the approximate direction in which your antenna should be turned.

If a radio receiver is picking up an interfering signal, run a test with the compact disc player and the receiver both on. Follow the same method for using a different outlet that was described for a TV set. If the interference is on AM, adjust the loopstick on the back of the radio receiver for minimum RFI pickup. If on FM and the receiver uses unshielded twin lead, follow the same procedure as you would for a TV set.

Computer Interference

If RFI is interfering with your computer, connect the computer to a different outlet, or use a line noise filter, or locate the computer in a different room as far from the compact disc player as possible. For further information you might find the following booklet prepared by the Federal Communications Commission helpful. It is entitled, "How to

Identify and Resolve Radio-TV Interference Problems," and is available from the U.S. Government Printing Office, Washington, DC 20403. Stock No. 004-000-00354-4.

TESTING CD PLAYERS

A CD player can be tested subjectively or objectively. A subjective test is a listening test with the ears of the auditor as the means of evaluation. An objective test is one made with instruments.

Subjective tests can be made in three ways. The first is by listening to the sound output of a player, possibly by using a disc that has been played repeatedly and so is very familiar. There is also the possibility of using a test disc. Still another subjective test can be an A/B type using a pair of CD players with one of these as a known standard in operating order.

Tests of this kind can be useful for determining faults that are fairly obvious. How useful they are depends on the age, sex, the musical background and frequency response of the listener's ears. While a compact disc can have a response to 20 kHz and a frequency response deviation of ± 0.5 dB, few if any of us have a hearing range extending that far, and it is also doubtful that the human ear and brain can be conscious of a frequency deviation of only 0.5 dB.

CD Test Records

There are two types of CD test discs. The first, intended for subjective evaluation tests, supplies musical tones and indicates their frequencies. The test record may also have short musical passages as a check on dynamic range, supplying some that are very quiet followed by peak audio signals, possibly those of percussion instruments.

The other type of test disc is for use with various test instruments such as a distortion analyzer, harmonic analyzer, a signal level meter and an oscilloscope. Some of these may be separate units or may be integrated.

There are a number of commercial test discs available. These include the Sony YEDS-2 and YEDS-7, Philips 410/055-2 and 410/056-2, and Denon DNC39-7147 and DN-3000F. The purpose of a test disc is to simulate faults to challenge the response of circuitry in compact disc players, specifically the laser optical tracking and error correction systems. The disc flaws do not have the same levels of severity and when using a test disc it is necessary to determine just how the flaws can be rated.

A test disc can also include left- and right-channel signals having a range from 20 Hz to 20 kHz. Instead of having a complete audio sweep, some test discs supply ten spot audio frequencies. A test disc could also have spot frequency signals at 1 kHz, 5 kHz and 16 kHz as a test of the ability of the de-emphasis network in the compact disc player to respond. A disc could also have specific frequencies not only for checking left- and right-channel sound separation but channel balance as well. Thus, a test disc not only tests the response of error and tracking circuits, but it can also be used as a check on a manufacturer's specifications and on circuit performance. Discs are also used to check on the audio performance of a player, including distortion measurements. A disc may contain a 0 dB reference tone for the measurement of signal-to-noise ratio because 0 dB represents the peak signal level that is recorded on compact discs.

Test discs have deliberately introduced faults that could be contained in a compact disc not properly cared for as a means of determining how well the compact disc player can overcome them. These test discs contain wedges consisting of a series of black dots which are not transparent. The dots are not the same size and gradually increase in diameter. The dots are meant to represent specks of dust of different sizes and also to simulate scratches. Since compact discs are also subject to fingerprints, test discs may contain a partially opaque smudge where fingerprints are usually most prevalent, near the edge of the disc. The black dots vary in width from 400 to 900 microns (micrometers or millionths of a meter) and are used to represent a scratch, while those that measure from 300 to 800 microns simulate a scratch or possibly a fingerprint.

One advantage of a test disc is that it can be used to simplify the A/B testing of compact disc players. Assuming a compact disc is in perfect condition, even a low-end player can produce good results. However, top quality players are much more able to take defects on discs in stride. In time and with continued use, compact discs can suffer the onslaught of dust, dirt, fingerprints and scratches. A low-end player will evidence the results of these defects; a top quality player will handle these discs as though they were taken out of the jewel box for the first time.

Test Disc Standards

At the time of this writing there are no standard test discs. Because of this, a test of a compact disc player has no meaning unless the test disc that was used is specified with the characteristics of that disc indicated. A standard test disc is obviously needed. A Compact Disc Subcommittee has been established to define the requirements for a test record to evaluate the performance of compact disc players. This effort to set up a standard method of measurement will result in a recommended procedure for measuring and reporting the performance of compact disc players. After a standard test disc has been made available, it would be helpful to consumers if manufacturers would put a label on the player to indicate it has successfully passed all tests using the standard.

The fact that a compact disc player will not work, will operate poorly or intermittently, or will exhibit mechanical or electronic difficulties, does not necessarily mean there is anything wrong with the player. There are a number of easy checks that will eliminate the time and expense of servicing.

Disc Does Not Rotate

It is entirely possible for one outlet to lose power since power lines in the home are subdivided into branches, each with its own fuse. Plug a lamp into the outlet being used by the compact disc player to determine if the outlet is live.

Make sure the power switch is turned on. Some users think that inserting the disc into the player turns power on automatically. Players generally have a glow lamp to indicate that power is being received.

If the player is being installed for the first time, check to make sure it is meeting its power input requirements. Some players have a switch to permit the unit to be operated by different line voltages. Check the switch to make sure it is set to its correct position for the line voltage in your area. For the U.S. and Canada that voltage should be 120V, 60 Hz. For all of Europe except the United Kingdom it is 220V, 50 Hz. For the United Kingdom and Australia it is 240V, 50 Hz. Some compact disc players are multipower switchable and can accommodate 110V/120V/220V/240V, 50 Hz/60 Hz. Always check the voltage selector before connecting the compact disc player and turning it on. On some compact disc players the variable input voltage control is adjustable with a screwdriver (Fig. 10-7). If you do not expect to use the compact disc player for a long time, disconnect its power cord from the outlet.

Voltage
Selector

Figure 10-7   Turn line-voltage selector to correct setting before plugging CD player into power outlet.

Make sure the disc drawer is operative. Even if power is being supplied to the player, it will not function until the disc drawer works correctly. Also check to make sure the disc has been properly inserted. If the disc is inserted upside down the player will not operate. Check to make sure the disc has been loaded with its label side up.

If the unit is a battery operated portable, slide open the battery compartment cover and replace the batteries. The player will be using two or more batteries. Do not try to economize by using just one new battery, even if this does solve the nonoperating condition. Be sure to put in all new batteries.

A compact disc player will not function unless a compact disc has been inserted and is in position. You may think you have left a compact disc in its drawer but in case of nonoperation, check to make sure. Sometimes, just as in the case of video cassette recorders, the formation of moisture inside the compact disc player will keep it from playing. Do not try to heat the player since this will only damage the unit. Keep it at room temperature for at least a half hour and then try again.

With some players there will be a nonoperative condition if the pause button has been depressed twice. Depress the pause button once again to see if this will restore operation.

Make sure the prongs of the plug on the power line cord are completely inserted into the outlet. Sometimes these prongs do not make good contact so spread them until they do. Some plugs are polarized so make sure they are inserted correctly into the outlet. Hold the molded part of the cord when plugging the cord into the AC outlet and when removing it. Power supply cords should be routed so they are not likely to be walked on or pinched by items placed on or against them. An indication that the compact disc player is not receiving line power is that while the power switch is turned on, none of the front panel indicators light.

Disc Is In Its Tray, But There Is No Sound

If the front panel indicators are lighted, then you know the compact disc player is receiving line power. Check to make sure the disc is label side up. Connect a pair of headphones. If you hear sound, the fault is not in the player but may be in the connecting cables to the following high-fidelity system or in the high-fidelity system itself. Try another sound source input to that system, preferably a phono record. If there is no sound, the fault is in the system. If there is sound, the problem lies in the connecting cables between the player and the system. Also make sure the output level control is not set to its maximum counterclockwise position. Rotate the control to determine if this produces sound output.

Make sure the sound source control on the high-fidelity system is set for compact disc playback. Check the volume control on the preamplifier or power amplifier of the high-fidelity system to make sure it is not in its completely counterclockwise setting.

Try transferring the connecting leads between the compact disc player and the aux or CD terminals on the high-fidelity system to a different sound source input such as phono. If this produces sound output, then the fault is at the aux terminals or the wiring from those terminals to amplifier circuitry inside the amplifier.

Disc Drawer Problems

If your fingers or a foreign object get caught in the disc drawer, press the open/close control to reopen the door. Do not try to force the drawer to open or to close and do not use any tools, such as a screwdriver, in an attempt to open or close the drawer.

The drawer is not a storage area and is designed for compact discs only. Do not try to put more than one disc into the drawer. When you have finished playing a disc, do not leave it in the drawer. Remove it and put it back in its jewel box or in any other storage device designed specifically for holding compact discs. You should be able to put the disc in the drawer easily and smoothly. If you cannot do this, examine the drawer to make sure someone has not inadvertently put something else in it.

When you are not using the compact disc player, keep the disc drawer closed. This will prevent dust from settling in the drawer; it will be transferred to the disc when it is inserted. Be sure to put the disc in the drawer with its label side up and hold the disc by its edge to keep the playing surface clean (Fig. 10-8).

Sound Is Heard But Is Intermittent

While the fault could be in the compact disc player or the following high-fidelity system, the most likely cause is a dirty or scratched disc. There is also a slim

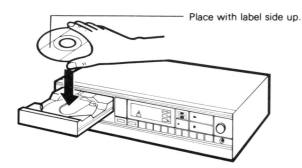

Place with label side up.

Figure 10-8 Correct method of inserting disc into drawer of player. (Courtesy RCA.)

possibility the disc is warped. Try a different disc, preferably one that has no prior history of playback problems.

Intermittent sound can also be due to a loose connection in the cable between the compact disc player and the high-fidelity system. With the compact disc player operating, move the connecting cable to see if it affects the sound. The cable should make positive contact with the input to the sound system.

Intermittent sound can also be due to a combination of factors involving both the disc and the compact disc player. A good quality player will probably be more tolerant of disc faults and will be able to compensate for them much more efficiently. The problem of intermittent sound is often much more prevalent with low-end compact disc players.

Remote Control Unit Does Not Work

The most common cause of failure is due to the batteries. Check to determine if the compact disc player works manually by direct control. The batteries are generally AA types. Be sure to insert them using the correct polarity. The flat bottom of the battery is the negative terminal; the metal tip in the center of the top area is the positive terminal. As in the case of portable compact disc players, replace both batteries. Batteries seldom wear out at the same time. If you put in a new battery while keeping one that is just partially discharged, the new battery will use much of its energy trying to charge the other. The battery compartment is generally marked so you can use this as a guide for the correct installation of the batteries. If the batteries are not put in properly, the remote control unit will not work. As the batteries become weaker, the operating range of the remote control becomes shorter. Do not use the remote control near fluorescent lamps since this could shorten the operating range of the remote control unit.

Unit Does Not Work When Function Buttons Are Pressed

This can happen if you depress a function button at the time the display is flashing on and off. Wait until the display turns on and remains on and then try again. The unit will not go into its play mode if more than one function control is depressed at the same time.

Unusually Long Search Time

This can be caused by some fault in the disc such as dirt or a scratch. A disc may appear clean but dirt that is microscopic and invisible to the naked eye can result in this problem. Try using a disc known to be in good working order and try cleaning the problem disc. A long search time without results can also be due to putting the disc into the disc drawer with the wrong side up. Check to make sure the disc has been inserted with its label side visible.

Brand New CD Player Does Not Work

Compact disc players are transported with shipping screws fastened into the unit to protect the optical scanning mechanism from any movement. These screws must be removed for the compact disc player to work (Fig. 10-9). Do not throw the screws away because you will need to use them if you must ship the compact disc player, possibly for servicing.

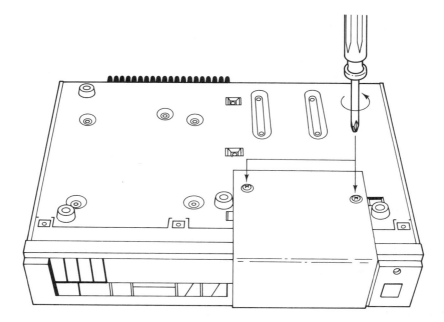

Figure 10-9 CD player will not work until shipping screws are removed. (Courtesy Marantz Company, Inc.)

PRECAUTIONS TO FOLLOW WITH COMPACT DISC PLAYERS

Because the compact disc player is so easy to use, it may create the false impression that it is immune to any adverse operating condition. The player is an extremely sophisticated instrument and both the discs and the player depend on the utmost precision. The usefulness of both can be extended by observing certain precautions.

Not all discs are made the same way and some of them have the one attractive feature of a low price in comparison with other discs. A qualifying label on the disc is a helpful guide (Fig. 10-10). There are also warning labels either on the compact disc player or in the accompanying instructional literature. One of these is a lightning bolt enclosed in a triangle. The purpose of this symbol is to alert the user to the presence of uninsulated dangerous voltages inside the player. Another symbol is an exclamation point, also enclosed inside a triangle. This is intended to alert the user to the presence of important operating and maintenance or servicing instructions in the literature accompanying the player (Fig. 10-11).

Figure 10-10 Compact disc player manufacturers suggest that only discs carrying this label be used in their components.

Figure 10-11 Compact disc player warning labels. The lightning flash means the presence of dangerous voltage. The exclamation mark refers to operating and maintenance information.

Disc Speed

While the compact disc player is designed to withstand shock and vibration, the extent to which it can do so depends on the design of the optical tracking system, the rigidity of its supporting elements, and its basic design. If the player is subjected to a sudden shock or jolt during playback, the speed of rotation may suddenly change or some noise may be produced. This is not a malfunction. If possible, stop the cause of vibration. While some testers of compact disc players have written about striking the units to see how they can tolerate such action, remember this is for evaluation purposes. It is not recommended as an operating condition. A compact disc player is much more tolerant of shock and vibration than an analog turntable, but unnecessary vibration is not recommended in either case.

If other audio components or their connecting cables are installed near the compact disc player, you may hear some hum. Try moving the connecting cables that join the player to the input of the following audio amplifier. It may also be necessary to move the player away from the high-fidelity system. If the connecting cables are not long enough, you can get an adapter plus an additional length of cable. Make sure to remove the compact disc from the drawer before moving the compact disc player.

The wide dynamic range of a compact disc generally comes as a surprise to those using it for the first time. Until you become accustomed to this feature, keep the volume control of the following amplifier turned down. An unexpected sound peak plus the high dynamic range can result in a sound volume capable of damaging the voice coil of a speaker. Even if you have acquired some experience with the player, it is always advisable when playing a new disc for the first time to play it through with reduced volume to become acquainted with its sonic characteristics.

If you are using a portable CD player and bring it in from a cold outdoor temperature to a warm inside temperature, you may get the condensation of a fine film of water on the lens and prism of the optical system. Give the player about 30 minutes of down time to let evaporation work for you.

Compact disc players use a power supply transformer which develops a moderate amount of heat. For this reason the units are equipped with ventilation holes or louvres. Do not install the player on top of units which become hot (such as audio power amplifiers) and do not surround the player with anything that will restrict the free flow of air.

Often enough, problems with compact disc players are due to external circumstances and can be attributed to the disc or the associated audio amplifier or other components of the high-fidelity system. Opening of the player's cabinet should only be done as a last resort and only by someone qualified as an electronics service technician. The optical pickup system, quite possibly the most important part of the compact disc player, is located inside the disc tray opening. For that reason you should not keep the door open for long periods of time.

A laser beam can emit hazardous radiation and can cause eye damage if not handled properly. This can happen if the player is removed from its case and should be done only by a trained technician.

LASER LENS CLEANERS

If a lens in the CD player becomes clouded by such airborne contaminants as dust, smoke, or moisture it may become prone to distortion, mistracking or the unnecessary engagement of error-correction circuitry.

If you are a service technician and want to clean the lens, do so only with lens tissues made for that purpose. These are obtainable in camera stores and are used for cleaning camera lenses. A special brush is also made for this purpose. Do not use an ordinary brush since it may scratch the lens surface. There is also an air blower brush designed for camera lenses but the usual lens tissue or brush is less expensive.

Mechanical Cleaner

It is possible to prevent these problems by using an accessory that resembles a compact disc in every way except that a brush protrudes from the inner edge of its bottom side (Fig. 10-12). The height of the brush is calculated for optimum effect without danger of misaligning or otherwise harming the lens of any CD player. Its bristles are man-made and contain a special fiber compound to ensure precision cleaning without damage to the delicate laser lens.

To use the laser lens cleaner put it in the drawer or well of any CD player and then activate the player's start control. Information encoded beneath the cleaner's disc surface commands the unit to stop automatically when the cleaning cycle is completed. The cleaner is supplied with a small brush for removing lint and other accumulations from its bristles.

Figure 10-12   CD laser lens cleaner. (Courtesy AudioSource.)

Dimmer Outlet

Occasionally, someone will plug the compact disc player into a wall outlet controlled by a dimmer switch. Often, both the dimmer and the player resent the connection, and one or the other fails to work. The solution is simple. Separate the antagonists and let each have its own, independent outlet.

Maintenance of Compact Disc Player

Normal maintenance of the compact disc player consists only of keeping the cabinet clean and dust free. You can keep the player cabinet clean by dusting it with a soft cloth or brush. Do not use furniture polish or any other kind of cleaner.

Disc Speed Changes

During playback, if the compact disc player is subjected to a sudden shock or jolt, the speed of rotation may change or some noise may be produced. This is not a malfunction.

Hum

If other audio components or their connecting cords are positioned near the player, you may hear a hum. In that case try moving the wiring, the CD player or the other components. Try moving the connecting cords first. If this helps, also try moving the component to which the cord is connected.

Disc Warpage

Compact discs are much less subject to warpage than analog phono records. However, this does not mean they are completely immune. Avoid storing discs in high-temperature, high-humidity locations. The discs may warp and become impossible to play. Also, discs with moisture on them may be unplayable. Wipe any moisture off with a soft, lint-free, dry cloth, and be sure discs are fully dry before using.

Disc Stabilizer

Disc warpage and vibration means the laser beam may be unable to accurately focus on every track on the compact disc. When this happens, the player's internal computer tries to fill the gap based on the preceding data. Depending on how serious the mistracking is the result can be digital harshness.

One curative method is to use a disc stabilizer (Fig. 10-13). This unit is made in black finished brass.

Figure 10-13　Disc stabilizer. (Courtesy Monster Cable.)

MODIFICATION PROCEDURES

From time to time manufacturers will issue modification procedures. Such changes are suggested so as to enhance some feature or function of a specific model of CD player. These changes are not intended for consumers but for qualified technicians. Figure 10-14 is a modification for enhancing tracking stability. Such changes are made when the compact disc player is brought in for servicing.

ORDERING REPLACEMENT PARTS

Replacement parts needed by service technicians can be ordered from the manufacturer's repair depots but the fastest response is obtained if the parts are clearly and specifically identified. This information can be obtained from the manufacturer's servicing manuals or are supplied by companies furnishing detailed servicing data along with schematics of the player. Parts are identified by a reference number, a part code,

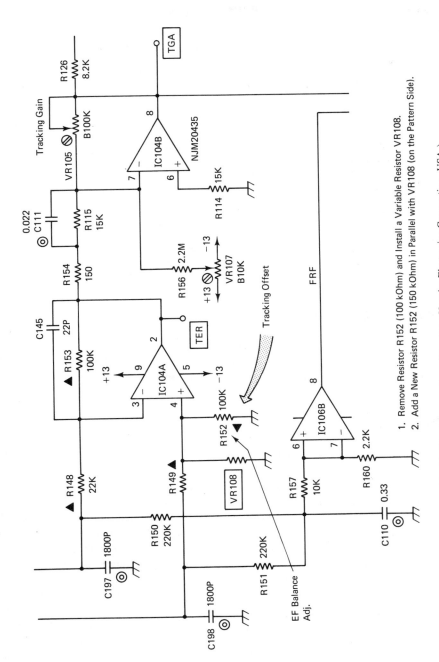

Figure 10-14 Modification procedure. (Courtesy Yamaha Electronics Corporation, USA.)

1. Remove Resistor R152 (100 kOhm) and Install a Variable Resistor VR108.
2. Add a New Resistor R152 (150 kOhm) in Parallel with VR108 (on the Pattern Side).

followed by a description (Fig. 10-15). In addition, supply information as to the CD player model number.

Ref. No.	Part Code	Description
U101	QQ020109AS	IC, CX20109
U102	QQ020108AS	IC, CX20108
U301	QQ023035AS	IC, CX23035
U302	QQ006116A&	IC, HM6116LP-4
U303	QQM05218BE	IC, M5218P
U304	QQM05221BE	IC, M5221P
U401	QQ000402KB	IC, HMCS402C
U402	QQ0004044B	IC, HMCS404C
U403	QQM05218BE	IC, M5218P
U501	QQ020152AS	IC, CX20152
U502	QQ004053B&	IC, 4053
U503	QQM05221BE	IC, M5221P
U504	QQM05221BE	IC, M5221P
U505	QQM04556AJ	IC, NJM4556D
X301	XAZ1E3001S	Xtal Osc., 8.4672 MHz
X401	CX4000001%	Ceramic Osc.
X501	XAZ3A4001S	Xtal, 35 MHz

Figure 10-15 Parts list for ordering replacements. (Courtesy Kyocera International Inc.)

TEST EQUIPMENT REQUIRED

The test equipment required for servicing compact disc players will include a DC voltmeter, an oscilloscope, and a frequency counter. One or more test discs will be needed for checking frequency response, dropouts and for adjusting the optical system.

FAILURE OF PARTS

Given enough time all parts may fail and there are no exceptions. There are different kinds of failure. A part may become completely defective, or it may change its electrical characteristics so that operation becomes intermittent. All parts are considered as having a figure of merit, a determination based on a statistical analysis of a previous history of failure. This type of analysis enables manufacturers to anticipate player operating problems and is also an aid in controlling parts inventory. The figure of merit is sometimes referred to as the mean time between failures and is abbreviated as MTBF. Transformers have the highest failure rate, followed by quartz crystals, transistors, capacitors, ICs and variable resistors.

Oddly enough, failures of compact disc players do not supply a straight line graph. Most failures occur when the item is either brand new or when it has been used for a long time. Brand new failures are caused by the use of parts which have barely passed electrical inspection tests in the factory. It does not take much of a change in their electrical characteristics to result in component disc player failure or poor operation. Old age failure is due to the fact that inevitably some parts will wear out, becoming nonfunctional due to temperature, humidity, vibration and improper handling.

OPERATIONAL
ANALYSIS

The compact disc and its associated compact disc player are not improvements on the transcription turntable and its associated analog phono record. Instead, they represent a complete breakaway utilizing an astonishing technology. The disc and its player are state of the art and are highly sophisticated components, not only in the way they are manufactured but also in the way they have managed to combine a mechanical structure and an optical structure with highly advanced electronic circuitry.

The compact disc and its player can be described in several ways. All of the preceding chapters supply an overall view that is essential to a more detailed analysis. In this chapter and in the one immediately following, there is a review of material presented earlier but in a different manner. With a general understanding as a background, we can now move ahead to a more in-depth understanding.

THE COMPACT DISC

On the compact disc signal information is recorded on the track in digital form. During its manufacture a cutting laser beam produces a series of pits which become a corresponding series of bumps on the reverse side which is ultimately scanned and read by a laser beam. These bumps are sometimes referred to as pits (Fig. 11-1), while those portions of the disc not affected by the laser cutting beam are called flats or land.

In drawing (a) the letter T indicates a transparent substrate, R is a reflecting layer, Pr a protective layer, and P the pits that are part of the track. In drawing (b) the pulses are plotted as a function of time. Although these pulses are shown as having smooth, sharply defined vertical lines, in reality they have rounded tops and sloping sides. The digital signal derived from this waveform is indicated as a series of channel bits, Ch.

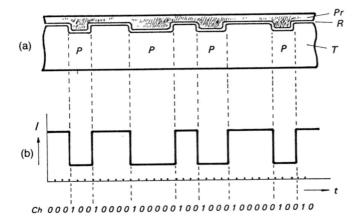

(a)

(b)

Ch 0001001000010000010010001000010010

Figure 11-1 Cross-section through a compact disc in the direction of the spiral track (a); the signal read by the optical pickup plotted as a function of time, *t*. (b).

The land area is that part of the disc that was not affected by the laser cutting beam. Note also in drawing (b) that neither a land nor a pit produce digit 1. The only time we have digit 1 is when we have a transition from a land to a pit. It is the vertical sides of the pulses that represent this transition. The left side of the pulse is the rising side; the right side of the pulse is the falling side. It is the relatively sharp pulse increase or decrease, the sharp change from land to pit or pit to land that gives us binary digit 1. All the areas of the bumps and the lands produce a binary 0 for they do not represent any change (Fig. 11-2)

Dimensional Details

The outside diameter of the **disc** is 120 mm as in item (a) in Figure 11-3. The clamping area ranges from a maximum of 33 mm (b) to a minimum of 26 mm (c). The center hole (d) measures 15 mm. The lead in area (e) and (f) is from 46 mm to 50 mm. The program area (g) is 33 mm and the maximum utilizable area indicated by (h) is 117 mm.

The details supplied in Figure 11-3 are for a disc prior to encoding. It is the flat area of the disc that is changed when signals are recorded on the disc (Fig. 11-4). What

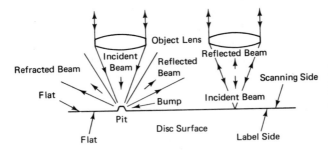

Figure 11-2 The transition from the refracted beam to the reflected beam produces binary digit 1. Refracted light from the bump or reflection from the flat results in binary 0. (Courtesy Kyocera International, Inc.)

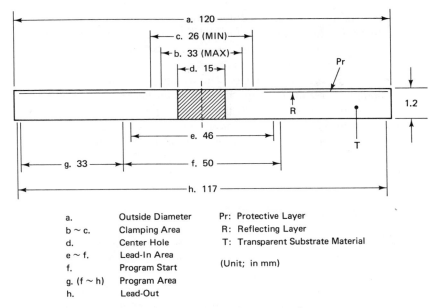

a.	Outside Diameter
b ~ c.	Clamping Area
d.	Center Hole
e ~ f.	Lead-In Area
f.	Program Start
g. (f ~ h)	Program Area
h.	Lead-Out

Pr: Protective Layer
R: Reflecting Layer
T: Transparent Substrate Material

(Unit; in mm)

Figure 11-3 Dimensions of a compact disc.

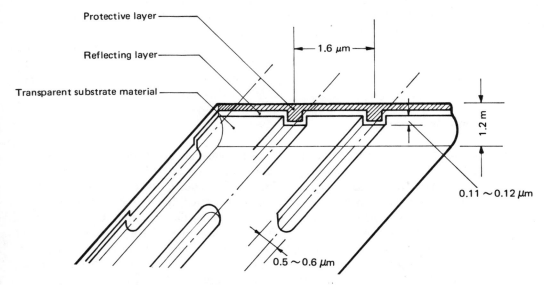

Figure 11-4 Encoding dimensions.

is unique in this process is the tremendous amount of data that is recorded; that is, the density of the information on the compact disc is very high, and this is based on the practically microscopic dimensions that are used.

The diameter of the scanning light-spot is only 1 micron (1 micrometer). The pitch of the track is 1.6 microns. The maximum length of a bump or the land between two bumps is 0.9 microns and the maximum length is 3.3 microns.

Referring to Figure 11-3, the track is optically scanned from below the disc at a constant velocity of 1.2 to approximately 1.4 meters/second (typically 1.25 m/s). The speed of rotation of the disc varies from about 500 rpm to about 200 rpm.

PROCESSING OF THE AUDIO SIGNAL

For converting the analog signal from the microphone into a digital signal, pulse code modulation (PCM) is used. In this system the signal is periodically sampled and each sample is translated into a binary number. From Nyquist's sampling theorem, the frequency of sampling should be at least twice as high as the highest frequency to be accounted for in the analog signal. The number of bits per sample determines the signal-to-noise ratio in the subsequent reproduction. In the compact disc system the analog signal in Figure 11-5(a) is sampled at a basic rate of 44.1 kHz as shown in Figure 11-5(b), which is sufficient for reproduction of the highest frequency in the audio spectrum, 20 kHz.

The signal is quantized by using uniform quantization as in Figure 11-5(c), the sampled amplitude is divided into equal parts. The number of bits per sample (called audio bits) is 32, that is, 16 bits for the left and 16 bits for the right audio channel as in Figure 11-5(d). This corresponds to a signal-to-noise ratio of more than 90 dB. The net bit rate is $44.1 \times 10^3 \times 32 = 1.41 \times 10^6$ audio bits per second. The time required between each sample can be calculated from $f = 1/t$, in which f is the frequency in hertz and t is the time in seconds. For a frequency of 44.1 kHz this can be calculated to be 1/ $44,100 = 0.0000226757$ second or 22.7×10^{-6} second.

Frame Arrangement

The audio bits are grouped into frames, each containing six of the original samples as shown in Figure 11-6(a). Successive blocks of audio bits have blocks of parity bits added to them in accordance with a coding system called CIRC (Cross-Interleave Reed-Solomon Code). This makes it possible to correct errors during the reproduction of the signal. The ratio of the number of bits before and after this operation is 3:4. Each frame has C and D bits (control and display bits) added to it; one of the functions of these bits is to provide information to the listener. After this operation the bits are called data bits.

The bit stream is then modulated; that is, the data bits are translated into channel bits suitable for storage on the disc. The EFM (Eight-to-Fourteen Modulation) code is used for this. In the EFM code blocks of eight bits are translated into blocks of fourteen

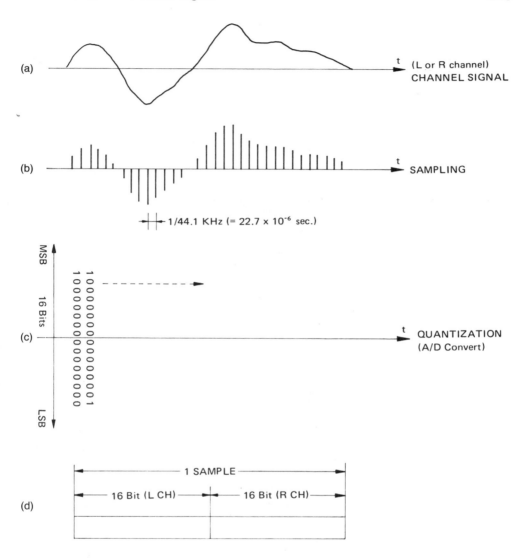

Figure 11-5 Analog form of left or right channel (a); sampling at a rate of 44.1 kHz (b); analog to digital conversion (c); total sample is 32 bits or 16 bits per channel (d).

bits (Fig. 11-6). The blocks of fourteen bits are linked by three merging bits. The ratio of the number of bits before and after modulation is 8:17.

For the synchronization (sync) of the bit stream, an identical synchronization pattern consisting of 27 channel bits is added to each frame. The total bit rate after all these manipulations is 4.32×10^6 channel bits per second.

The illustration in Figure 11-6 shows one frame of the successive bit streams. There are six sampling periods for one frame as in drawing (a), with 32 bits per

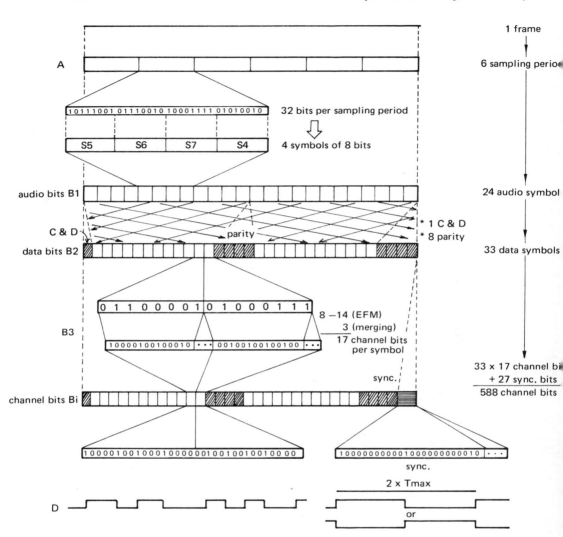

Figure 11-6 Bit streams in the encoding system.

sampling period; that is, 16 bits for each of the two sound channels. These 32 bits are divided to make four symbols in the audio bit stream, identified as audio bits B1 in the illustration. In the data bit stream (B2) eight parity and one C and D symbols have been added to the 24 audio symbols. To scatter possible errors, the symbols of different frames in B1 are interleaved so that the audio signals in one frame of B2 originate from different frames in B1. The modulation translates the eight data bits of a symbol of B2 into fourteen channel bits, to which three merging bits are added, as indicated in B3. The frames are marked with a sync signal of the form shown at the bottom right in

Figure 11-6. The final result is the channel bit stream, Bi, which is used for encoding on the master disc. This is done in such a way that each digit 1 indicates the transition between a flat and a bump. An idealized arrangement appears in drawing (d).

Table 11-1 gives a survey of the successive operations with the associated bit rates with their names. From the magnitude of the channel bit rate and the scanning speed of 1.25 meters per second, it follows that the length of a channel bit on the disc is approximately 0.3 microns.

TABLE 11-1 Names of the succesive signals, the associated bit rates and operations during the processing of the audio signal

Name	Bit rate in 10^6 bits/s	Operations
Audio signal		PCM (44.1 KHz)
Audio bit stream	1.41	CIRC (+ parity bits)
		Addition to C&D bits
		EFM
Data bit stream	1.94	Addition of merging bits
		Addition of synchronization patterns
Channel bit stream	4.32	

Disc Encoding

The signal produced in this way is used by the disc manufacturer to switch on and off the laser beam that illuminates the light-sensitive layer on a rotating glass disc, called the "master." A pattern of pits is produced on the disc by a photographic developing process. After the surface has been coated with a thin layer of silver, an electroplating process is applied to produce a nickel impression, called the "metal father." From the father disc, impressions called "mother" discs are produced in a similar manner. The impressions of the mother discs, called "sons" or "stampers," are used as tools with which the pits, P, as indicated previously in Figure 11-1, are impressed into the thermoplastic transparent carrier material (T) of the disc.

Disc Readout

The disc is optically scanned by an AlGaAs semiconductor laser. Figure 11-7 shows the optical part of the pickup. The light from the laser having a wavelength of about 800 nm is focused through a beamsplitter prism and an object (objective) lens onto the reflecting layer of the disc. The diameter of the light spot is about 1 micron. When the spot falls into the interval between two pits (bumps), it is almost totally reflected and reaches the four photodiodes.

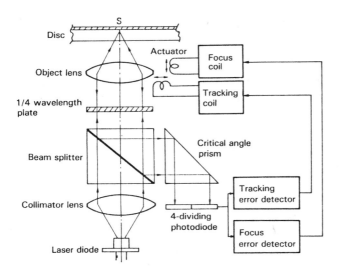

Figure 11-7 Optical system. (Courtesy Kyocera International, Inc.)

The depth of a pit (or the height of a bump) is about 1/4 of a wavelength in the transparent substrate material. When the light spot lands on a bump, interference causes less light to be reflected and an appreciably smaller amount reaches the photodiodes. When the ouput signals from the four photodiodes are added, the result is a fairly rough approximation of the rectangular pulse pattern on the disc in the form of pits and flats.

The optical pickup is very small and is mounted in a motor-driven carriage that enables the pickup to track across the radius of the disc so that it can scan the complete spiral track. The lens assembly within the optical head is mounted on a linear motor that consists of a combination of a coil and a permanent magnet. When the coil is energized the pickup can be directed to any required part of the track, the locational information being provided by the C and D bits added to each frame on the disc. Thus the pickup is able to find any particular musical selection chosen by the listener.

When the selection has been found, the pickup must then follow the track accurately to within ± 0.1 micron without being affected by the next or previous track. Since the track on the disc may have some slight eccentricity and since the suspension of the turntable is not perfect, the track may have a maximum side-to-side swing of 300 microns. A tracking servosystem is therefore necessary to ensure that the deviation between the pickup and the track is smaller than the permitted value of ± 0.1 micron and must also be able to absorb the consequences of small vibrations of the player.

The depth of focus of the optical pickup at position S (Fig. 11-7) is about 4 microns. The axial deviation of the disc owing to various mechanical effects can have a maximum of 1 micron. It is evident that a servosystem is necessary to give correct focusing of the pickup on the reflecting layer. The object lens can therefore be displaced in the direction of its optical axis by a combination of a coil and a permanent magnet, somewhat in the manner of a voice coil/permanent magnet assembly in a loudspeaker.

FOCUS CONTROL

The reflected laser beam from a disc is polarized 90 degrees with the beam splitter (Fig. 11-8) and sent to the photodiodes via the cylindrical lens. The beam passed through this lens gradually varies its shape along its path, first as an oval in a longitudinal direction, then as a circle, and finally as an oval in a transverse direction.

The beam shape varies with the distance from the disc. The photodiodes are divided into four sections, all of which provide outputs when the beam is in focus. However, when the disc is too close the longitudinal direction oval beam supplies a light signal to the upper and lower photodiodes, causing only these two diodes to provide outputs. On the other hand, if the disc is too far, only the left and right diodes provide an output. By amplifying the difference in output derived from these four-

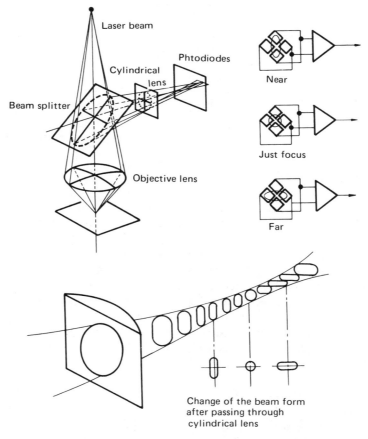

Figure 11-8 Polarization of the reflected scanning beam. (Courtesy Kyocera International, Inc.)

division diodes, a focus error signal can be obtained. This focus error signal is amplified and fed to the object lens for focus correction and in this way always maintains an in-focus state. The focus correction is handled in the focus servo control circuit.

Photodiode Array

The optical pickup comprises six-division photodiodes, A through F (Fig. 11-9). The four photodiodes at the center $(A + C)$ and $(B + D)$ provide both focus error detection by means of a main beam spot and main signal pickup. The two remaining diodes (E and F) provide tracking error detection by means of subbeam spots.

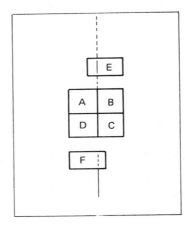

Figure 11-9   Photodiode assembly for focusing and tracking error detection. (Courtesy Kyocera International, Inc.)

Focus Error Detector

The output of the photodiodes used for focusing are delivered to an op amp which not only works to strengthen the weak signal input but also functions as a comparator (Fig. 11-10). When the beam is in focus equal signal voltages are delivered to the op amp and the unit has no output, as in drawing (a). If the beam is out of focus as in drawings (b) and (c) whether before the focal point or after it, the voltages delivered to the op amp are not equal and therefore the amp supplies a signal ouput. The polarity of this output is either plus or minus, and it is this polarity which determines whether the focusing coil will move in one direction or the other. As the focusing coil moves, the output of the comparator becomes less and less and finally reaches zero. When this happens the focusing coil stops its motion.

THE TRACKING SERVO

For some compact disc players the tracking error detection method employed is called the heterodyne method. This method involves monitoring whether or not the laser beam is applied equally to the four-division photodiode assembly. When the beam is located

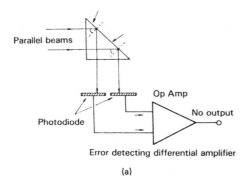

Error detecting differential amplifier

(a)

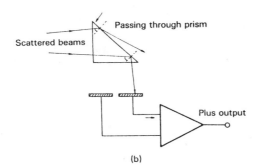

(b)

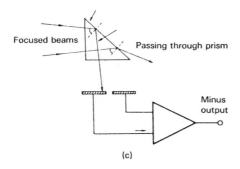

Figure 11-10 Focus error detection. (Courtesy Kyocera International, Inc.)

at the center of a track, the output of $(A + C) - (B + D)$ becomes zero (Fig 11-11). However, if the beam is deflected from the center of the track the waveform of $(A + C) - (B + D)$ changes based on the direction and extent of the deflection (Fig. 11-12). This signal is called a differential (DL) signal. In this method, the sizes of the DL signal rising from 0 volt and falling are held as samples. We can call the sample at rising S1 and that at falling S2 (Fig. 11-13).

S1–S2 is the tracking error signal and its effect is to move the pickup lens to the left or right until this signal becomes zero. The photodiode output is supplied to a pair

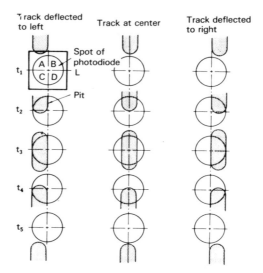

Figure 11-11 Tracking error detection. (Courtesy Kyocera International Inc.)

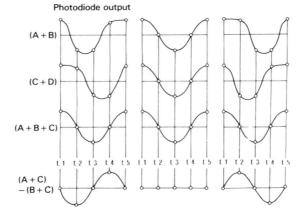

Figure 11-12 Variations in photodiode output due to tracking error. (Courtesy Kyocera International, Inc.)

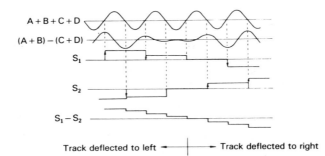

Figure 11-13 Differential signal. (Courtesy Kyocera International, Inc.)

256

of op amps (Fig. 11-14). The output of these two amplifiers is integrated by an R-C network and is applied as a triangular wave signal to the output op amp. It is amplified here and then sent to the tracking servo. The laser pickup returns inward little by little, so as not to go out of the disc during this period.

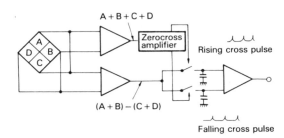

Figure 11-14 Development of tracking pulses. (Courtesy Kyocera International, Inc.)

Tracking Adjustment

Tracking consists of a number of subsections, both electronic and mechanical. These include a tracking error detector, a servo amplifier, a tracking adjustment device and a tracking servo control section.

Tracking adjustment can be handled by using a track-following mirror (Fig. 11-15). The actual amount of physical movement of this mirror is extremely small with the mirror behaving as though it were pivoted on a central axis. Light from the laser in drawing (a) is reflected by the track-following mirror onto the disc. The returned beam also strikes this mirror, and then using another mirror, it is directed toward an optical sensor. Details of the movement of the track-following mirror show the relationship of the scanning beam to the disc being scanned in drawing (b).

Tracking Servo Circuit

In the tracking servo circuit (Fig. 11-16) the reflected beam is picked up by two pairs of shunted diodes, indicated here by the letters E and F. The electrical outputs of these diodes are fed into a tracking error detection and phase correction amplifier, identified in the drawing as IClO4. This IC contains two op amplifiers, with the output of the first supplied to pin 7 of the second. The second amplifier supplies phase correction and also inverts the signal, and it is this signal that is brought out from pin 8. IC104 can be regarded as a voltage amplifier. Now the signal is further amplified by the next integrated circuit, IC102, and then subsequently power amplified by the following IC, IC103. The amount of signal input to IC102 is controlled by variable resistor R149. This is a factory adjustment and once the correct amount of IClO2 driving voltage has been established the resistor is locked.

IC103 is analogous to the power amplifier used in an audio power amplifier. The audio amplifier must deliver power to the voice coils of the speaker system. IC103 must deliver power to the system's tracking coil. Both the voice coil in a speaker and the

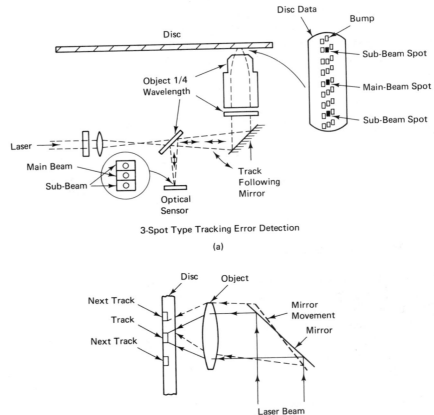

Figure 11-15 Three-spot type tracking error detection (a); mirror movement (b).
(Courtesy Kyocera International, Inc.)

tracking coil in the CD player are current-operated devices and depend on the magnetic field supplied by a current.

In addition to the ICs, various independent transistors are used in the tracking servo circuitry. Transistors TR110, TR111 and TR112 function as a voltage limiter for the tracking coil. When a large tracking signal is present that may cause the tracking coil mirror to move beyond its normal motion swing these transistors are turned on, disabling the tracking servo.

Tracking Servo Control

Tracking servo control is performed by causing transistors TR107, TR108 and TR109 to turn on and off through the application of voltages or pulses to the following terminals: TS (tracking servo stop); TG (tracking gain); TH (tracking hold); and KP (kick pulse).

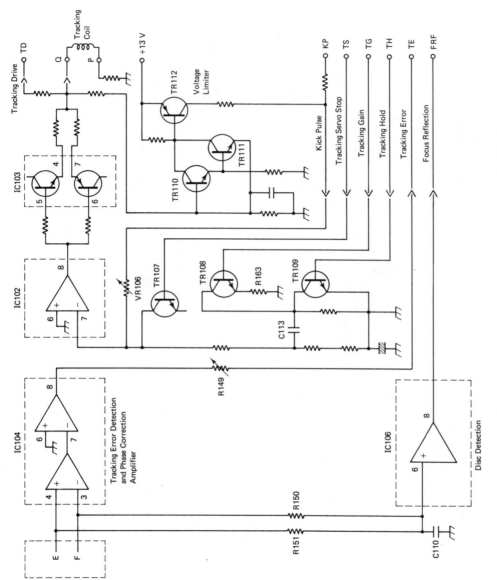

Figure 11-16 Tracking servo circuit. (Courtesy Kyocera International, Inc.)

Input terminal \ Mode in operation	Play	Slow Search (One track kick)	Fast Search (10 track kicks)	Fastest Search
KP	Not generated	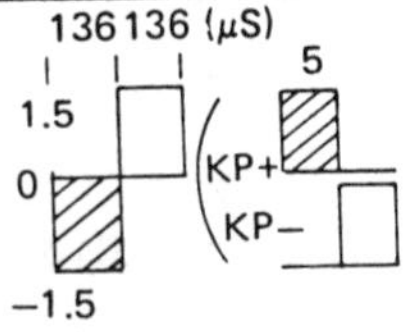 136 136 (µS), 1.5, 0, −1.5, (KP+ / KP−), 5	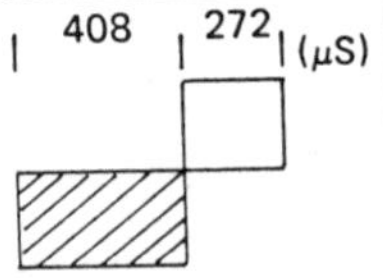 408, 272 (µS)	Not generated
TS	"L" (TR107-OFF)			Tracking Servo-ON Emitting "H" voltage periodically.
TG	"H" TR108-ON Tracking gain-LOW	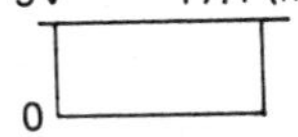 5V, 0, 17.4 (mS) TR108-OFF (Tracking gain-HIGH)	 17.4 (mS)	
TH	"L" (TR109-OFF / Tracking hold-OFF)	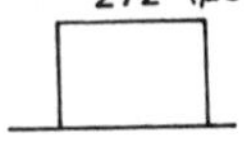 272 (µS) (TR109-ON / Tracking hold-ON)	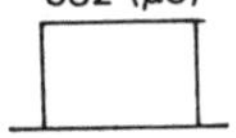 682 (µS)	

Figure 11-17 Modes of tracking. (Courtesy Kyocera International, Inc.)

The modes of operation can be classified as play, slow search, fast search, and fastest search (Fig. 11-17).

The kick pulse for slow search is an AC pulse and its positive and negative excursions each have a time duration of 136 microseconds. For fast search ten-track kicks are used.

DISC MOTOR SERVO

The speed of the disc motor rotation is controlled by comparing the signal extracted in accordance with the linear velocity from the disc reproduction signal with a reference signal (Fig. 11-18). This comparison operation is made within the servo control (SVC). The signal to be used for controlling the speed of disc motor rotation is output in the form of a pulse from pin 10 or pin 1 of IC105 (the drive motor IC amplifier) or the plus terminal of the disc drive motor. Although not directly indicated in Figure 11-18, the pulse signal output from pins 1 or 10 is fed back to pins 3 or 4 of IC109.

The output of this IC (inverted when inputting to pin 3) is obtained from pin 2 which is converted to an analog voltage by the integrating circuit of R253 and C132. This voltage is sent to pin 7 of IC106, working as a preamplifier and is then power amplified by IC105 to drive the disc motor. The direction of motor drive depends on the polarity of the voltage reaching the drive motor, M. If the output is from pins 1 or 10 of IC105 the voltage will be positive and rotation will be in one direction. If the input voltage is from pin 2 of IC109 it will be negative and the motor shaft will rotate in the opposite direction.

IC106 and IC105 can be regarded as being in series with the drive motor shunted across this combination. The polarity of the voltage at the point identified as DR is

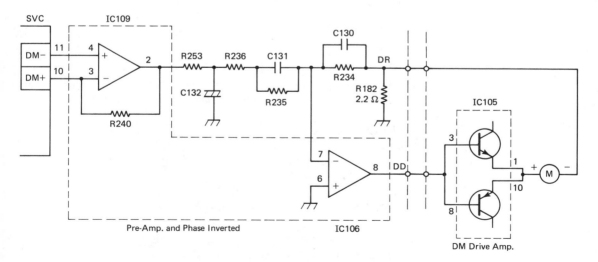

Figure 11-18 Motor control circuit. (Courtesy Kyocera International, Inc.)

negative and that at the input to pin 7 of IC106 is also negative. However, IC106 can phase invert the motor drive voltage so it is positive at the point marked *DD*.

Pulse Motor Control

When the pulse signal is output from pin 10 of the servo control, as indicated in Figure 11-18, the disc motor starts to rotate. AFC (automatic frequency control) operation causes the motor rotation to be pulled within $\pm$ 10 percent of its constant speed rotation. The time duration of the pulse at pin 10 is in the range of 118 to 147 microseconds followed by a no-pulse time of 18 microseconds to the beginning of the next pulse (Fig. 11-19). The disc reproduction signal is read and the calculation is made in the disc servocontrol circuit. If the width of the EFM signal is wider than 11T (clock pulses) the rotation speed is lower than required. Thus, pulses must be generated

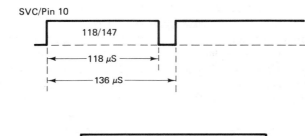

Figure 11-19 Comparison of clock pulses with EFM signal. (Courtesy Kyocera International, Inc.)

continuously until the necessary speed is obtained. When the frame synchronization with the clock is established, the AFC operation changes to PLL (phase locked loop) operation.

The pulses shown in Figure 11-19 are those generated by a 4.3218 MHz crystal clock. In this illustration the EFM signal is being compared to the number of clock pulses. 11T refers to the time required for the formation of 11 pulses, each of equal time duration.

Constant Speed Rotation with Constant Linear Velocity

When the rotational speed of the disc becomes lower, the width of the pulse from pin 10 (DM + in Figure 11-18) is made wider and if the speed becomes higher the pulse width is made narrower, thus holding the linear velocity constant (Fig. 11-20).

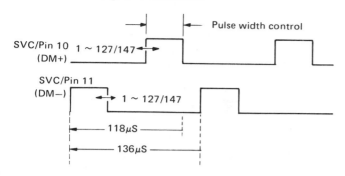

Figure 11-20 If disc speed becomes higher, pulse width is narrowed. (Courtesy Kyocera International, Inc.)

Disc Motor Brake

The pulse signal is output from pin 11 (DM− in Figure 11-18). A braking action is obtained by applying a reverse voltage to the disc motor. The EFM signal is read into the servo control and as a result the speed of rotation is decreased. If the EFM signal does not produce a reverse action in one frame, a single count is made and after the elapse of four counts the pulse signal from pin 11 (DM−) is stopped (Fig. 11-21).

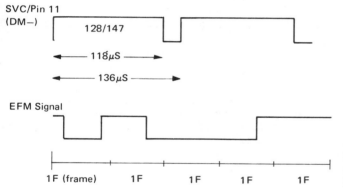

Figure 11-21 EFM signal is used for producing braking action. (Courtesy Kyocera International, Inc.)

AUDIO SIGNAL PRODUCTION

The audio signal in binary form must ultimately be converted to its audio equivalent so the signal must be processed in the compact disc player (Fig. 11-22).

In clock regeneration a bit clock signal is developed to supply synchronization to the input signal read by the optical pickup.

In the demultiplexer and EFM circuitry, conversion follows the same rules that were applied to EFM modulation, but now in the opposite sense. The information is then temporarily stored in the RAM and reaches the error-detection and correction circuits. The parity bits can be used here to correct errors or to detect errors if correction is found to be impossible. These errors can originate from defects in the disc

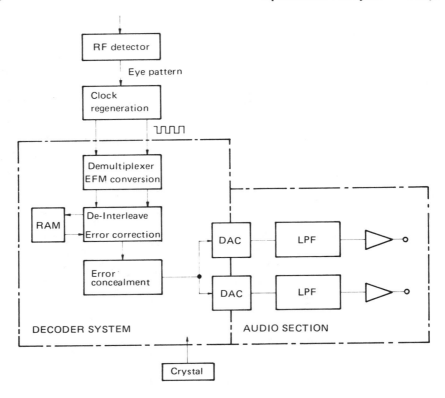

Figure 11-22 Decoder system and audio section for the development of the analog audio signal. Code: RF (radio frequency); RAM (random access memory); EFM (eight-t fourteen modulation); DAC (digital to analog conversion); LPF (low pass filter). (Courtesy Kyocera International, Inc.)

manufacturing process, damage during use, or fingerprints or dust on the disc. Since the information with the CIRC code is interleaved in time, errors that occur at the input of the decoder in one frame are spread over a large number of frames during decoding. This increases the probability that the maximum number of correctable errors per frame will not be exceeded. A flaw such as a scratch can often produce a train of errors called an error burst. The error-correction code used in the decoder can correct a burst of up to 4,000 data bits, largely because the errors are spread out in this way. If more errors than the permitted maximum occur, they can only be detected. In the error concealment and muting block the errors detected are then masked. If the value of a sample indicates an error, a new value is determined by linear interpolation between the preceding value and the next one. If two or more successive sample values indicate an error, the preceding value will be held.

THE EYE PATTERN

The quality of the data channel is evaluated by an eye pattern, obtained by connecting a scope to the output of the high-frequency (RF) amplifier. The signals from the different lands and bumps are superimposed on the screen; they are strongly rounded, mainly because the spot diameter is not zero and the pit walls are not precisely vertical. If the transmission quality is adequate, however, it is always possible to determine whether the signal is positive or negative at clock times. The lozenge or diamond shaped pattern is called the eye. Because of channel imperfections, the eye can become obscured and due to phase jitter of the signal relative to the clock, an eye becomes narrower and noise reduces its height.

CROSS-INTERLEAVE ERROR CORRECTION

When analog audio signals are recorded on conventional analog phono records it is difficult to correct signal errors that have occurred in the path from the source to reproduction. With suitably coded digital signals on compact discs, however, a practical means of error correction does exist (Fig. 11-23).

Drawing (a) shows the digital information on a compact disc and it is represented in this example by the 26 letters of the alphabet arranged in their correct order from A to Z. Drawing (b), shows a few random errors which we can call signal dropouts. The sequential arrangement of the letters remains and it is correct, but a few of the letters, such as C, G, M and N, and a few others have disappeared. The number of letters in drawing (b) that have disappeared are relatively few but in drawing (c) a much larger amount are no longer present.

Drawing (d) illustrates the concept behind the Cross-Interleave technique. Consider the group of letters at the left in this drawing. They are still arranged in their original sequence but now have a series of straight lines at a small slant connecting the letters. Start with the letter A and you will see that this line joins these letters: A, G, M, S and Y. If you look at the third row in the letters at the right you will see them rearranged. Start with the letter F and following the slant line we have the letters F, L, R, X and K from the beginning of the next slant line. On the right side, these now appear in this order and form the fourth row.

This technique, using letters as an example, is Cross-Interleaving, since the letters on one line are interleaved with the letters on another. If we consider each of these letters as representing a data bit, then when encoded on a disc, they would appear as in drawing (e). Drawing (f) shows the data as they would be encoded without interleaving. The left side of drawing (d) corresponds to the arrangement in drawing (f). The right side of drawing (d) corresponds to the arrangement in drawing (e). It is from this method of use and the names of the inventors that we obtain the name: Cross-Interleave Reed-Solomon Code (CIRC).

Figure 11-24 is a block diagram representing the decoding circuit for CIRC. The 32 symbols (Si1...Si32) of a frame (24 audio symbols and 8 parity symbols) are applied

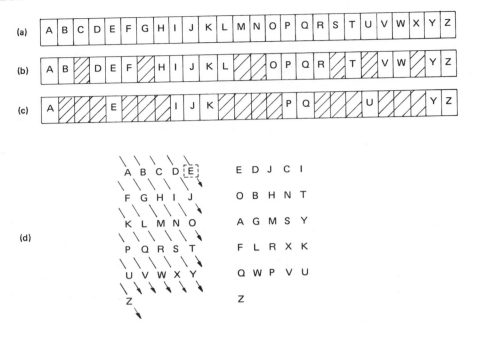

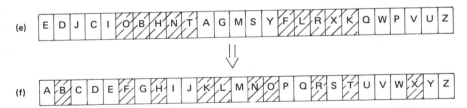

Figure 11-23   Cross-Interleave error correction. (Courtesy Kyocera International, Inc.)

in parallel to the 32 inputs. The delay lines D2i (i = 1...16) have a delay equal to the duration of one symbol, so that the information of the even symbols of a frame is cross-interleaved with that of the odd symbols of the next frame. The decoder DEC1 is designed in accordance with the encoding rules for a Reed-Solomon code. It corrects a maximum of two errors and if multiple errors occur passes them on unchanged, attaching to all 28 symbols a Cl flag sent via the dashed lines. Owing to the different lengths of the delay lines Dj (j = 1...28) errors that occur in one word at the output of DEC1 are spread over a number of words at the input of DEC2. This has the effect of reducing the number of errors per DEC3 word. The decoder DEC2 is designed in accordance with the encoding rules for a Reed-Solomon code. It can correct a maxi-

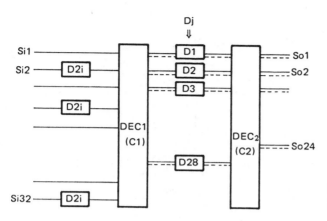

Figure 11-24 CIRC error correction. (Courtesy Kyocera International, Inc.)

mum of two errors with reference to Cl and if it cannot do so, 24 symbol values are passed on unchanged and the associated positions are given a flag via the dashed lines; So1...So24 are outgoing symbols.

ERROR CONCEALMENT

The purpose of error concealment is to make the errors that have been detected but not corrected by the CIRC decoder virtually inaudible. Depending on the magnitude of the error to be concealed, this is done by interpolation or by previous word holding.

Two consecutive 8-bit symbols delivered by the decoder together form a 16-bit sample value. Since a sample value in the case of a detected error carries an erasure flag, the concealment mechanism "knows" whether a particular value is reliable or not. A reliable sample value undergoes no further processing but an unreliable one is replaced by a new value obtained by a linear interpolation between reliable immediate neighbors. Sharp clicks are thus avoided. All that happens is a short-lived slight increase in the distortion of the audio signal. With alternate correct and incorrect sample values, the bandwidth of the audio signal is halved during the interpolation (10 kHz). If the decoder delivers a sequence of wrong sample values, a linear interpolation does not help. In that case the previous word would be held.

CONTROL AND DISPLAY

The control and display block is constructed of 98 frames (Fig. 11-25). Each frame has one control and display symbol which consists of eight bits of P, Q, R, S, T, U, V and W channels. At the present only the P and Q channels are fixed for use; the other channels are not as yet assigned.

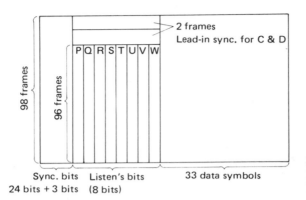

Sync. bits   Listen's bits   33 data symbols

24 bits + 3 bits   (8 bits)

Figure 11-25 Control and display (C and D) block. (Courtesy Kyocera International, Inc.)

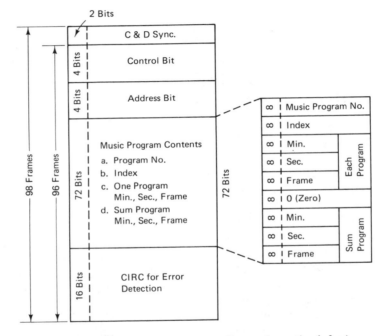

Figure 11-26 Q channel. (Courtesy Kyocera International, Inc.)

The P and Q Channels

P channel: The music program is on or not.

P = 0 in the music program. P = 1 in the interval of a music program.

Q channel (Fig. 11-26). Control bits (4 bits): Audio channels (4 or 2) and pre-emphasis (in or not).

1. Audio signal without pre-emphasis:
   2-channel . . . 0000
   4-channel . . . 1000
2. Audio channel with pre-emphasis:
   2-channel . . . 0001
   4-channel . . . 1001

Pre-emphasis:

T1 = 50 microseconds at f1, approximately 3.18 kHz

T2 = 15 microseconds at f2, approximately 10.6 kHz

QUICK TROUBLESHOOTING

Troubleshooting involves narrowing servicing down to a specific component. The best way to do this is to consider the compact disc player as composed of a series of blocks and then to concentrate on those blocks that could be in the trouble path. You can determine what those areas are by considering the symptoms. As an extreme example, if the disc does not rotate it would be futile to consider the D/A converter as a possible trouble source.

DATA AND SIGNAL PATHS

Every compact disc player can be considered to be a two-part component. One section of the player is involved with data flow and by data we mean the audio signal, whether that signal is in binary form or analog (Fig. 12-1). The other part of the compact disc player consists of circuits in the control signal flow path. The dashed lines in the illustration indicate the data flow path; the solid lines represent control signal flow.

FLOWCHART ANALYSIS

Narrowing a servicing problem to a specific area involves making a number of decisions to find the defect through a process of elimination. This can be done by using a flowcharting technique, a method commonly used by computer programmers as an initial step in the preparation of a computer program.

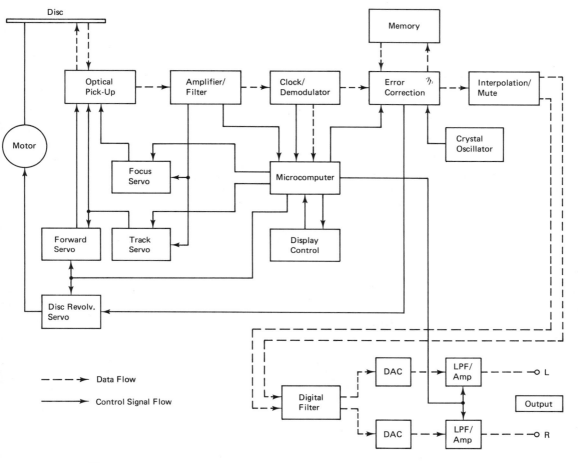

Figure 12-1 Chart of data and signal current flow. (Courtesy Kyocera International, Inc.)

A flowchart of all the possible problems that could occur in a compact disc player could be quite complicated. The one shown in Figure 12-2 is just a small portion of the overall flowchart.

Not all servicing flowcharts are alike. Those followed by factory servicing technicians (Fig. 12-3) make strong use of part numbers or reference numbers and these are intelligible only to those supplied with lists of such numbers containing identification of what these numbers represent. For these technicians servicing is much easier than for those who do general electronic repairs. They can identify the parts, the replacement units are readily available, and a servicing procedure is set up for them. Furthermore, they need work only on compact disc players made by their company.

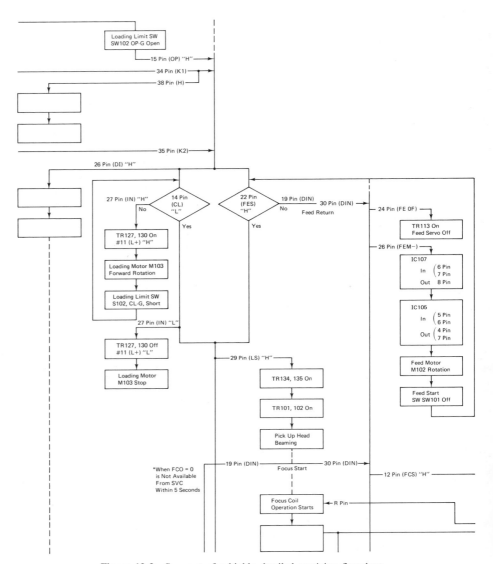

Figure 12-2   Segment of a highly detailed servicing flowchart.

The type of flowchart used by general service technicians is quite different because each block is more clearly identified (Fig. 12-4). These flowcharts often use abbreviations, such as D/A, PLL, Sync, AF, RF, but most of these are either well known or can be interpreted. If a service technician's flowchart does use part numbers, they are often supplied as supplementary information to allow easy ordering of replacements.

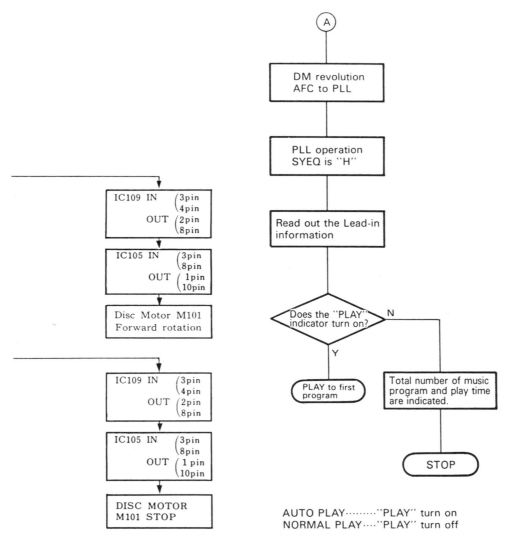

Figure 12-3 Portion of flowchart used by factory service technicians.

Figure 12-4 Flowchart for service technicians not factory associated.

Flowchart Symbols

There are about 20 different symbols used by computer programmers for the preparation of their flowcharts but for the most part, a compact disc player flowchart requires only four (Fig. 12-5).

The first one (a) is a terminal symbol used to indicate the start or end of an action. It could represent turning a compact disc player on, and later in the same

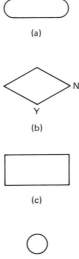

Figure 12-5 Flowcharting symbols used in compact disc player servicing.

flowchart for turning the compact disc player off. It can also be used to indicate the start of any action, such as the beginning of play of a particular track. The terminal symbol is often the first and last symbol used in a compact disc player servicing chart but it can occasionally be found elsewhere.

The diamond-shaped symbol (b) is the decision symbol and is accompanied by the letters Y (yes) and N (no). With a no answer the flow of action follows one path; with a yes answer a different path is followed.

The symbol in drawing (c) has the outline of a rectangle and is a processing symbol. The wording inside this symbol indicates some action. This action could be focus search, disc rotation, or an indicator turning on, among others.

The final symbol (d) is a small circle and is known as a connector. Generally a letter is written inside the circle to indicate a connection to another part of the compact disc player servicing flowchart (Fig. 12-6). The connector marked A on the left side is joined to the other connector, also marked A, on the right side. Each symbol is connected by a straight line called a flowline. These lines indicate the path to be followed in a servicing procedure.

The Flowchart

The symbols to be used in a servicing flowchart can be drawn freehand but a better method is to use a template. Since not all compact disc players are alike, it is helpful to prepare a servicing flowchart on all those you service. While you can depend on your memory, having a set of flowcharts handy can shorten servicing time.

Another aid in compact disc flowchart servicing is the pre-prepared flowchart (Fig. 12-7). These are much easier to use and are neater than a self-prepared chart.

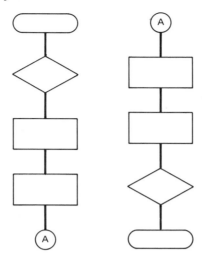

Figure 12-6 Use of a connector. The movement or flow is from A on the bottom left to A at the top right.

These blank flowcharts are available in pad form, and the pads plus a template are all that are needed to start flowchart servicing. The pads and the template should be available in larger art supply stores.

The flowchart consists of blank rectangles arranged in columns and rows and identified by numbers and letters. The first column is known as the 1 column, the second as 2, and so on. The first row is A, the second is B, the third is C, and so forth. Each rectangle or block has a letter and a number. Thus block B3 is the second rectangle in column 3, row B. Each block is clearly identified by its alphanumeric designation, printed on the flowcharting form.

Flowcharting Abbreviations

Since there is limited room within each flowcharting block, abbreviations are commonly used. Unfortunately, there is no standardization for these abbreviations and those used in the servicing flowchart of one manufacturer may not correspond to those used by other manufacturers. The following list of abbreviations is typical.

AFC	automatic frequency control
DD	disc detection
DM	disc motor
DT	disc tracking
EFM	eight-to-fourteen modulation
FCS	focus in operation signal
FEO	focus error output
FES	focus error signal
FRF	focus error on confirm signal. Focus refraction.

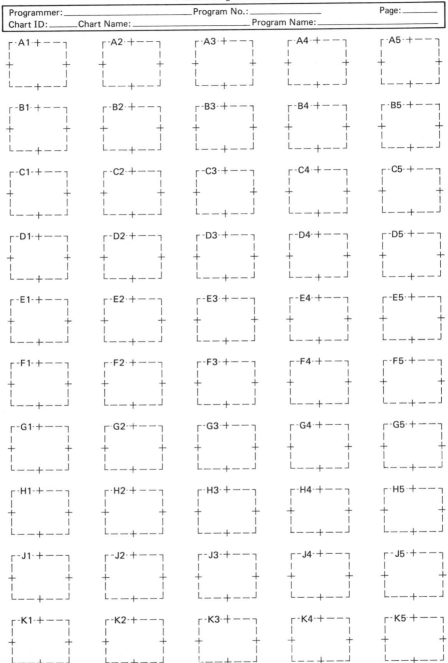

Figure 12-7 Blank flowchart.

FZC	focus zero correction (or focus zero crosspoint signal)
H	also written as H voltage. A hold voltage. A focus pulling indication signal. A voltage applied to the FCS terminal.
HF	high frequency (RF)
HS	hold signal
IC	integrated circuit
KP	kick pulse
L	a reference voltage
PCO	phase controlled output
PLL	phase lock loop
SL	slice level
SVC	servo controller
SYNC	synchronization
T	clock pulse
TEO	tracking error output
TG	tracking gain
TH	tracking hold
TR	transistor
TROF	tracking servo off
VCO	voltage controlled oscillator

The question of which flowchart to use will depend on the specific trouble symptoms. Based on these the flowchart may be simple or detailed and lengthy. In some instances more than one flowchart may be required if the symptoms are in different areas of the compact disc player or if the symptoms require a more detailed analysis. These faults may or may not be related.

NO SOUND: THE PLAYER DOES NOT WORK

Since this condition can mean trouble anywhere in the player, an overall flowchart (Fig. 12-8) is required. Finding the fault is a process of elimination and so a large number of decision symbols are used. By following the yes and no connections on these symbols, it should be possible to narrow the search in a logical and orderly manner.

If the player does not function, do not immediately assume the fault is in the player. It may seem obvious but check to make sure there is power available at the outlet and if there is that the power switch is turned on. Failure of the compact disc player to work is possibly one of the most common complaints.

While the flowchart shows the testing steps to follow, no chart can cover every possible contingency. For example, a player may not work if no disc has been inserted,

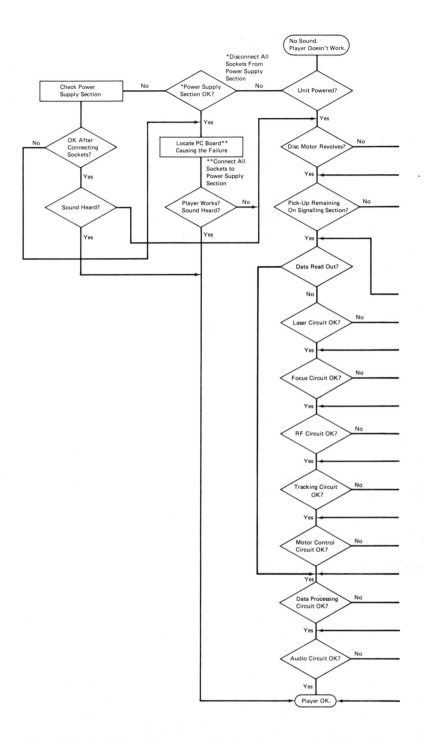

Figure 12-8 Servicing problem: no sound, player does not work. (Courtesy Kyocera International, Inc.)

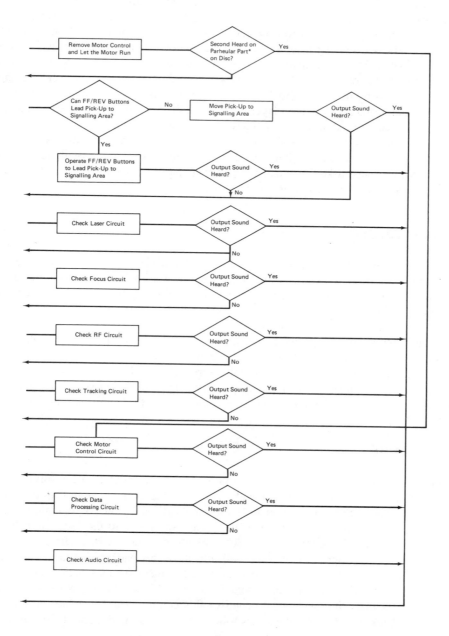

Figure 12-8 (cont.)

or if it has been inserted upside down, or if two discs are in the loading tray, or if the loading tray is mechanically operated and has not been fully closed. None of these are covered in the flowchart and therefore a physical examination of the player is the first step. Open the compact disc player only after you have made some preliminary tests of your own including: Is line power available? Is operating switch turned on? Is loading tray clear? Has a disc been inserted into the loading tray and has the disc been inserted with the label side up? Are there any foreign objects in the loading tray and has anyone tampered with the loading tray? Has the player been dropped or become water-damaged or been affected by high humidity? Does the player work when operated manually but not with remote control? If the player will not deliver sound to an external amplifier will it still operate headphones, or is the connecting cable from the player to the high-fidelity system satisfactory and will operation be restored if a new cable is used? Are the plugs on the connecting cable corroded? You can answer some of these questions but if you have been asked to repair the player as part of your work, do not expect to get all the answers honestly from the user.

LASER CIRCUIT FAILURE

Assume you have followed the overall block diagram (Fig. 12-8) and that when you reach the block marked "laser circuit OK?" you have a "no" answer. This means you must now move to the block reading "check laser circuit." By itself that instruction is inadequate. What we need at this point is another flowchart detailing the instructions to follow in the event of laser circuit failure (Fig. 12-9).

The abbreviations in this flowchart are Q (for transistors); U (for integrated circuits) and D (for diodes). To be able to identify these components you will need a circuit diagram or be familiar with the transistors, ICs and diodes that are used. Circuit diagrams are available in the manufacturers' servicing manuals but you will probably be able to get one more easily and quickly from a company that publishes such diagrams.

RF CIRCUIT FAILURE

In this circuit the signal picked up by the photodiodes, arranged as a four-division unit and used for focus error detection and main signal pickup is amplified by several transistors. One of these transistors works in an emitter-follower configuration and the output signal taken from the emitter of this transistor is sent to the HF terminal as an eye-pattern signal, also known as the EFM waveform (Fig. 12-10). The peak-to-peak voltage of the eye pattern is two volts. Adjustment of this pattern should be made near the center area of a standard test disc with the adjustment for maximum clarity of the eye pattern signal. The adjustment is done by a potentiometer whose range is limited to ± 45 degrees from the mechanical center of this control. The procedure in the flow-chart is to check the first four amplifiers following the photodiodes and the mixer circuit (Fig. 12-11).

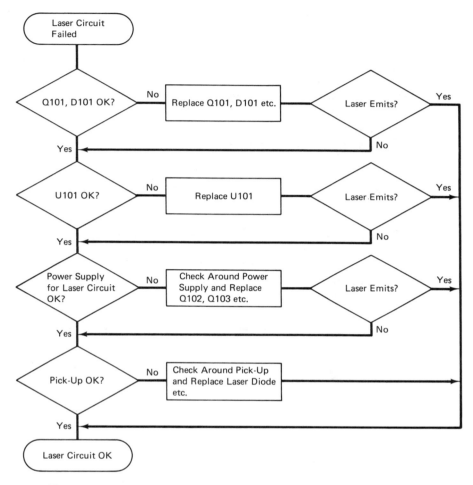

Figure 12-9 Flowchart for laser circuit failure. (Courtesy Kyocera International, Inc.)

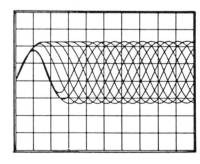

Figure 12-10 Eye pattern (EFM) waveform. (Courtesy Kyocera International, Inc.)

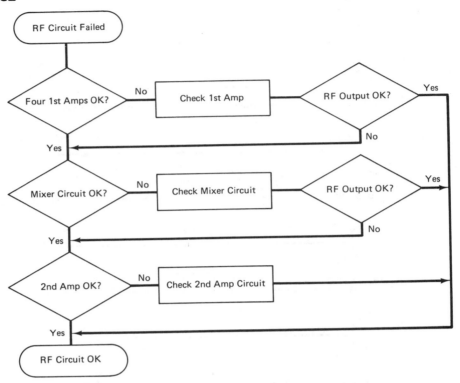

Figure 12-11 Flowchart for RF circuit failure. (Courtesy Kyocera International, Inc.)

FOCUS CIRCUIT FAILURE

When the disc scanning beams are focused, the same quantity of light is applied to the photodiodes and the error signal becomes zero. However, if the beams are out of focus, the error signal does not become zero and is coupled to the focus coil (Fig. 12-12).

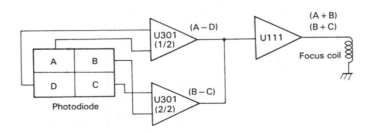

Figure 12-12 Focus servo circuit.

Although two ICs are indicated here it is just one unit. The identification number, U301, and U111 in the following IC may not have these identification numbers in a different CD player.

In the event of focus circuit failure, the flowchart indicates that the first amplifier, the logic circuit, the second amplifier and the focus coil should be checked in turn (Fig. 12-13).

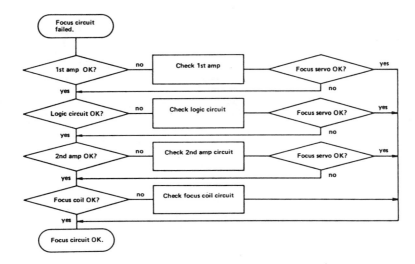

Figure 12-13 Flowchart for focus circuit failure. (Courtesy Kyocera International, Inc.)

TRACKING CIRCUIT FAILURE

The tracking circuit uses a number of ICs and various transistors (Fig. 12-14). Depending on the operation mode selected, tracking servo control is achieved by making certain transistors (TR107, TR108 and TR109) turn on and off through the application of voltages or pulses to the terminals identified as TS, TG, TH and KP.

When an H signal is input to terminal TS, transistor TR107 is turned on which disables the servo. If the H signal is applied to the TG terminal, transistor TR108 is turned on. This lowers the tracking gain by grounding through resistor R163 and capacitor C113. When the H signal is input to terminal TH, transistor TR109 is turned on. This holds the tracking coil in place by the charge on capacitor C113. The kick pulse is input to this terminal. According to the manner in which this pulse is generated from the servo control, high- or low-speed kick or continuous kick operation is selected. Search operation for forward or reverse is performed in sequence depending on the generation of a plus or minus kick pulse.

Transistors TR110, TR111 and TR112 function as a limiter for the tracking coil. When a large tracking signal that may cause the tracking coil to move beyond its

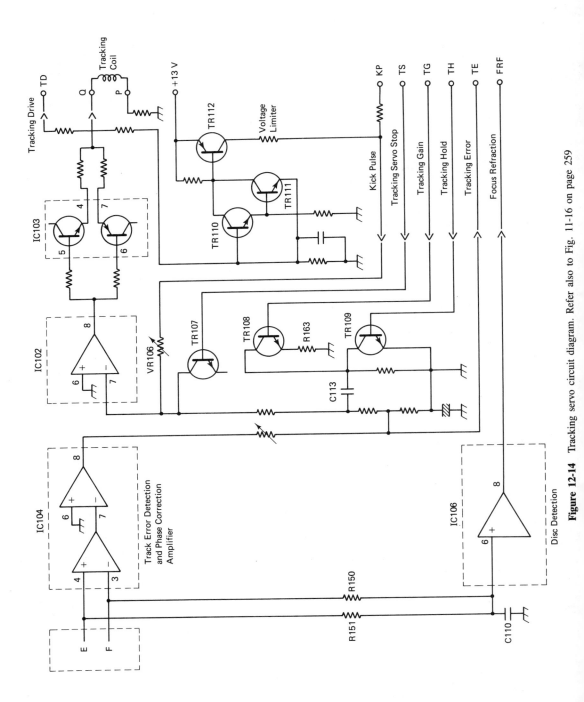

Figure 12-14 Tracking servo circuit diagram. Refer also to Fig. 11-16 on page 259

operating range is output from pins 4 and 7 of integrated circuit IC103, these transistors are turned on, disabling the tracking servo. This is equivalent to the application of an H signal to the TS (tracking servo stop) terminal.

Figure 12-15 is the flowchart for tracking circuit failure.

MOTOR CONTROL FAILURE

An explanation of the disc motor servo was previously explained in Chapter 11 and a circuit diagram was supplied in Fig. 11-18. Servicing of the motor control system can be handled in flowchart form (Fig. 12-16). The ICs are checked in turn and as a final step it may be necessary to replace the crystal clock.

DATA PROCESSOR FAILURE

For the most part the data processor (Fig. 12-17) is made up of integrated circuits. Integrated circuit modules cannot be handled as you would a resistor or capacitor. They are affected by electrostatic charges and are also temperature sensitive. It is best to avoid touching the terminals on the IC with your fingers or with any tools which do not have insulated handles. Special tools are available for inserting or removing an IC from a printed circuit board. Avoid using a soldering iron without precautions. There are special soldering irons for this purpose that have grounded tips that prevent electrostatic charge buildup. And when inserting a new IC always be sure to use an exact replacement. The fact that a pair of ICs looks alike does not mean they are the same.

Replacing resistors, capacitors, coils, diodes and transistors means unsoldering and resoldering. With the exception of the transistors and some coils, these are two terminal devices. It should not take more than about five seconds to unsolder each terminal. A good operating practice is to use a heat sink. This can be a tool such as a pair of long-nose pliers positioned between the component and the printed circuit board. The sink should be as close to the component and as far from the board as possible. You can use a rubber band around the handle of the tool to hold it in place. Use as much metal of the tool in contact with the lead of the component as possible. And not only components, but the printed circuit board itself can be damaged by too much heat.

AUDIO CIRCUIT FAILURE

Audio circuit failure does not necessarily mean a complete absence of sound. There are two sound output channels, left and right, and there is always the possibility that just one of these channels has been affected.

The chain of servicing events as indicated in the flowchart (Fig. 12-18) involves moving step by step from the digital-to-analog converter to the audio output. In this

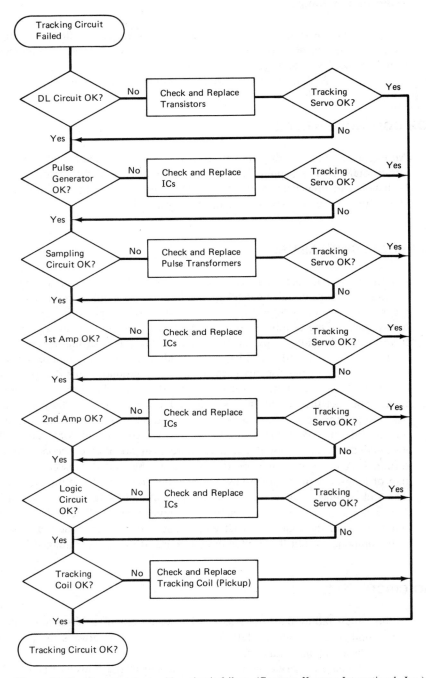

Figure 12-15 Flowchart for tracking circuit failure. (Courtesy Kyocera International, Inc.)

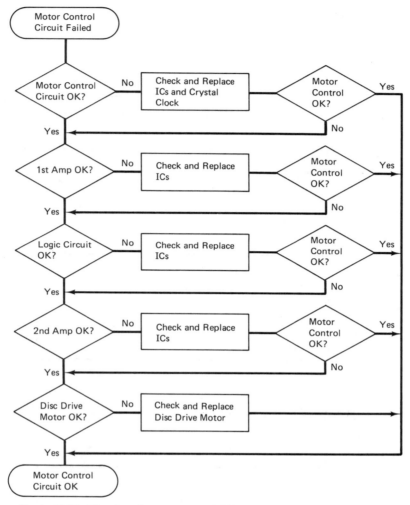

Figure 12-16 Flowchart for motor control failure. (Courtesy Kyocera International, Inc.)

case it would involve checking the filters, as well as the integrated circuits containing audio amplifiers.

There is always the possibility that lack of sound may be due to factors outside the compact disc player. The audio connecting cables and the following hi-fi amplifier may be at fault. Plug in a pair of headphones and if you get sound output, external trouble may be indicated. If you have a spare speaker try connecting it to the audio output terminals of the player. The sound will be weak but at least you will know that audio exists at the output.

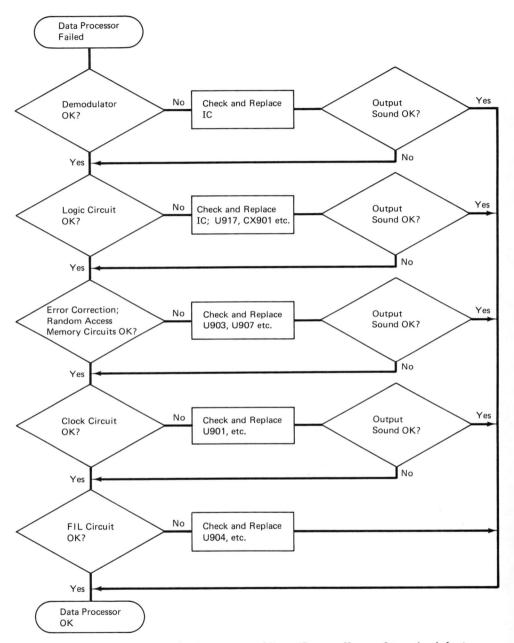

Figure 12-17 Flowchart for data processor failure. (Courtesy Kyocera International, Inc.)

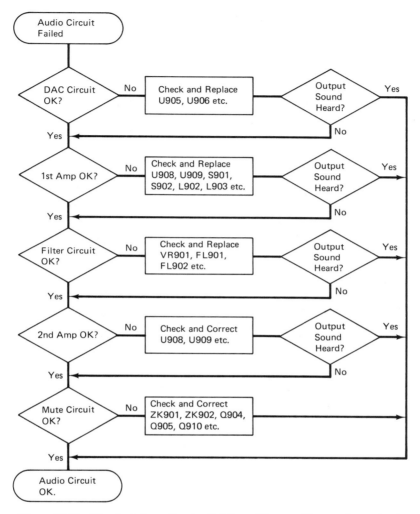

Figure 12-18 Flowchart for audio circuit failure. (Courtesy Kyocera International, Inc.)

The Op Amp

An IC can contain a number of cascaded individual amplifiers capable of supplying a large amount of signal gain, sometimes as much as 50,000. Known as an operational amplifier, usually abbreviated as op amp, it is arranged with an external feedback loop as in Figure 12-19(a). The gain of the op amp is the ratio of its input resistance, Rin, to its feedback resistance, Rf.

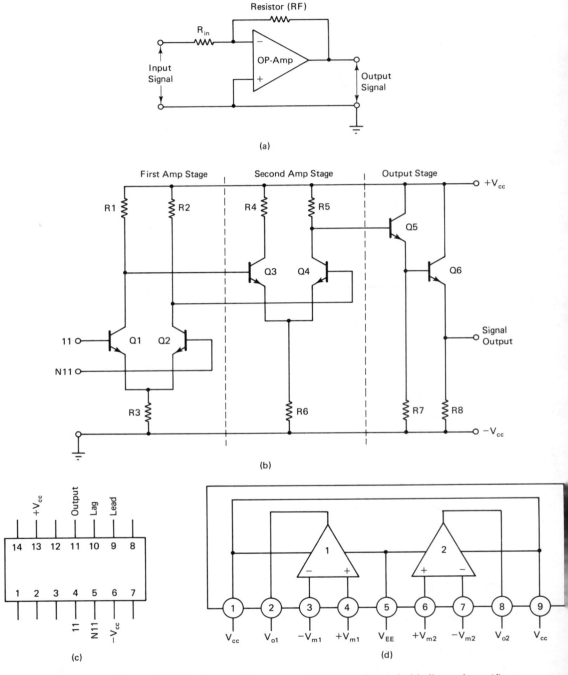

Figure 12-19(a) Op amp IC arrangement; (b) schematic; (c) dual in-line package; (d) single in-line package.

The op amp circuit in drawing (b) is built into a chip (c). Sometimes a single chip may contain more than one op amp as in Figure 12-19(d). This is a single in-line package with all the connections to one side of the chip.

Characteristically, an op amp has a very high input impedance which is advantageous since this imposes a very light load on the preceding driving circuit. The output impedance is extremely low. While the op amp can be found in the audio section of the compact disc player it can be used elsewhere in the compact disc player as a preamplifier following the laser head, as an HF amplifier, as a drive amplifier, or as an audio amplifier. It can function as a comparator arrangement, using its two input terminals for this purpose. The two signals brought into these terminals will be compared in the op amp, with the smaller signal level subtracted from the larger and the resulting difference appearing as an output voltage. This can then be used as a signal control.

One of the inputs to the op amp in a comparator arrangement can be grounded. This simply indicates that the grounded input is to be used as the reference.

ADJUSTMENTS

Every compact disc player requires various adjustments to get optimum functioning from various systems. These could include focus offset, the correct adjustment of various mechanisms, vertical adjustment, balance, disc motor, radial gain, pulse width, phase lock loop and output level, feed motor gain, and servo adjustments. It should not be necessary to make these adjustments since they are done at the factory. Furthermore, the adjustments are held in place by means of lock screws (Fig. 12-20). However, under conditions of extreme and repeated vibration these screws may become loose. An improper adjustment can mean an inoperative compact disc player or one that works poorly or intermittently, giving symptoms of some defect. Adjustments are made using a scope and/or voltmeter to make sure the waveforms and voltages correspond to those suggested by the manufacturer.

The adjustment screws are Allen set screws and require the use of an Allen wrench. To determine if the screw needs some rotation, insert the screw and try turning it gently. If the screw is firmly in position, it is unlikely that any adjustment is required. If the screw appears to be loose and turns easily, it very possibly needs attention. If you have determined that you must turn the screw, be sure to loosen the associated locking screw first.

INTEGRATED CIRCUITS

Every compact disc player depends on integrated circuits (ICs) and were it not for these extremely compact arrangements, it is doubtful if the players could exist at the current size and price.

Most of the components in the IC are solid state and are either transistors or diodes. The next most common components are resistors and conductors for connecting

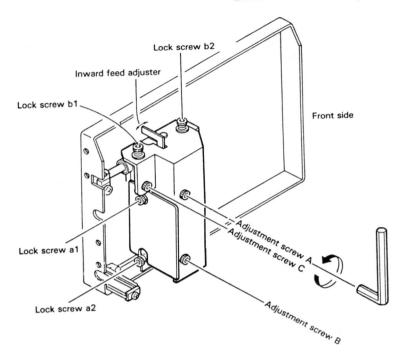

Figure 12-20 Operating adjustments are fastened by lock screws. (Courtesy Kyocera International, Inc.)

the components. Some ICs include capacitors but coils are discrete parts and are wired externally.

ICs can be categorized in many ways but most often they can be described as analog or digital. Digital ICs have binary inputs and outputs, or are analog when these are in analog form.

The Discrete IC

While an IC can contain a relatively large number of components, especially solid-state units, it is generally considered as a single unit rather than a collection of separate parts.

13

DIGITAL AUDIO
TAPE/PLAYER

Whether the compact disc will eliminate the phono record or whether it will take its place as just another sound source is debatable. The technology of the compact disc will affect not only the phono record but other components associated with a high-fidelity system. One of these is the audio cassette.

The present audio cassette system is analog. However, just as the CD player is an alternative to the phono turntable, so too will we have a digital tape recorder/player. The sound input to this component will be analog. In the player, that sound will be converted to digital, recorded on tape in digital form, and will then be changed back to analog immediately prior to the output.

Digital audio tape cassettes, commonly known as DATs, will represent the next step in combining digital data with a high density, magnetic storage medium. DATs can be classified into two types of system: R-DATs, which use a rotary head, and S-DATs, characterized by a fixed head. As in the case of video-cassette recorders, the rotary head technique is preferable.

ADVANTAGES OF DAT

In the future, tape recorders will not only be capable of recording pulse code modulation sound, but will be able to do many things that conventional tape recorders cannot do with compact audio cassettes. These advantages are:

1. The DAT technique will permit about a 50% reduction in the size of the cassette. As a consequence, the cassette recorder/player will be more adaptable for portable and auto use.

2. C-180 audio cassette tapes do have a 3-hour recording and playback time, but achieve this only by making the tape extremely thin, with the danger of the tape's stretching or tearing. Digital audio tape should be able to record for three hours without this problem.

3. As in the case of the CD player, the R-DAT will have a rapid search function, making it easy to find the start of each track. Further, by using subcodes you can expect a diversity of features.

4. With the R-DAT tape, speed is reduced to 8.15 mm/sec, or 1/4-inch/sec and the writing speed is 3.133 mm/sec. The tape speed of a conventional audio cassette is 47.6 mm/sec or 1-7/8 ips. For equivalent sound recording and playback, the R-DAT tape will run at about one-sixth the speed of audio cassettes. As a consequence, less tape will be required for the recording and playback of music.

The R-DAT unit will have a sampling frequency of 48 kHz, a little higher than that used by a compact disc player, and it will use 16-bit linear quantization.

R-DAT TAPE FORMAT

To examine the way in which a digitized audio signal is recorded on magnetic tape, note the tape format in Fig. 13-1. The track width is 13.591 μm (microns), about one-tenth the thickness of a human hair, and the length of the track is only 23.501 mm. Within this length, each bit of data occupies an extremely short distance of 0.67 μm, so as to achieve a recording density of 114 megabits/in^2. This is the first time such a high recording density has been achieved.

Data Quality

A general assumption is always made that our hearing range is from 20 Hz to 20 kHz. Most of us have a hearing ability well within that frequency band, but it was selected to cover every human hearing possibility.

To digitize signals in this range, the signal must be sampled at a frequency at least twice as great as the highest frequency in that range. In the R-DAT, sampling is done at 48 kHz, supplying a margin of 8 kHz. Stereo requires two channels, and since we will be using 16 bits we have $48{,}000 \times 16 \times 2 = 1{,}536{,}000$ bits/sec. or 1.536 megabits /sec.

This is not the final requirement. We need to compensate for errors, especially for dropouts when the signal is recorded and played back from a tape and so the signal is subjected to special error correction processing. To accomplish this, extra information amounting to 37.5% of the original signal is added to the signal, which raises the required signal data rate to 2.46 megabits. Subcodes are also added to the signal to enable various functions to be controlled, so the signal ultimately has a data-rate of

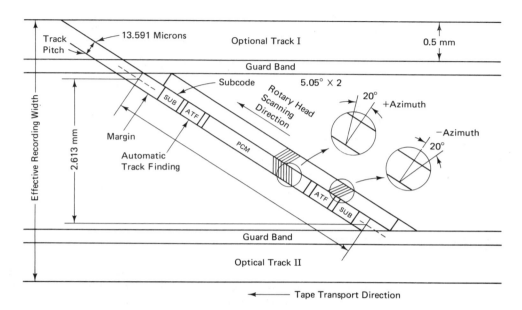

Figure 13-1 DAT format. (Courtesy Sony Corporation of America.)

2.77 megabits. The advantage of digital signal processing is that the use of a buffer makes real-time processing unnecessary.

R-DAT HEADS

Either two or four recording/playback heads are used. The diameter of the drum in which the heads are mounted (Fig. 13-2) is 30 mm and the magnetic tape is in contact with the drum over an arc of 90 degrees or one-fourth of the circumference of the drum. The advantage of a 90-degree wrap means that only a short length of tape is in contact with the drum, reducing the possibility of tape damage. It also allows high-speed transport and search while the tape is in contact with the drum. Further, a low tape tension can be used, a factor which ensures long head life.

There is still an additional advantage. The fact that only a short length of tape contacts the drum means a reduced chance of damage during high-speed search performed without removing the tape from the drum. Accordingly, even if 100 times normal tape speed is used, and this would be 8.15 mm/sec × 100 = 81.5 cm/sec, the tape would be strong enough to withstand this treatment. Furthermore, if signals can be read during high speed transport, it is also possible for data to be read during high-speed search, permitting quick access to a desired portion of the tape.

When four heads are used (Fig. 13-3) they can be separated by 90 degrees to allow simultaneous monitoring.

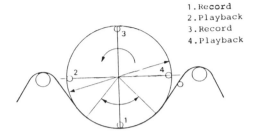

```
1.Record
2.Playback
3.Record
4.Playback
```

Figure 13-2 Drum makes 90-degree wiping contact with the tape. (Courtesy Sony Corporation of America.)

Figure 13-3 When four heads are used, they are spaced 90 degrees apart. (Courtesy Sony Corporation of America.)

ROTARY HEAD PROBLEMS

The head used in the R-DAT is similar to that in a video cassette recorder. The magnetically recorded tape can be considered as a transformer winding and the coil used in the head a winding as well, and so the head is sometimes referred to as a rotary transformer.

The output from this rotary transformer has a poor frequency characteristic in the low-frequency range necessitating its conversion to a higher-frequency.

In the standard R-DAT format, the 30-mm diameter drum is rotated at 2,000 rpm. To overcome the low-frequency range problem and, in particular, to eliminate direct-current components, the system uses 8-10 conversion in which an 8-bit signal is converted to one consisting of 10 bits. This method has the advantage of reducing the range of signal wavelengths to be handled with the result that the maximum wavelength is four times longer than the minimum wavelength. It also makes overwriting possible, eliminating the need for a separate erase head. This is necessary to limit the wavelength components so short wavelength signals can erase previously recorded long wavelength signals.

ERROR CORRECTION

In the R-DAT system, the error correction method is able to correct both "burst errors" and "random errors" that may occur in recording. Burst error refers to dropouts caused by dust, scratches on the tape or by clogging of the head with dirt. Random error can be caused by crosstalk from an adjacent track, remaining traces of an imperfectly erased signal, or mechanical instability. To cope with these errors, the R-DAT format is provided with double Reed-Solomon codes that are highly effective for error detection, correction and interpolation. Furthermore, the signal is rearranged as interleaved blocks. To make playback possible, even if one head is blocked, the blocks are recorded straddled across two tracks (Fig. 13-4).

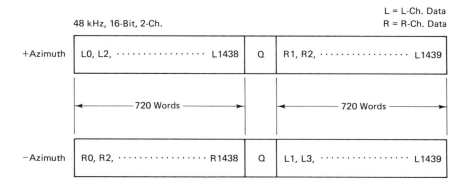

Figure 13-4 Interleave with two tracks completely joined. (Courtesy Sony Corporation of America.)

SIGNAL FORMAT

The data that has been subject to 8-10 conversion, double Reed-Solomon encoding, interleaving and other processing also has a block format in which each block consists of 288 bits (Fig. 13-5). A close look at the block format shows that with the exception of the sync byte, all block address interleaved contents can be checked by means of 8 × 3 = 24 bits. This is also useful for accurate identification of the start of tracks. The 256 bits of data consist of 32 symbols with one symbol represented by 8 bits. One track contains 128 blocks consisting of these symbols for a total of 4,096 symbols. Of these, 1,184 symbols are used for error correction, which leaves 2,912 symbols for use as data. There is also an area reserved for subcodes.

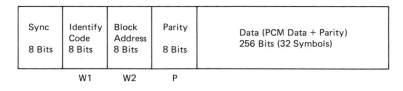

Figure 13-5 Pulse code modulation block format. (Courtesy Sony Corporation of America.)

TRACK FORMAT

With regard to track format, one track is subjected to time division (Fig. 13-6). Different areas are then allocated to each respective signal. To avoid interference between blocks, interblock gaps (IBG) are also provided. When performing after recording, certain areas are partially rewritten in accordance with the setting of this IBG. Rewriting can be performed without writing over adjacent areas. The subcode areas in

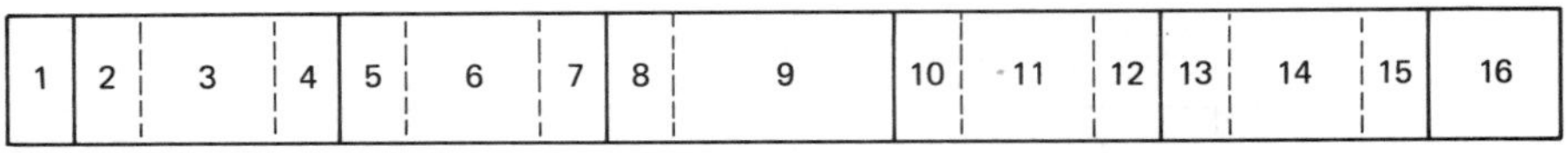

1	2	3	4	5	6	7	8	9	10	·11	12	13	14	15	16

		Signal	Angle (Deg.)	Number of Blocks
1	Margin	1/2f ch	5.051	11
2	PLL (Sub)	1/2f ch	0.918	2
3	Sub − 1		3.673	8
4	Post Amble	1/2f ch	0.459	1
5	IBG	1/6f ch	1.378	3
6	ATF		2.296	5
7	IBG	1/6f ch	1.378	3
8	PLL (PCM)	1/2f ch	0.918	2
9	PCM		58.776	128
10	IBG	1/6f ch	1.378	3
11	ATF		2.296	5
12	IBG	1/6f ch	1.378	3
13	PLL	1/2f ch	0.918	2
14	Sub − 2		3.673	8
15	Post Amble	1/2f ch	0.459	1
16	Margin	1/2f ch	5.051	11
	Total		90	196

Recording Density — 61.0 kBPI

f ch* — 9.408 MHz

*Calculated Under the Condition That 30 mm
Diameter — 90° Wrap Angle, 2000 rpm Cylinder
is Used

Figure 13-6 Pulse code modulation track format. (Courtesy Sony Corporation of America.)

which detailed data on program contents is written and the main PCM data areas are separate, allowing independent editing of the areas.

AUTOMATIC TRACK FINDING

Areas are provided within the track format to enable automatic track finding (ATF). ATF (Fig. 13-7) uses a pilot signal (f1), sync signal 1 (f2), sync signal 3 (f3), and erase

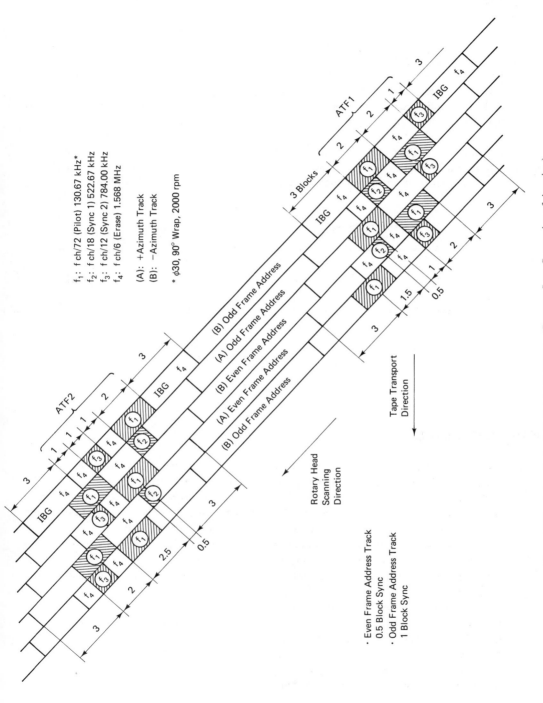

f_1: f ch/72 (Pilot) 130.67 kHz*
f_2: f ch/18 (Sync 1) 522.67 kHz
f_3: f ch/12 (Sync 2) 784.00 kHz
f_4: f ch/6 (Erase) 1.568 MHz

(A): +Azimuth Track
(B): −Azimuth Track

* ø30, 90° Wrap, 2000 rpm

ATF1

3 Blocks

IBG f_4

ATF2

IBG f_4

Tape Transport
Direction

Rotary Head
Scanning
Direction

· Even Frame Address Track
  0.5 Block Sync
· Odd Frame Address Track
  1 Block Sync

(B) Odd Frame Address
(A) Odd Frame Address
(B) Even Frame Address
(A) Even Frame Address
(B) Odd Frame Address

Figure 13-7 Automatic track finding track pattern. (Courtesy Sony Corporation of America.)

signal (f4). When the head advances in the direction of the arrow, the presence of an ATF signal is detected by picking up either the f2 or f3 sync signals.

The adjacent pilot signals (f1) on both sides are then immediately compared, and a decision is made whether the tracking is correct or not. The f1 signal components use low-range frequencies that are not affected by the azimuth setting, so crosstalk can be picked up and detected from both sides. Since this ATF system compares the crosstalk using an analog method, the processing is different than for other areas. The ATF area is clearly divided into two parts in the track format, so a small amount of track curvature does not result in tracking errors. This, together with the use of wide heads has resulted in a system in which compatibility is easy to achieve (Fig. 13-8). A tracking control head (CTL) such as that used for video is not required.

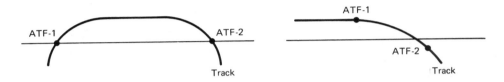

Figure 13-8   ATF data are in two locations. (Courtesy Sony Corporation of America.)

HIGH-SPEED SEARCH

The high-speed search function is also a key feature of the R-DAT format. As tape speed is only 8.15 mm/sec and the drum wrap only 90 degrees, the tape can be transported at high speed while still in contact with the drum. The width and thickness of the magnetic tape are the same as those of the tape used in audio cassettes, so the physical strength of the tape can be considered to be the same also.

If we suppose that the practical limit is 50 times the normal speed for audio cassettes (4.76 cm/sec × 50 = 2.38 m/sec); this speed, if recalculated for R-DATs is 300 times normal speed, an important factor in the realization of the high-speed search function (Fig. 13-9).

In addition, the tape format is arranged so the data for control purposes can be read from the location by the heads during high-speed search. As a result, although there is some dependency on recording time, search speeds not previously attainable have been achieved. The accuracy of high-speed search is guaranteed by specifying an address within the block format. This means that locations within tracks can be accurately cued, so the tape recorder is convenient and easy to use.

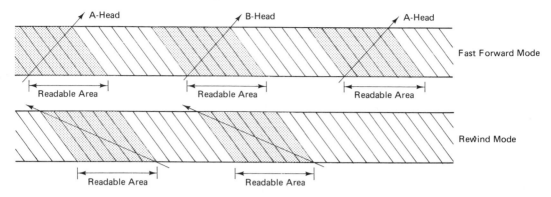

Figure 13-9 Head trace in fast forward and rewind modes. (Courtesy Sony Corporation of America.)

SUBCODES

The subcode areas are mainly used for recording program numbers and time codes. The subcode capacity is 273.1 KB or about 4.5 times the 60 KB capacity of a compact disc. The subcodes are in two locations above and below the tracks making them resistant to dropout. Other areas are used for recording various items in the same manner as compact discs, such as sampling frequency, channel number, quantization number, tape speed, copy protection, and use or non-use of preemphasis.

THE R-DAT CASSETTE

The R-DAT cassette is a completely sealed structure and measures $73 \times 54 \times 10.5$ mm and weighs about 20 grams. To prevent accidental touching of the tape surface, the lid, called a slider, is double-locked and as long as it is not deliberately opened, the tape inside is protected from fingerprints and dirt. (Fig. 13-10). To avoid tape slackness, provisions for a brake have been included, along with a photodiode for tape end detection. These may be required for future developments.

POSSIBILITIES FOR FUTURE DEVELOPMENT

If a very small drum could be produced, an even smaller digital tape recorder that could fit into the palm of the hand would be possible. By halving the tape speed and changing the sampling frequency, the recording time could be 4 to 6 hours or four channels could

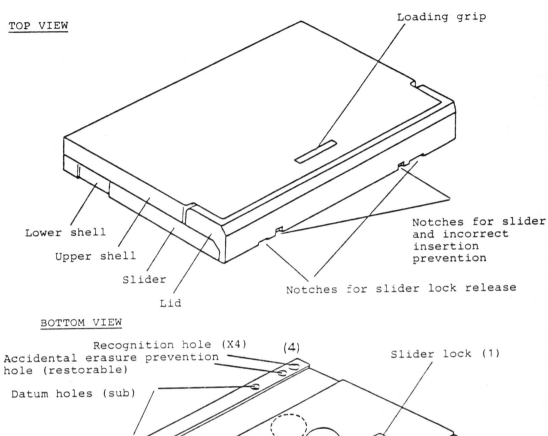

TOP VIEW

Loading grip

Lower shell

Upper shell

Slider

Lid

Notches for slider
and incorrect
insertion
prevention

Notches for slider lock release

BOTTOM VIEW

Recognition hole (X4)   (4)

Accidental erasure prevention
hole (restorable)

Datum holes (sub)

Slider lock (1)

(1)(2)(3)

Slider lock (2)

Hub holes
(covered by slider)

Lid lock
(locked by slider)

Figure 13-10 Construction of the R-DAT cassette. (Courtesy Sony Corporation of America.)

be provided. Further, by arranging for automatic mode selection by means of subcodes, the tape recorder could have many new applications, including use as an inexpensive data recorder. Table 13-1 lists the basic specifications of an R-DAT system.

TABLE 13-1 Basic Specifications of the R-DAT System.

Number of Channels	(ch)	2	2	2	4	2
Sampling Frequency	(kHz)	48	44.1	32		
Quantization	(bit)	16	16	16	12	
Tape Width	(mm)	3.81 (+0 / −0.02)				
Type of Tapes		MP	Oxide	MP		
Tape Thickness	(μm)	13 ± 1				
Tape Speed	(mm/s)	8.15	12.225	8.15	8.15	4.075
Track Pitch	(μm)	13.59	20.41	13.59		
Track Angle (Tape Runs)	(deg)	6°22′59.5″				
Recording Time	(min)	120	80	120	120	240
Head Gap Azimuth Angle	(deg)	± 20				
Recommended Cylinder Specifications		ø30, 90° Wrap 2000 rpm			1000 rpm	
Writing Speed	(m/s)	3.133	3.129	3.133	3.133	1.567
Modulation Scheme		8 - 10				
Recording Density		61kBPI				
Error Detection and Correction Code		Doubly-Encoded RSC				
Redundancy	(%)	37.5	42.6	58.3	37.5	37.5
Transmission Rate	(MBPS)	2.46				1.23
Sub-coding (Capacity)	(kBPS)	273.1				136.5
Tracking System		ATF				
Dimension of the Cassette	(mm)	73 × 54 × 10.5 (W × D × H)				

(Courtesy Sony Corporation of America)

INDEX